# Safety Symbols

These symbols appear in laboratory activities.
They alert you to possible dangers and remind
you to work carefully.

**General Safety Awareness** Read all directions for an experiment several times. Follow the directions exactly as they are written. If you are in doubt, ask your teacher for assistance.

**Physical Safety** If the lab includes physical activity, use caution to avoid injuring yourself or others. Tell your teacher if there is a reason that you should not participate.

**Safety Goggles** Always wear safety goggles to protect your eyes in any activity involving chemicals, heating, or the possibility of broken glassware.

**Lab Apron** Wear a laboratory apron to protect your skin and clothing from harmful chemicals or hot materials.

**Plastic Gloves** Wear disposable plastic gloves to protect yourself from contact with chemicals that can be harmful. Keep your hands away from your face. Dispose of gloves according to your teacher's instructions.

**Heating** Use a clamp or tongs to hold hot objects. Test an object by first holding the back of your hand near it. If you feel heat, the object may be too hot to handle.

**Heat-Resistant Gloves** Hot plates, hot water, and hot glassware can cause burns. Never touch hot objects with your bare hands. Use an oven mitt or other hand protection.

**Flames** Tie back long hair and loose clothing, and put on safety goggles before using a burner. Follow instructions from your teacher for lighting and extinguishing burners.

**No Flames** If flammable materials are present, make sure there are no flames, sparks, or exposed sources of heat.

**Electric Shock** To avoid an electric shock, never use electrical equipment near water, or when the equipment or your hands are wet. Use only sockets that accept a three-prong plug. Be sure cords are untangled and cannot trip anyone. Disconnect equipment that is not in use.

**Fragile Glassware** Handle fragile glassware, such as thermometers, test tubes, and beakers, with care. Do not touch broken glass. Notify your teacher if glassware breaks. Never use chipped or cracked glassware.

**Corrosive Chemical** Avoid getting corrosive chemicals on your skin or clothing, or in your eyes. Do not inhale the vapors. Wash your hands after completing the activity.

**Poison** Do not let any poisonous chemical get on your skin, and do not inhale its vapor. Wash your hands after completing the activity.

**Fumes** When working with poisonous or irritating vapors, work in a well-ventilated area. Never test for an odor unless instructed to do so by your teacher. Avoid inhaling a vapor directly. Use a wafting motion to direct vapor toward your nose.

**Sharp Object** Use sharp instruments only as directed. Scissors, scalpels, pins, and knives are sharp and can cut or puncture your skin. Always direct a sharp edge or points away from yourself and others.

**Disposal** All chemicals and other materials used in the laboratory must be disposed of safely. Follow your teacher's instructions.

**Hand Washing** Before leaving the lab, wash your hands thoroughly with soap or detergent, and warm water. Lather both sides of your hands and between your fingers. Rinse well.

Inside Earth

PRENTICE HALL Science Explorer

PEARSON
Prentice
Hall

Boston, Massachusetts
Upper Saddle River, New Jersey

# Inside Earth

## Book-Specific Resources

Student Edition
StudentExpress™ with Interactive Textbook
Teacher's Edition
All-in-One Teaching Resources
Color Transparencies
Guided Reading and Study Workbook
Student Edition on Audio CD
Discovery Channel School® Video
Lab Activity Video
Consumable and Nonconsumable Materials Kits

## Program Print Resources

Integrated Science Laboratory Manual
Computer Microscope Lab Manual
Inquiry Skills Activity Books
Progress Monitoring Assessments
Test Preparation Workbook
Test-Taking Tips With Transparencies
Teacher's ELL Handbook
Reading Strategies for Science Content

## Differentiated Instruction Resources

Adapted Reading and Study Workbook
Adapted Tests
Differentiated Instruction Guide for Labs and Activities

## Program Technology Resources

TeacherExpress™ CD-ROM
Interactive Textbooks Online
PresentationExpress™ CD-ROM
*ExamView*®, Computer Test Bank CD-ROM
Lab zone™ Easy Planner CD-ROM
Probeware Lab Manual With CD-ROM
Computer Microscope and Lab Manual
Materials Ordering CD-ROM
Discovery Channel School® DVD Library
Lab Activity DVD Library
Web Site at PHSchool.com

## Spanish Print Resources

Spanish Student Edition
Spanish Guided Reading and Study Workbook
Spanish Teaching Guide With Tests

**Acknowledgments** appear on p. 214, which constitutes an extension of this copyright page.

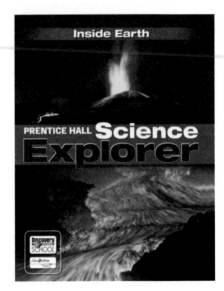

**Cover**
Lava flows down Mount Etna on the island of Sicily.

ISBN 0-13-201149-2
5 6 7 8 9 10    10 09 08 07

## Program Authors

**Michael J. Padilla, Ph.D.**
Professor of Science Education
University of Georgia
Athens, Georgia

Michael Padilla is a leader in middle school science education. He has served as an author and elected officer for the National Science Teachers Association and as a writer of the National Science Education Standards. As lead author of Science Explorer, Mike has inspired the team in developing a program that meets the needs of middle grades students, promotes science inquiry, and is aligned with the National Science Education Standards.

**Ioannis Miaoulis, Ph.D.**
President
Museum of Science
Boston, Massachusetts

Originally trained as a mechanical engineer, Ioannis Miaoulis is in the forefront of the national movement to increase technological literacy. As dean of the Tufts University School of Engineering, Dr. Miaoulis spearheaded the introduction of engineering into the Massachusetts curriculum. Currently he is working with school systems across the country to engage students in engineering activities and to foster discussions on the impact of science and technology on society.

**Martha Cyr, Ph.D.**
Director of K–12 Outreach
Worcester Polytechnic Institute
Worcester, Massachusetts

Martha Cyr is a noted expert in engineering outreach. She has over nine years of experience with programs and activities that emphasize the use of engineering principles, through hands-on projects, to excite and motivate students and teachers of mathematics and science in grades K–12. Her goal is to stimulate a continued interest in science and mathematics through engineering.

## Book Authors

**Carole Garbuny Vogel**
Science Writer
Lexington, Massachusetts

**Michael Wysession, Ph.D.**
Associate Professsor of
 Earth and Planetary Sciences
Washington University
St. Louis, Missouri

## Contributing Writers

**Sharon M. Stroud**
Science Instructor
Widefield High School
Colorado Springs, Colorado

**Thomas R. Wellnitz**
Science Instructor
The Paideia School
Atlanta, Georgia

## Consultants

**Reading Consultant**

**Nancy Romance, Ph.D.**
Professor of Science
 Education
Florida Atlantic University
Fort Lauderdale, Florida

**Mathematics Consultant**

**William Tate, Ph.D.**
Professor of Education and
 Applied Statistics and
 Computation
Washington University
St. Louis, Missouri

# Reviewers

## Tufts University Content Reviewers

Faculty from Tufts University in Medford, Massachusetts, developed *Science Explorer* chapter projects and reviewed the student books.

**Astier M. Almedom, Ph.D.**
Department of Biology

**Wayne Chudyk, Ph.D.**
Department of Civil and Environmental Engineering

**John L. Durant, Ph.D.**
Department of Civil and Environmental Engineering

**George S. Ellmore, Ph.D.**
Department of Biology

**David Kaplan, Ph.D.**
Department of Biomedical Engineering

**Samuel Kounaves, Ph.D.**
Department of Chemistry

**David H. Lee, Ph.D.**
Department of Chemistry

**Douglas Matson, Ph.D.**
Department of Mechanical Engineering

**Karen Panetta, Ph.D.**
Department of Electrical Engineering and Computer Science

**Jan A. Pechenik, Ph.D.**
Department of Biology

**John C. Ridge, Ph.D.**
Department of Geology

**William Waller, Ph.D.**
Department of Astronomy

## Content Reviewers

**Paul Beale, Ph.D.**
Department of Physics
University of Colorado
Boulder, Colorado

**Jeff Bodart, Ph.D.**
Chipola Junior College
Marianna, Florida

**Michael Castellani, Ph.D.**
Department of Chemistry
Marshall University
Huntington, West Virginia

**Eugene Chiang, Ph.D.**
Department of Astronomy
University of California – Berkeley
Berkeley, California

**Charles C. Curtis, Ph.D.**
Department of Physics
University of Arizona
Tucson, Arizona

**Daniel Kirk-Davidoff, Ph.D.**
Department of Meteorology
University of Maryland
College Park, Maryland

**Diane T. Doser, Ph.D.**
Department of Geological Sciences
University of Texas at El Paso
El Paso, Texas

**R. E. Duhrkopf, Ph.D.**
Department of Biology
Baylor University
Waco, Texas

**Michael Hacker**
Co-director, Center for Technological Literacy
Hofstra University
Hempstead, New York

**Michael W. Hamburger, Ph.D.**
Department of Geological Sciences
Indiana University
Bloomington, Indiana

**Alice K. Hankla, Ph.D.**
The Galloway School
Atlanta, Georgia

**Donald C. Jackson, Ph.D.**
Department of Molecular Pharmacology, Physiology, & Biotechnology
Brown University
Providence, Rhode Island

**Jeremiah N. Jarrett, Ph.D.**
Department of Biological Sciences
Central Connecticut State University
New Britain, Connecticut

**David Lederman, Ph.D.**
Department of Physics
West Virginia University
Morgantown, West Virginia

**Becky Mansfield, Ph.D.**
Department of Geography
Ohio State University
Columbus, Ohio

**Elizabeth M. Martin, M.S.**
Department of Chemistry and Biochemistry
College of Charleston
Charleston, South Carolina

**Joe McCullough, Ph.D.**
Department of Natural and Applied Sciences
Cabrillo College
Aptos, California

**Robert J. Mellors, Ph.D.**
Department of Geological Sciences
San Diego State University
San Diego, California

**Joseph M. Moran, Ph.D.**
American Meteorological Society
Washington, D.C.

**David J. Morrissey, Ph.D.**
Department of Chemistry
Michigan State University
East Lansing, Michigan

**Philip A. Reed, Ph.D.**
Department of Occupational & Technical Studies
Old Dominion University
Norfolk, Virginia

**Scott M. Rochette, Ph.D.**
Department of the Earth Sciences
State University of New York, College at Brockport
Brockport, New York

**Laurence D. Rosenhein, Ph.D.**
Department of Chemistry
Indiana State University
Terre Haute, Indiana

**Ronald Sass, Ph.D.**
Department of Biology and Chemistry
Rice University
Houston, Texas

**George Schatz, Ph.D.**
Department of Chemistry
Northwestern University
Evanston, Illinois

**Sara Seager, Ph.D.**
Carnegie Institution of Washington
Washington, D.C.

**Robert M. Thornton, Ph.D.**
Section of Plant Biology
University of California
Davis, California

**John R. Villarreal, Ph.D.**
College of Science and Engineering
The University of Texas – Pan American
Edinburg, Texas

**Kenneth Welty, Ph.D.**
School of Education
University of Wisconsin–Stout
Menomonie, Wisconsin

**Edward J. Zalisko, Ph.D.**
Department of Biology
Blackburn College
Carlinville, Illinois

## Teacher Reviewers

**David R. Blakely**
Arlington High School
Arlington, Massachusetts

**Jane E. Callery**
Two Rivers Magnet Middle
    School
East Hartford, Connecticut

**Melissa Lynn Cook**
Oakland Mills High School
Columbia, Maryland

**James Fattic**
Southside Middle School
Anderson, Indiana

**Dan Gabel**
Hoover Middle School
Rockville, Maryland

**Wayne Goates**
Eisenhower Middle School
Goddard, Kansas

**Katherine Bobay Graser**
Mint Hill Middle School
Charlotte, North Carolina

**Darcy Hampton**
Deal Junior High School
Washington, D.C.

**Karen Kelly**
Pierce Middle School
Waterford, Michigan

**David Kelso**
Manchester High School Central
Manchester, New Hampshire

**Benigno Lopez, Jr.**
Sleepy Hill Middle School
Lakeland, Florida

**Angie L. Matamoros, Ph.D.**
ALM Consulting, INC.
Weston, Florida

**Tim McCollum**
Charleston Middle School
Charleston, Illinois

**Bruce A. Mellin**
Brooks School
North Andover, Massachusetts

**Ella Jay Parfitt**
Southeast Middle School
Baltimore, Maryland

**Evelyn A. Pizzarello**
Louis M. Klein Middle School
Harrison, New York

**Kathleen M. Poe**
Fletcher Middle School
Jacksonville, Florida

**Shirley Rose**
Lewis and Clark Middle School
Tulsa, Oklahoma

**Linda Sandersen**
Greenfield Middle School
Greenfield, Wisconsin

**Mary E. Solan**
Southwest Middle School
Charlotte, North Carolina

**Mary Stewart**
University of Tulsa
Tulsa, Oklahoma

**Paul Swenson**
Billings West High School
Billings, Montana

**Thomas Vaughn**
Arlington High School
Arlington, Massachusetts

**Susan C. Zibell**
Central Elementary
Simsbury, Connecticut

## Safety Reviewers

**W. H. Breazeale, Ph.D.**
Department of Chemistry
College of Charleston
Charleston, South Carolina

**Ruth Hathaway, Ph.D.**
Hathaway Consulting
Cape Girardeau, Missouri

**Douglas Mandt, M.S.**
Science Education Consultant
Edgewood, Washington

## Activity Field Testers

**Nicki Bibbo**
Witchcraft Heights School
Salem, Massachusetts

**Rose-Marie Botting**
Broward County Schools
Fort Lauderdale, Florida

**Colleen Campos**
Laredo Middle School
Aurora, Colorado

**Elizabeth Chait**
W. L. Chenery Middle School
Belmont, Massachusetts

**Holly Estes**
Hale Middle School
Stow, Massachusetts

**Laura Hapgood**
Plymouth Community
    Intermediate School
Plymouth, Massachusetts

**Mary F. Lavin**
Plymouth Community
    Intermediate School
Plymouth, Massachusetts

**James MacNeil, Ph.D.**
Cambridge, Massachusetts

**Lauren Magruder**
St. Michael's Country
    Day School
Newport, Rhode Island

**Jeanne Maurand**
Austin Preparatory School
Reading, Massachusetts

**Joanne Jackson-Pelletier**
Winman Junior High School
Warwick, Rhode Island

**Warren Phillips**
Plymouth Public Schools
Plymouth, Massachusetts

**Carol Pirtle**
Hale Middle School
Stow, Massachusetts

**Kathleen M. Poe**
Fletcher Middle School
Jacksonville, Florida

**Cynthia B. Pope**
Norfolk Public Schools
Norfolk, Virginia

**Anne Scammell**
Geneva Middle School
Geneva, New York

**Karen Riley Sievers**
Callanan Middle School
Des Moines, Iowa

**David M. Smith**
Eyer Middle School
Allentown, Pennsylvania

**Gene Vitale**
Parkland School
McHenry, Illinois

# Contents

# Inside Earth

# Reference Section

**Enhance understanding through dynamic video.**

**Preview** Get motivated with this introduction to the chapter content.

**Field Trip** Explore a real-world story related to the chapter content.

**Assessment** Review content and take an assessment.

**Get connected to exciting Web resources in every lesson.**

*SciLINKS®* Find Web links on topics relating to every section.

**Active Art** Interact with selected visuals from every chapter online.

**Planet Diary®** Explore news and natural phenomena through weekly reports.

**Science News®** Keep up to date with the latest science discoveries.

**Experience the complete textbook online and on CD-ROM.**

**Activities** Practice skills and learn content.

**Videos** Explore content and learn important lab skills.

**Audio Support** Hear key terms spoken and defined.

**Self-Assessment** Use instant feedback to help you track your progress.

# Activities

# Dancing With Volcanoes

A helicopter moves toward the top of an erupting volcano. With care and speed, a team of scientists gets out to do their work.

"I've been out there sometimes when lava is shooting out of the ground 100 meters high," says volcanologist Margaret Mangan. "The main thing you're struck with is the sound. It's like the roaring of many jet engines. Then there's the smell of sulfur, which is choking. The wind can blow particles from the lava fountain over you, little bits of congealed lava. It feels like a hot sandstorm."

Other times, the eruption is gentler. Lava flows out of the ground in a single channel. "You can walk right up to the channel, just like you'd walk up to a river's edge. We wear what's like a ski mask to keep our faces from getting burnt by the radiant heat. We wear fire-retardant cloth and thick shoes and gloves, to keep our clothes from catching fire. It's hot and sweaty, but you're too excited about what you're doing to think about it."

As a helicopter hovers nearby, lava oozes down Mount Kilauea, a volcano on the island of Hawaii.

Margaret Mangan grew up in Washington, D.C., and received a Ph.D. from Johns Hopkins University in Baltimore, Maryland. She is a geologist with the Volcano Hazards Team of the U.S. Geological Survey in Menlo Park, California. Formerly, she was the scientist-in-charge of the Hawaiian Volcano Observatory. Maggie has two daughters. She enjoys giving talks and hands-on workshops for middle school science students.

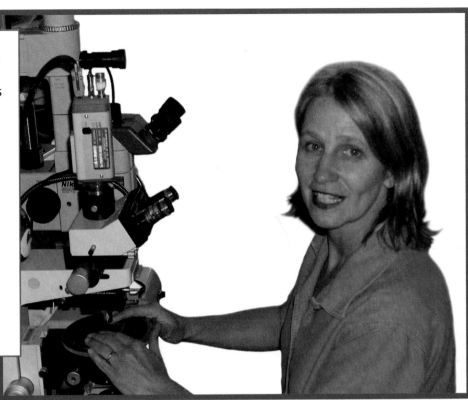

Dr. Margaret Mangan studies lava samples.

*Talking With*
# Dr. Margaret Mangan

## ? How did you get interested in science?

When I was little, I had no interest in science. I wanted to be a dancer. But I did have a good teacher in high school who taught earth science. He was amazingly interesting and funny. In the back of my mind, that stuck with me. After high school, I worked and studied dance. Then I decided to go to college. Because of that earth science course, I took geology and really liked it. But I had to catch up. I had never taken chemistry, physics, or precalculus in high school. So I did some "quick study" work and got up to speed.

## ? How did you choose volcanology?

When I became a graduate student in geology, I studied crystals and mineral science. It appealed to the artist in me because the study of crystals has a lot to do with symmetry and structure—how things are put together. When I needed to support myself, I got a job with the U.S. Geological Survey. I worked as an assistant to a volcanologist in an area of Oregon and Washington called the Columbia River flood basalts.

## ? What are flood basalts?

Beneath Earth's crust, molten rock, or magma, collects in pockets called magma chambers. On top of magma chambers, cracks can open in the ground. We call them fissures. The underground magma is so hot and so fluid that it runs out as a flood of lava, eventually forming a flood basalt. Millions of years ago in the part of Washington where I was working, fissures opened up and lava began to flow west. Our research was to find out how big the lava flows were and how far they traveled.

We hiked into beautiful canyons, which look like birthday cakes with layers of basalt lava stacked one on top of another, hundreds of meters deep. I loved being outside in the middle of canyons and rolling hills. In the midst of that amazing outpouring of volcanism, I learned I wanted to do science outdoors and to study volcanoes.

I kept working for the U.S. Geological Survey, but also started my Ph.D. thesis research on magma chambers. After completing my degree, I hopped on a plane with my husband and daughters to live and work in Hawaii.

Layers of basalt lava

Layers of lava formed these flood basalts in Columbia Gorge, Washington.

## ? What was your work like in Hawaii?

I had two main jobs. One was to keep track of the eruption that's gone on at Kilauea volcano since 1983. We wanted to make sure that people coming to the volcano and living near the volcano were safe. We observed the volcano closely and then passed information to the local government and the National Park Service.

I also started a research project related to the Kilauea eruption. I wanted to know why some explosions are bigger than others. You start with the same volcano, the same type of magma underneath. But sometimes it'll come oozing out of the ground and other times it'll erupt in big explosions. My research, which I'm still doing here in California, takes me back and forth between the real volcanoes and the laboratory. I try to simulate or model a volcanic eruption by making a very small magma chamber right in the lab.

In the laboratory, I put a small piece of lava and some water inside a capsule about as big as my index finger. Then I subject it to the temperature and pressures that would be underneath a volcano. After a few days, I lower the temperature and pressure. This simulates the way the pressure lessens and the magma starts to cool as it rises to the surface of a volcano. Finally, I put the capsule in contact with ice. This stops the process in its tracks, and simulates how magma suddenly cools when it comes out of a vent into the atmosphere.

## ? What are you learning from your research?

I'm looking for what affects how explosive an eruption is. Right now, the research is very much focused on the "soda can model." You take a soda can, shake it a tad, open it, and the soda kind of wells over your hand. But if you shake it a lot, then open it, it flies up to the ceiling. There's no difference in the carbonation. The percentage of $CO_2$ gas is the same in both cans. What is different is the rate of degassing—the rate at which the bubbles of gas form. That's what makes the "eruption" strong or gentle.

**Maggie collects lava samples from Mount Kilauea.**

## ? Isn't studying volcanoes dangerous?

Well, the danger is a drawback. There's always a concern for safety, even in the lab work. When I do field work, I ask myself: What are the conditions I'm approaching? There's a level of danger, but I'm very careful to think it through and act in ways that keep me safe. Once you make a decision to do something, you move in, you do it. You can't let the fear affect your actions, because then you get clumsy. You have to be controlled and organized.

## Writing in Science

**Career Link** Maggie says her training as a dancer gave her a sense of discipline. She feels that learning about practice, self-control, and organization have helped her be a better scientist. What interests, experiences, or parts of your personality might make you a good scientist? Why do you think so?

Go Online
PHSchool.com

**For:** More on this career
**Visit:** PHSchool.com
**Web Code:** cfb-1000

# Plate Tectonics

## Chapter Preview

**interactive Textbook**

The huge gash in the ground is a rift valley formed where the mid-Atlantic ridge cuts through Iceland. ▶

## Lab zone™ Chapter **Project**

### Make a Model of Earth

In this chapter, you will learn how movements deep within Earth help to create mountains and other surface features. As you read this chapter, you will build a model that shows Earth's interior.

**Your Goal** To build a three-dimensional model that shows Earth's surface features, as well as a cutaway view of Earth's interior

Your model must

● be built to scale to show the layers of Earth's interior

● include at least three of the plates that form Earth's surface, as well as two landmasses or continents

● show how the plates push together, pull apart, or slide past each other and indicate their direction of movement

● follow the safety guidelines in Appendix A

**Plan It!** Think about the materials you could use to make a three-dimensional model. How will you show what happens beneath the crust? As you learn about sea-floor spreading and plate tectonics, add the appropriate features to your model.

# Earth's Interior

## Reading Preview

### Key Concepts
- How have geologists learned about Earth's inner structure?
- What are the characteristics of Earth's crust, mantle, and core?

### Key Terms
- seismic waves • pressure
- crust • basalt • granite
- mantle • lithosphere
- asthenosphere • outer core
- inner core

### ⊙ Target Reading Skill

**Using Prior Knowledge** Before you read, look at the section headings and visuals to see what this section is about. Then write what you know about Earth's interior in a graphic organizer like the one below. As you read, write what you learn.

| What You Know |
|---|
| 1. Earth's crust is made of rock. |
| 2. |

| What You Learned |
|---|
| 1. |
| 2. |

---

### Lab zone — Discover **Activity**

#### How Do Scientists Find Out What's Inside Earth?

1. Your teacher will provide you with three closed film canisters. Each canister contains a different material. Your goal is to determine what is inside each canister—even though you can't directly observe what it contains.
2. Tape a paper label on each canister.
3. To gather evidence about what is in the canisters, you may tap, roll, shake, or weigh them. Record your observations.
4. What differences do you notice between the canisters? Apart from their appearance on the outside, are the canisters similar in any way? How did you obtain this evidence?

**Think It Over**
**Inferring** From your observations, what can you infer about the contents of the canisters? How is a canister like Earth?

---

Imagine watching an island grow! That's exactly what you can do on the island of Hawaii. On the south side of the island, molten material pours out of cracks in Mount Kilauea (kee loo AY uh) and flows into the ocean. As this lava flows over the land, it cools and hardens into rock.

The most recent eruptions of Mount Kilauea began in 1983. An area of cracks 7 kilometers long opened in Earth's surface. Through the cracks spurted "curtains of fire"—fountains of hot liquid rock from deep inside Earth. Since that time, the lava has covered more than 100 square kilometers of land with a layer of rock. When the lava reaches the sea, it extends the borders of the island into the Pacific Ocean.

FIGURE 1
**Lava Flows in Hawaii**
These people are watching lava from vents in Kilauea flow into the Pacific Ocean.

FIGURE 2
**Getting Beneath the Surface**
Geologists (left) examine rocks for
clues about what's inside Earth.
Even though caves like this one in
Georgia (below) may seem deep,
they reach only a relatively short
distance beneath the surface.

# Exploring Inside Earth

Earth's surface is constantly changing. Throughout
our planet's long history, its surface has been lifted
up, pushed down, bent, and broken. Thus Earth
looks different today from the way it did millions
of years ago.

Volcanic eruptions like those at Mount
Kilauea make people wonder, What's inside
Earth? Yet this question is very difficult to
answer. Much as geologists would like to, they
cannot dig a hole to the center of Earth. The
extreme conditions in Earth's interior prevent
exploration far below the surface.

The deepest mine in the world, a gold mine
in South Africa, reaches a depth of 3.8 kilometers. But that mine only scratches the surface.
You would have to travel more than 1,600 times
that distance—over 6,000 kilometers—to reach
Earth's center. **Geologists have used two main
types of evidence to learn about Earth's
interior: direct evidence from rock samples
and indirect evidence from seismic waves.** The
geologists in Figure 2 are observing rock on
Earth's surface.

**Evidence From Rock Samples**   Rocks from inside Earth give geologists clues about Earth's structure. Geologists have drilled holes as much as 12 kilometers into Earth. The drills bring up samples of rock. From these samples, geologists can make inferences about conditions deep inside Earth, where these rocks formed. In addition, forces inside Earth sometimes blast rock to the surface from depths of more than 100 kilometers. These rocks provide more information about the interior.

**Evidence From Seismic Waves**   Geologists cannot look inside Earth. Instead, they must rely on indirect methods of observation. Have you ever hung a heavy picture on a wall? If you have, you know that you can knock on the wall to locate the wooden beam underneath the plaster that will support the picture. When you knock on the wall, you listen carefully for a change in the sound.

To study Earth's interior, geologists also use an indirect method. But instead of knocking on walls, they use seismic waves. When earthquakes occur, they produce **seismic waves** (SYZ mik). Geologists record the seismic waves and study how they travel through Earth. The speed of seismic waves and the paths they take reveal the structure of the planet.

Using data from seismic waves, geologists have learned that Earth's interior is made up of several layers. Each layer surrounds the layers beneath it, much like the layers of an onion. In Figure 3, you can see how seismic waves travel through the layers that make up Earth.

 Reading Checkpoint   **What causes seismic waves?**

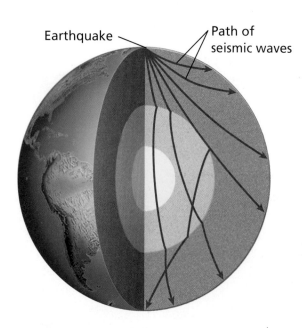

Earthquake — Path of seismic waves

**FIGURE 3**
**Seismic Waves**
Scientists infer Earth's inner structure by recording and studying how seismic waves travel through Earth.

Depth
0
0.5 m
1 m

**Pressure Increases**

1.5 m
2 m

# A Journey to the Center of Earth

**The three main layers of Earth are the crust, the mantle, and the core. These layers vary greatly in size, composition, temperature, and pressure.** If you could travel through these layers to the center of Earth, what would your trip be like? To begin, you will need a vehicle that can travel through solid rock. The vehicle will carry scientific instruments to record changes in temperature and pressure as you descend.

**Temperature** As you start to tunnel beneath the surface, the surrounding rock is cool. Then at about 20 meters down, your instruments report that the rock is getting warmer. For every 40 meters that you descend from that point, the temperature rises 1 Celsius degree. This rapid rise in temperature continues for several tens of kilometers. After that, the temperature increases more slowly, but steadily. The high temperatures inside Earth are the result of heat left over from the formation of the planet. In addition, radioactive substances inside Earth release energy. This further heats the interior.

**Pressure** During your journey to the center of Earth, your instruments record an increase in pressure in the surrounding rock. **Pressure** results from a force pressing on an area. Because of the weight of the rock above, pressure inside Earth increases as you go deeper. The deeper you go, the greater the pressure. Pressure inside Earth increases much as it does in the swimming pool in Figure 4.

FIGURE 4
**Pressure and Depth**
The deeper this swimmer goes, the greater the pressure from the surrounding water.
**Comparing and Contrasting** *How is the water in the swimming pool similar to Earth's interior? How is it different?*

# The Crust

Your journey to the center of Earth begins in the crust. The **crust** is the layer of rock that forms Earth's outer skin. **The crust is a layer of solid rock that includes both dry land and the ocean floor.** On the crust you find rocks and mountains. The crust also includes the soil and water that cover large parts of Earth's surface.

This outer rind of rock is much thinner than the layer that lies beneath it. In fact, you can think of Earth's crust as being similar to the paper-thin skin of an onion. The crust is thickest under high mountains and thinnest beneath the ocean. In most places, the crust is between 5 and 40 kilometers thick. But it can be up to 70 kilometers thick beneath mountains.

The crust beneath the ocean is called oceanic crust. Oceanic crust consists mostly of rocks such as basalt. **Basalt** (buh SAWLT) is dark rock with a fine texture. Continental crust, the crust that forms the continents, consists mainly of rocks such as granite. **Granite** is a rock that usually is a light color and has a coarse texture.

**✓ Reading Checkpoint** What is the main type of rock in oceanic crust?

**FIGURE 5**
**Earth's Interior**
Earth's interior is divided into layers: the crust, mantle, outer core, and inner core.
**Interpreting Diagrams** *Which of Earth's layers is the thickest?*

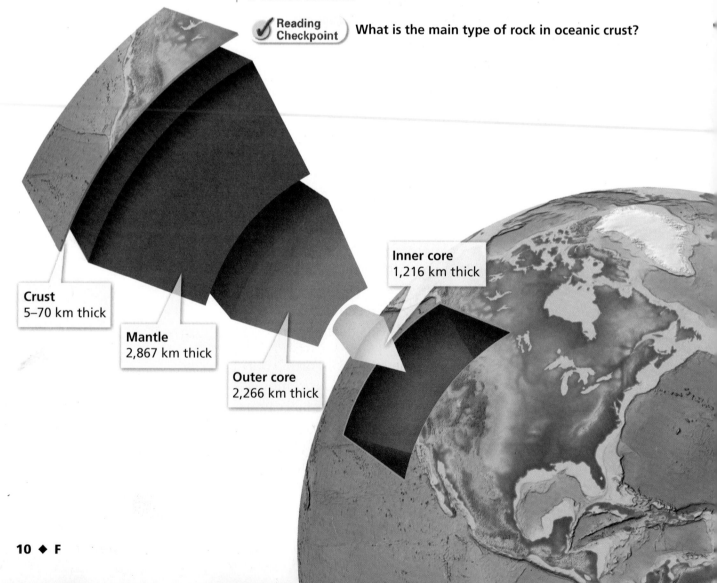

Crust
5–70 km thick

Mantle
2,867 km thick

Outer core
2,266 km thick

Inner core
1,216 km thick

# The Mantle

Your journey downward continues. About 40 kilometers beneath the surface, you cross a boundary. Below the boundary is the solid material of the **mantle,** a layer of hot rock. **Earth's mantle is made up of rock that is very hot, but solid. Scientists divide the mantle into layers based on the physical characteristics of those layers. Overall, the mantle is nearly 3,000 kilometers thick.**

**The Lithosphere** The uppermost part of the mantle is very similar to the crust. The uppermost part of the mantle and the crust together form a rigid layer called the **lithosphere** (LITH uh sfeer). In Greek, *lithos* means "stone." As you can see in Figure 6, the lithosphere averages about 100 kilometers thick.

**The Asthenosphere** Below the lithosphere, your vehicle encounters material that is hotter and under increasing pressure. As a result, the part of the mantle just beneath the lithosphere is less rigid than the rock above. Like road tar softened by the heat of the sun, this part of the mantle is somewhat soft—it can bend like plastic. This soft layer is called the **asthenosphere** (as THEN uh sfeer). In Greek, *asthenes* means "weak." Although the asthenosphere is softer than the rest of the mantle, it's still solid. If you kicked it, you would stub your toe.

**The Lower Mantle** Beneath the asthenosphere, the mantle is solid. This solid material extends all the way to Earth's core.

 **Reading Checkpoint** **What is the asthenosphere?**

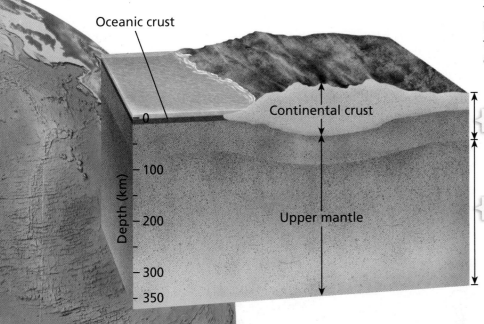

**FIGURE 6**
**Lithosphere and Asthenosphere**
The rigid lithosphere, which includes the crust, rests on the softer material of the asthenosphere.

## Temperature Inside Earth

The graph shows how temperatures change between Earth's surface and the bottom of the mantle. On this graph, the temperature at Earth's surface is 0°C. Study the graph carefully and then answer the questions.

1. **Reading Graphs** As you move from left to right on the x-axis, how does depth inside Earth change?

2. **Estimating** What is the temperature at the boundary between the lithosphere and the asthenosphere?

3. **Estimating** What is the temperature at the boundary between the lower mantle and the core?

4. **Interpreting Data** How does temperature change with depth in Earth's interior?

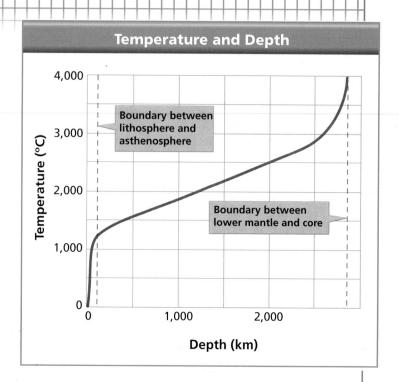

**Temperature and Depth**

Boundary between lithosphere and asthenosphere

Boundary between lower mantle and core

Temperature (°C)

Depth (km)

## The Core

After traveling through the mantle, you reach Earth's core. **The core is made mostly of the metals iron and nickel. It consists of two parts—a liquid outer core and a solid inner core.** Together, the inner and outer core are 3,486 kilometers thick.

**Outer Core and Inner Core** The **outer core** is a layer of molten metal that surrounds the inner core. Despite enormous pressure, the outer core is liquid. The **inner core** is a dense ball of solid metal. In the inner core, extreme pressure squeezes the atoms of iron and nickel so much that they cannot spread out and become liquid.

Most of the current evidence suggests that both parts of the core are made of iron and nickel. But scientists have found data suggesting that the core also contains substances such as oxygen, sulfur, and silicon. Scientists must seek more data before they decide which of these other substances is most important.

 **Reading Checkpoint** What is the main difference between the outer core and the inner core?

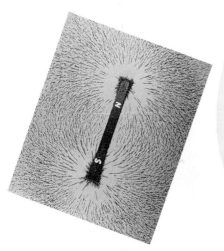

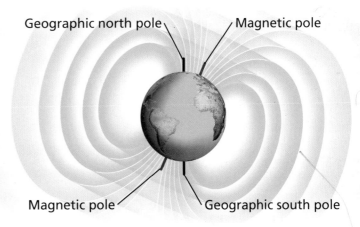

Geographic north pole · Magnetic pole

Magnetic pole · Geographic south pole

**Bar Magnet's Magnetic Field**
The pattern of iron filings was made by sprinkling them on paper placed under a bar magnet.

**Earth's Magnetic Field**
Like a magnet, Earth's magnetic field has north and south poles.

**The Core and Earth's Magnetic Field** Scientists think that movements in the liquid outer core create Earth's magnetic field. Because Earth has a magnetic field, the planet acts like a giant bar magnet. As you can see in Figure 7, the magnetic field affects the whole Earth.

Consider an ordinary bar magnet. If you place it on a piece of paper and sprinkle iron filings on the paper, the iron filings line up with the bar's magnetic field. If you could cover the entire planet with iron filings, they would form a similar pattern. When you use a compass, the compass needle aligns with the lines of force in Earth's magnetic field.

**FIGURE 7**
**Earth's Magnetic Field**
Just as a bar magnet is surrounded by its own magnetic field, Earth's magnetic field surrounds the planet.
**Relating Cause and Effect** *If you shifted the magnet beneath the paper, what would happen to the iron filings?*

---

## Section 1 Assessment

**Target Reading Skill** **Using Prior Knowledge**
Review your graphic organizer and revise it based on what you just learned in the section.

### Reviewing Key Concepts

**1. a. Explaining** Why is it difficult to determine Earth's inner structure?
   **b. Inferring** How are seismic waves used to provide evidence about Earth's interior?
**2. a. Listing** List Earth's three main layers.
   **b. Comparing and Contrasting** What is the difference between the lithosphere and the asthenosphere? In which layer is each located?

**c. Classifying** Classify each of the following layers as liquid, solid, or solid but able to flow slowly: lithosphere, asthenosphere, lower mantle, outer core, inner core.

## Writing in Science

**Narrative** Write a narrative of your own imaginary journey to the center of Earth. Your narrative should describe the layers of Earth through which you travel and how temperature and pressure change beneath the surface.

# Convection and the Mantle

## Reading Preview

### Key Concepts
- How is heat transferred?
- What causes convection currents?
- What causes convection currents in Earth's mantle?

### Key Terms
- radiation • conduction
- convection • density
- convection current

### 🎯 Target Reading Skill
**Outlining** An outline shows the relationship between major ideas and supporting ideas. As you read, make an outline about heat transfer. Use the red headings for the main topics and the blue headings for the subtopics.

| Convection and the Mantle |
|---|
| I. Types of Heat Transfer |
|   A. Radiation |
|   B. |
|   C. |
| II. Convection Currents |

## Lab zone Discover **Activity**

### How Can Heat Cause Motion in a Liquid?

1. Carefully pour some hot water into a small, shallow pan. Fill a clear, plastic cup about half full with cold water. Place the cup in the pan.
2. Allow the water to stand for two minutes until all motion stops.
3. Fill a plastic dropper with some food coloring. Then, holding the dropper under the water's surface and slightly away from the edge of the cup, gently squeeze a small droplet of the food coloring into the water.
4. Observe the water for one minute.
5. Add another droplet at the water's surface in the middle of the cup and observe again.

**Think It Over**
**Inferring** How do you explain what happened to the droplets of food coloring? Why do you think the second droplet moved in a way that was different from the way the first droplet moved?

Earth's molten outer core is nearly as hot as the surface of the sun. What makes an object hot? Whether the object is Earth's core or a cooking pot, the cause is the same. When an object is heated, the particles that make up the object move faster. The faster-moving particles have more energy.

If you have ever touched a hot pot accidentally, you have discovered for yourself (in a painful way) that heat moves. In this case, it moved from the hot pot to your hand. The movement of energy from a warmer object to a cooler object is called heat transfer. To explain how heat moves from Earth's core through the mantle, you need to know how heat is transferred.

# Types of Heat Transfer

Heat always moves from a warmer substance to a cooler substance. For example, holding an ice cube will make your hand begin to feel cold in a few seconds. But is the coldness in the ice cube moving to your hand? No! Since cold is the absence of heat, it's the heat in your hand that moves to the ice cube. This is one of the ways that heat is transferred. **There are three types of heat transfer: radiation, conduction, and convection.**

**Radiation** The transfer of energy through space is called **radiation.** Heat transfer by radiation takes place with no direct contact between a heat source and an object. Sunlight is radiation that warms Earth's surface. Other familiar forms of radiation include the heat you feel around a flame or open fire.

**Conduction** Heat transfer within a material or between materials that are touching is called **conduction.** For example, a spoon in a pot of soup heats up by conduction, as shown in Figure 8. Heat moves from the hot soup and the pot to the particles that make up the spoon. The particles near the bottom of the spoon vibrate faster as they are heated, so they bump into other particles and heat them, too. Gradually the entire spoon heats up. When your hand touches the spoon, conduction transfers heat from the spoon directly to your skin. Then you feel the heat. Conduction is responsible for some of the heat transfer inside Earth.

✓ Reading Checkpoint  **What is conduction?**

**FIGURE 8**
**Conduction**
In conduction, the heated particles of a substance transfer heat through contact with other particles in the substance. Conduction heats the spoon and the pot itself. That's why you need a mitt to protect your hand from the hot handle.

# Go Online

PHSchool.com

**For:** More on convection currents in the mantle
**Visit:** PHSchool.com
**Web Code:** cfd-1012

**Convection** Heat can also be transferred by the movement of fluids—liquids and gases. **Convection** is heat transfer by the movement of currents within a fluid. During convection, heated particles of fluid begin to flow. This flow transfers heat from one part of the fluid to another.

Heat transfer by convection is caused by differences of temperature and density within a fluid. **Density** is a measure of how much mass there is in a volume of a substance. For example, rock is more dense than water because a given volume of rock has more mass than the same volume of water.

When a liquid or gas is heated, the particles move faster and spread apart. As a result, the particles of the heated fluid occupy more space. The fluid's density decreases. But when a fluid cools, its particles move more slowly and settle together more closely. As the fluid becomes cooler, its density increases.

## Convection Currents

When you heat soup on a stove, convection occurs in the soup, as shown in Figure 9. As the soup at the bottom of the pot gets hot, it expands and therefore becomes less dense. The warm, less dense soup moves upward and floats over the cooler, denser soup. At the surface, the warm soup cools, becoming denser. Then gravity pulls this cooler, denser soup back down to the bottom of the pot, where it is heated again.

A constant flow begins as the cooler, denser soup sinks to the bottom of the pot and the warmer, less dense soup rises. A **convection current** is the flow that transfers heat within a fluid. **Heating and cooling of the fluid, changes in the fluid's density, and the force of gravity combine to set convection currents in motion.** Convection currents continue as long as heat is added. Without heat, convection currents eventually stop.

**Reading Checkpoint** What is the role of gravity in creating convection currents?

**FIGURE 9**
**Convection Currents**
Differences in temperature and density cause convection currents. In the pot, convection currents arise because the soup close to the heat source is hotter and less dense than the soup near the surface.

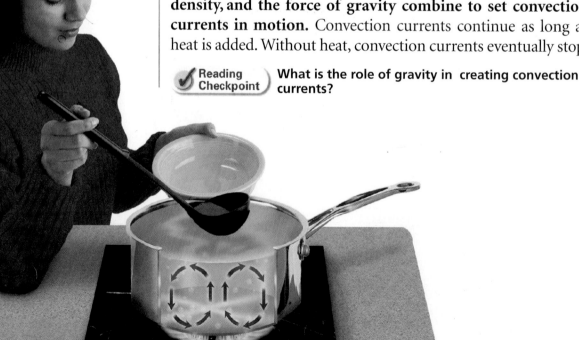

# Convection Currents in Earth

In Earth's mantle, large amounts of heat are transferred by convection currents, as shown in Figure 10. **Heat from the core and the mantle itself causes convection currents in the mantle.**

How is it possible for mantle rock to flow? Over millions of years, the great heat and pressure in the mantle cause solid mantle rock to flow very slowly. Many geologists think that plumes of mantle rock rise slowly from the bottom of the mantle toward the top. The hot rock eventually cools and sinks back through the mantle. Over and over, the cycle of rising and sinking takes place. Convection currents like these have been moving inside Earth for more than four billion years!

There are also convection currents in the outer core. These convection currents cause Earth's magnetic field.

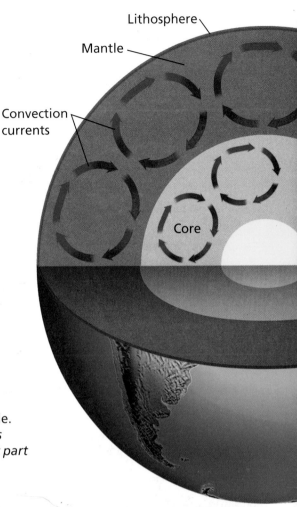

Lithosphere

Mantle

Convection currents

Core

FIGURE 10
**Mantle Convection**
Most geologists think that convection currents rise and sink through the mantle.
**Applying Concepts** *What part of Earth's interior is like the soup in the pot? What part is like the burner on the stove?*

# Section 2 Assessment

**Target Reading Skill** Outlining Use the information in your outline about heat transfer to help you answer the questions below.

## Reviewing Key Concepts

1. **a. Listing** What are the three types of heat transfer?
   **b. Explaining** How is heat transferred through space?
2. **a. Defining** What is a convection current?
   **b. Relating Cause and Effect** In general, what happens to the density of a fluid as it becomes hotter?
   **c. Summarizing** Describe how convection currents form.
3. **a. Identifying** Name two layers of Earth in which convection currents take place.
   **b. Relating Cause and Effect** What causes convection currents in the mantle?
   **c. Predicting** What will happen to the convection currents in the mantle if Earth's interior eventually cools down? Explain.

**Lab zone** At-Home **Activity**

**Tracing Heat Flow** Convection currents may keep the air inside your home at a comfortable temperature. Air is made up of gases, so it is a fluid. Regardless of the type of home heating system, heated air circulates through a room by convection. You may have tried to adjust the flow of air in a stuffy room by opening a window. When you did so, you were making use of convection currents. With an adult family member, study how your home is heated. Look for evidence of convection currents.

# Drifting Continents

## Reading Preview

### Key Concepts
- What was Alfred Wegener's hypothesis about the continents?
- What evidence supported Wegener's hypothesis?
- Why was Wegener's hypothesis rejected by most scientists of his day?

### Key Terms
- continental drift
- Pangaea
- fossil

### Target Reading Skill

**Identifying Supporting Evidence** As you read, identify the evidence that supports the hypothesis of continental drift. Write the evidence in a graphic organizer like the one below.

Evidence

Hypothesis

Shape of continents

Earth's continents have moved.

## Lab zone — Discover **Activity**

### How Are Earth's Continents Linked Together?

1. Find the oceans and the seven continents on a globe showing Earth's physical features.
2. How much of the globe is occupied by the Pacific Ocean? Does most of Earth's dry land lie in the Northern or Southern Hemisphere?
3. Find the points or areas where most of the continents are connected. Find the points at which several of the continents almost touch, but are not connected.
4. Examine the globe more closely. Find the great belt of mountains running from north to south along the western side of North and South America. Can you find another great belt of mountains on the globe?

**Think It Over**
**Posing Questions** What questions can you pose about how oceans, continents, and mountains are distributed on Earth's surface?

Five hundred years ago, the sea voyages of Columbus and other explorers changed the map of the world. The continents of Europe, Asia, and Africa were already known to mapmakers. Soon mapmakers were also showing the outlines of the continents of North and South America. Looking at these world maps, many people wondered why the coasts of several continents matched so neatly. For example, the coasts of Africa and South America look as if they could fit together like jigsaw-puzzle pieces. In the 1700s, geologists thought that the continents had always remained in the same place. But early in the 1900s, one scientist began to think that the continents could have once been joined in a single landmass.

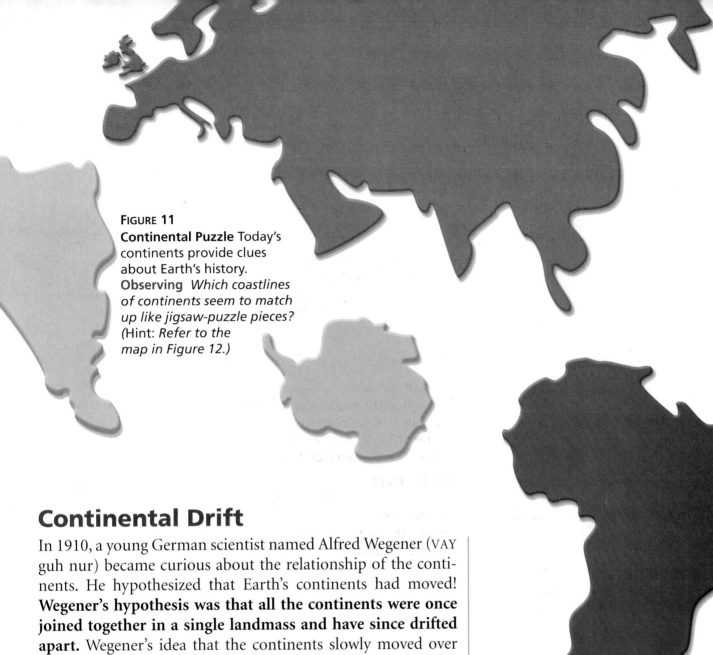

**FIGURE 11**
**Continental Puzzle** Today's continents provide clues about Earth's history.
**Observing** *Which coastlines of continents seem to match up like jigsaw-puzzle pieces?* (Hint: *Refer to the map in Figure 12.*)

# Continental Drift

In 1910, a young German scientist named Alfred Wegener (VAY guh nur) became curious about the relationship of the continents. He hypothesized that Earth's continents had moved! **Wegener's hypothesis was that all the continents were once joined together in a single landmass and have since drifted apart.** Wegener's idea that the continents slowly moved over Earth's surface became known as **continental drift.**

According to Wegener, the continents drifted together to form the supercontinent **Pangaea** (pan JEEuh). *Pangaea* means "all lands." According to Wegener, Pangaea existed about 300 million years ago. This was the time when reptiles and winged insects first appeared. Tropical forests, which later formed coal deposits, covered large parts of Earth's surface.

Over tens of millions of years, Pangaea began to break apart. The pieces of Pangaea slowly moved toward their present-day locations. These pieces became the continents as they are today.

**Wegener gathered evidence from different scientific fields to support his ideas about continental drift. He studied land features, fossils, and evidence of climate change.** In 1915, Wegener published his evidence for continental drift in a book called *The Origin of Continents and Oceans.*

**For:** Links on continental drift
**Visit:** www.SciLinks.org
**Web Code:** scn-1013

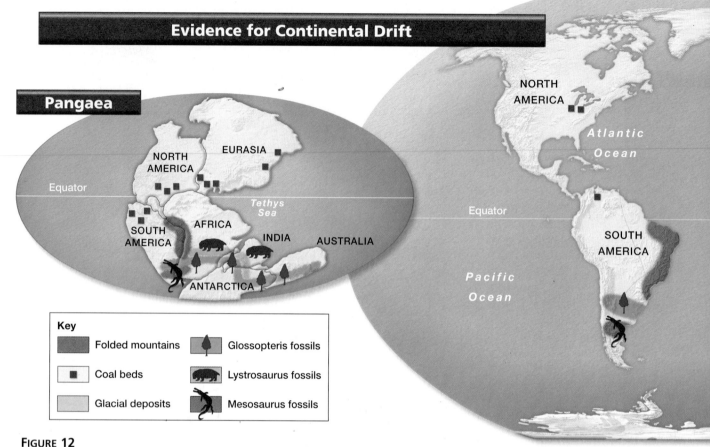

**Pangaea**

FIGURE 12

Fossils and rocks found on different continents provide evidence that Earth's landmasses once were joined together in the supercontinent Pangaea.

**Inferring** *What do the matching mountain ranges in Africa and South America show, according to Wegener's hypothesis?*

**Evidence From Land Features** As shown in Figure 12, mountains and other features on the continents provided evidence for continental drift. For example, when Wegener pieced together maps of Africa and South America, he noticed that mountain ranges on both continents line up. He noticed that European coal fields match up with coal fields in North America.

**Evidence From Fossils** Wegener also used fossils to support his argument for continental drift. A **fossil** is any trace of an ancient organism that has been preserved in rock. For example, *Glossopteris* (glaw SAHP tuh ris), was a fernlike plant that lived 250 million years ago. *Glossopteris* fossils have been found in rocks in Africa, South America, Australia, India, and Antarctica. The occurrence of *Glossopteris* on these widely separated landmasses convinced Wegener that Pangaea had existed.

Other examples include fossils of the freshwater reptiles *Mesosaurus* and *Lystrosaurus*. These fossils have also been found in places now separated by oceans. Neither reptile could have swum great distances across salt water. Wegener inferred that these reptiles lived on a single landmass that has since split apart.

**Lystrosaurus**

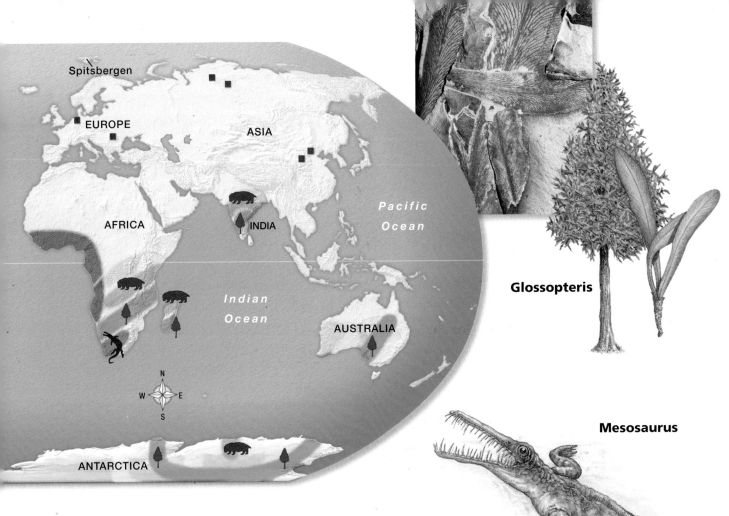

Glossopteris

Mesosaurus

**Evidence From Climate** Wegener used evidence of climate change to support his hypothesis. As a continent moves toward the equator, its climate becomes warmer. As a continent moves toward the poles, its climate becomes colder. But the continent carries with it the fossils and rocks that formed at its previous locations. For example, fossils of tropical plants are found on Spitsbergen, an island in the Arctic Ocean. When these plants lived about 300 million years ago, the island must have had a warm and mild climate. According to Wegener, Spitsbergen must have been located closer to the equator.

Geologists found evidence that when it was warm in Spitsbergen, the climate was much colder in South Africa. Deep scratches in rocks showed that continental glaciers once covered South Africa. Continental glaciers are thick layers of ice that cover hundreds of thousands of square kilometers. But the climate of South Africa is too mild today for continental glaciers to form. Wegener concluded that when Pangaea existed, South Africa was much closer to the South Pole. According to Wegener, the climates of Spitsbergen and South Africa changed because these landmasses had moved.

 **Reading Checkpoint** How would continental drift affect a continent's climate?

# Wegener's Hypothesis Rejected

Wegener attempted to explain how continental drift took place. He suggested that the continents plowed across the ocean floors. **Unfortunately, Wegener could not provide a satisfactory explanation for the force that pushes or pulls the continents.** Because Wegener could not identify the cause of continental drift, most geologists rejected his idea.

For geologists to accept continental drift, they would also have had to change their ideas about how mountains form. In the early 1900s, many geologists thought that mountains formed because Earth was slowly cooling and shrinking. According to this hypothesis, mountains formed when the crust wrinkled like the skin of a dried-up apple.

Wegener said that if these geologists were correct, then mountains should be found all over Earth's surface. But mountains usually occur in narrow bands along the edges of continents. Wegener developed a hypothesis that better explained where mountains occur and how they form. Wegener proposed that when continents collide, their edges crumple and fold. The folding continents push up huge mountains.

 **Reading Checkpoint** According to Wegener, how do mountains form?

**FIGURE 13**
**Alfred Wegener**
Although scientists rejected his theory, Wegener continued to collect evidence on continental drift and to update his book. He died in 1930 on an expedition to explore Greenland's continental glacier.

## Section 3 Assessment

### Target Reading Skill

**Identifying Supporting Evidence** Refer to your graphic organizer about continental drift as you answer Question 2 below.

### Reviewing Key Concepts

1. a. **Identifying** Who proposed the concept of continental drift?
   b. **Summarizing** According to the hypothesis of continental drift, how would a world map have changed over the last 250 million years?
2. a. **Reviewing** What evidence supported the hypothesis of continental drift?
   b. **Explaining** How did fossils provide evidence for continental drift?
   c. **Forming Hypotheses** Deposits of coal have been found beneath the ice of Antarctica. But coal only forms in warm swamps. Use Wegener's hypothesis to explain how coal could be found so near to the South Pole.

3. a. **Explaining** Why did most scientists reject Wegener's hypothesis of continental drift?
   b. **Making Judgments** Do you think the scientists of Wegener's time should have accepted his hypothesis? Why or why not?

**Lab zone** At-Home **Activity**

**Moving the Continents** Using a world map and tracing paper, trace the outlines of the continents that border the Atlantic Ocean. Label the continents. Then use scissors to carefully cut your map along the edges of the continents. Throw away the Atlantic Ocean. Place the two remaining pieces on a dark surface and ask family members to try to fit the two halves together. Explain to them about continental drift and Pangaea.

# Sea-Floor Spreading

## Reading Preview

### Key Concepts
- What is the process of sea-floor spreading?
- What is the evidence for sea-floor spreading?
- What happens at deep-ocean trenches?

### Key Terms
- mid-ocean ridge • sonar
- sea-floor spreading
- deep-ocean trench
- subduction

### ⊙ Target Reading Skill
**Sequencing** Make a flowchart to show the process of sea-floor spreading.

| Magma erupts along mid-ocean ridge |
| --- |

↓

| |
| --- |

↓

| |
| --- |

### What Is the Effect of a Change in Density?

1. Partially fill a sink or dishpan with water.
2. Open up a dry washcloth in your hand. Does the washcloth feel light or heavy?
3. Moisten one edge of the washcloth in the water. Then gently place the washcloth so that it floats on the water's surface. Observe the washcloth carefully (especially at its edges) as it starts to sink.
4. Remove the washcloth from the water and open it up in your hand. Is the mass of the washcloth the same as, less than, or greater than when it was dry?

**Think It Over**
**Observing** How did the washcloth's density change? What effect did this change in density have on the washcloth?

Deep in the ocean, the temperature is near freezing. There is no light, and living things are generally scarce. Yet some areas of the deep-ocean floor are teeming with life. One of these areas is the East Pacific Rise. This area forms part of the Pacific Ocean floor off the coasts of Mexico and South America. Here, ocean water sinks through cracks, or vents, in the crust. The water is heated by contact with hot material from the mantle. The hot water then spurts back into the ocean.

Around these hot-water vents live some of the most bizarre creatures ever discovered. Giant, red-tipped tube worms sway in the water. Nearby sit giant clams nearly a meter across. Strange spider-like crabs scuttle by. Surprisingly, the geological features of this strange environment provided some of the best evidence for Wegener's hypothesis of continental drift.

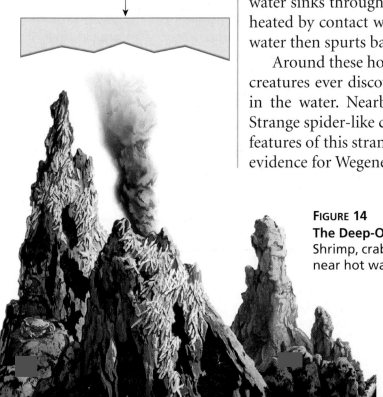

**FIGURE 14**
**The Deep-Ocean Floor**
Shrimp, crabs, and other organisms cluster near hot water vents in the ocean floor.

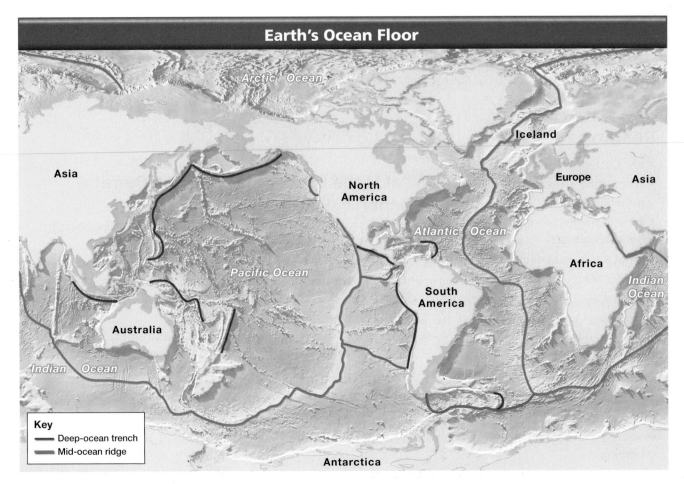

**FIGURE 15**
The mid-ocean ridge system is more than 50,000 kilometers long.
**Interpreting Maps** *What is unusual about Iceland?*

# Mid-Ocean Ridges

The East Pacific Rise is just one of many **mid-ocean ridges** that wind beneath Earth's oceans. In the mid-1900s, scientists mapped the mid-ocean ridges using sonar. **Sonar** is a device that bounces sound waves off underwater objects and then records the echoes of these sound waves. The time it takes for the echo to arrive indicates the distance to the object.

Mid-ocean ridges curve like the seam of a baseball along the sea floor. They extend into all of Earth's oceans. Figure 15 shows the location of these ridges. Most of the mountains in the mid-ocean ridge system lie hidden under hundreds of meters of water. But in a few places the ridge pokes above the surface. For example, the island of Iceland is a part of the mid-ocean ridge that rises above the surface in the North Atlantic Ocean. A steep-sided valley splits the top of some mid-ocean ridges.

The mapping of mid-ocean ridges made scientists curious to know more about them. What are the ridges? How do they form?

 **Reading Checkpoint** ) **What device is used to map the ocean floor?**

# What Is Sea-Floor Spreading?

Harry Hess, an American geologist, was one of the scientists who studied mid-ocean ridges. Hess carefully examined maps of the mid-ocean ridge system. Then he began to think about the ocean floor in relation to the problem of continental drift. Finally, he reached a startling conclusion: Maybe Wegener was right! Perhaps the continents do move.

In 1960, Hess proposed a radical idea. He suggested that a process he called **sea-floor spreading** continually adds new material to the ocean floor. **In sea-floor spreading, the sea floor spreads apart along both sides of a mid-ocean ridge as new crust is added. As a result, the ocean floors move like conveyor belts, carrying the continents along with them.** Look at Figure 16 to see the process of sea-floor spreading.

Sea-floor spreading begins at a mid-ocean ridge, which forms along a crack in the oceanic crust. Along the ridge, molten material that forms several kilometers beneath the surface rises and erupts. At the same time, older rock moves outward on both sides of the ridge. As the molten material cools, it forms a strip of solid rock in the center of the ridge. When more molten material flows into the crack, it forms a new strip of rock.

 **Reading Checkpoint** **How does new oceanic crust form?**

**Go Online**
PHSchool.com

**For:** More on sea-floor spreading
**Visit:** PHSchool.com
**Web Code:** cfd-1014

FIGURE 16
**Sea-Floor Spreading**
Molten material erupts through the valley that runs along the center of some mid-ocean ridges. This material hardens to form the rock of the ocean floor.
**Applying Concepts** *What happens to the rock along the ridge when new molten material erupts?*

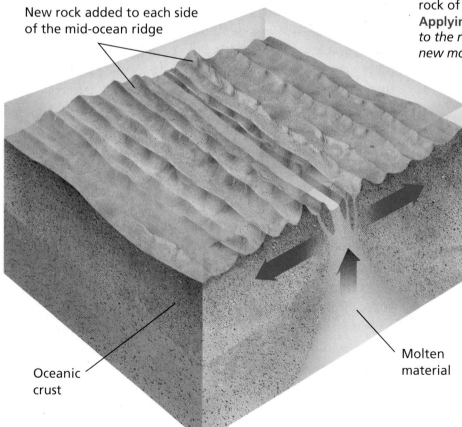

New rock added to each side of the mid-ocean ridge

Oceanic crust

Molten material

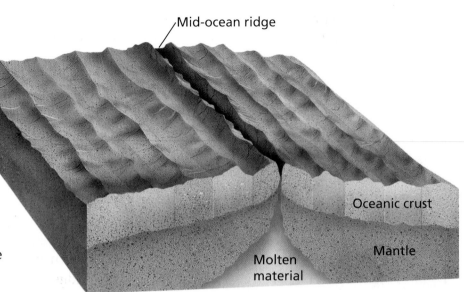

Mid-ocean ridge

Oceanic crust

Mantle

Molten material

Rock formed when Earth's magnetic field was normal

Rock formed when Earth's magnetic field was reversed

**FIGURE 17**
**Magnetic Stripes**
Magnetic stripes in the rock of the ocean floor show the direction of Earth's magnetic field at the time the rock hardened.
**Interpreting Diagrams** *How are these matching stripes evidence of sea-floor spreading?*

# Evidence for Sea-Floor Spreading

**Several types of evidence supported Hess's theory of sea-floor spreading: eruptions of molten material, magnetic stripes in the rock of the ocean floor, and the ages of the rocks themselves.** This evidence led scientists to look again at Wegener's hypothesis of continental drift.

**Evidence From Molten Material** In the 1960s, scientists found evidence that new material is indeed erupting along mid-ocean ridges. The scientists dived to the ocean floor in *Alvin,* a small submarine built to withstand the crushing pressures four kilometers down in the ocean. In a ridge's central valley, *Alvin's* crew found strange rocks shaped like pillows or like toothpaste squeezed from a tube. Such rocks form only when molten material hardens quickly after erupting under water. These rocks showed that molten material has erupted again and again along the mid-ocean ridge.

**Evidence From Magnetic Stripes** When scientists studied patterns in the rocks of the ocean floor, they found more support for sea-floor spreading. You read earlier that Earth behaves like a giant magnet, with a north pole and a south pole. Surprisingly, Earth's magnetic poles have reversed themselves many times during Earth's history. The last reversal happened 780,000 years ago. If the magnetic poles suddenly reversed themselves today, you would find that your compass needle points south.

Scientists discovered that the rock that makes up the ocean floor lies in a pattern of magnetized "stripes." These stripes hold a record of reversals in Earth's magnetic field. The rock of the ocean floor contains iron. The rock began as molten material that cooled and hardened. As the rock cooled, the iron bits inside lined up in the direction of Earth's magnetic poles. This locked the iron bits in place, giving the rocks a permanent "magnetic memory."

Using sensitive instruments, scientists recorded the magnetic memory of rocks on both sides of a mid-ocean ridge. They found that stripes of rock that formed when Earth's magnetic field pointed north alternate with stripes of rock that formed when the magnetic field pointed south. As shown in Figure 17, the pattern is the same on both sides of the ridge.

**Evidence From Drilling Samples**  The final proof of sea-floor spreading came from rock samples obtained by drilling into the ocean floor. The *Glomar Challenger,* a drilling ship built in 1968, gathered the samples. The *Glomar Challenger* sent drilling pipes through water six kilometers deep to drill holes in the ocean floor. This feat has been compared to using a sharp-ended wire to dig a hole into a sidewalk from the top of the Empire State Building.

Samples from the sea floor were brought up through the pipes. Then the scientists determined the age of the rocks in the samples. They found that the farther away from a ridge the samples were taken, the older the rocks were. The youngest rocks were always in the center of the ridges. This showed that sea-floor spreading really has taken place.

**Reading Checkpoint**  Why does the rock of the ocean floor have a pattern of magnetic stripes?

**Lab zone  Try This Activity**

## Reversing Poles

1. Cut six short pieces, each about 2.5 cm long, from a length of audiotape.
2. Tape one end of each piece of audiotape to a flat surface. The pieces should be spaced 1 cm apart and lined up lengthwise in a single row.
3. Touch a bar magnet's north pole to the first piece of audiotape. Then reverse the magnet and touch its south pole to the next piece.
4. Repeat Step 3 until you have applied the magnet to each piece of audiotape.
5. Sweep one end of the magnet about 1 cm above the line of audiotape pieces. Observe what happens.

**Making Models**  What characteristic of the ocean floor did you observe as you swept the magnet along the line of audiotape pieces?

**FIGURE 18**
**Sea-Floor Drilling**
The *Glomar Challenger* was the first research ship designed to drill samples of rock from the deep-ocean floor.

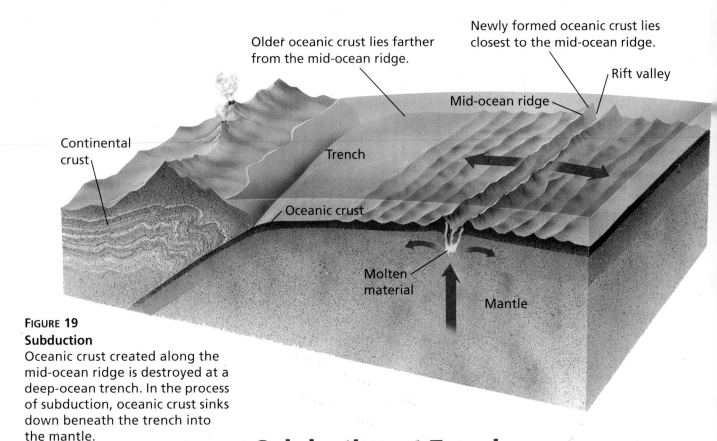

Older oceanic crust lies farther from the mid-ocean ridge.

Newly formed oceanic crust lies closest to the mid-ocean ridge.

Rift valley

Mid-ocean ridge

Continental crust

Trench

Oceanic crust

Molten material

Mantle

**FIGURE 19**
**Subduction**
Oceanic crust created along the mid-ocean ridge is destroyed at a deep-ocean trench. In the process of subduction, oceanic crust sinks down beneath the trench into the mantle.
**Drawing Conclusions** *Where would the densest oceanic crust be found?*

**Discovery CHANNEL SCHOOL**

*Plate Tectonics*

Video Preview
▶ Video Field Trip
Video Assessment

# Subduction at Trenches

How can the ocean floor keep getting wider and wider? The answer is that the ocean floor generally does not just keep spreading. Instead, the ocean floor plunges into deep underwater canyons called **deep-ocean trenches.** At a deep-ocean trench, the oceanic crust bends downward. What occurs at trenches? **In a process taking tens of millions of years, part of the ocean floor sinks back into the mantle at deep-ocean trenches.**

**The Process of Subduction** The process by which ocean floor sinks beneath a deep-ocean trench and back into the mantle is called **subduction** (sub DUK shun). As subduction occurs, crust closer to a mid-ocean ridge moves away from the ridge and toward a deep-ocean trench. Sea-floor spreading and subduction work together. They move the ocean floor as if it were on a giant conveyor belt.

New oceanic crust is hot. But as it moves away from the mid-ocean ridge, it cools and becomes more dense. Eventually, as shown in Figure 19, gravity pulls this older, denser oceanic crust down beneath the trench. The sinking crust is like the washcloth in the Discover activity at the beginning of this section. As the dry washcloth floating on the water gets wet, its density increases and it begins to sink.

**Subduction and Earth's Oceans** The processes of subduction and sea-floor spreading can change the size and shape of the oceans. Because of these processes, the ocean floor is renewed about every 200 million years. That is the time it takes for new rock to form at the mid-ocean ridge, move across the ocean, and sink into a trench.

The vast Pacific Ocean covers almost one third of the planet. And yet it is shrinking. How can that be? Sometimes a deep ocean trench swallows more oceanic crust than a mid-ocean ridge can produce. Then, if the ridge does not add new crust fast enough, the width of the ocean will shrink. In the Pacific Ocean, subduction through the many trenches that ring the ocean is occurring faster than new crust can be added.

On the other hand, the Atlantic Ocean is expanding. Unlike the Pacific Ocean, the Atlantic Ocean has only a few short trenches. As a result, the spreading ocean floor has virtually nowhere to go. In most places, the oceanic crust of the Atlantic Ocean floor is attached to the continental crust of the continents around the ocean. So as the Atlantic's ocean floor spreads, the continents along its edges also move. Over time, the whole ocean gets wider.

**FIGURE 20**
**Growing an Ocean**
Because of sea-floor spreading, the distance between Europe and North America is increasing by a few centimeters per year.

 **Reading Checkpoint** **Why is the Pacific Ocean shrinking?**

---

## Section 4 Assessment

**⊙ Target Reading Skill** Sequencing Refer to your flowchart on sea-floor spreading as you answer the questions below.

### Reviewing Key Concepts

1. a. **Naming** What scientist helped to discover the process of sea-floor spreading?
   b. **Identifying** Along what feature of the ocean floor does sea-floor spreading begin?
   c. **Sequencing** What are the steps in the process of sea-floor spreading?
2. a. **Reviewing** What three types of evidence provided support for the theory of sea-floor spreading?
   b. **Applying Concepts** How do rocks along the central valley of the mid-ocean ridge provide evidence of sea-floor spreading?
   c. **Predicting** Where would you expect to find the oldest rock on the ocean floor?

3. a. **Defining** What is a deep-ocean trench?
   b. **Relating Cause and Effect** What happens to oceanic crust at a deep-ocean trench?

## Writing in Science

**Description** Write a description of what you might see if you could explore a mid-ocean ridge in a vessel like the *Alvin*. In your description, be sure to include the main features of the ocean floor along and near the ridge.

**Skills Lab**

# Modeling Sea-Floor Spreading

## Problem

How does sea-floor spreading add material to the ocean floor?

## Skills Focus

making models

## Materials

- scissors
- colored marker
- metric ruler
- 2 sheets of unlined paper

## Procedure

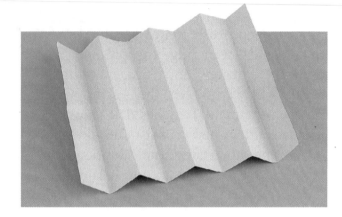

1. Draw stripes across one sheet of paper, parallel to the short sides of the paper. The stripes should vary in spacing and thickness.

2. Fold the paper in half lengthwise and write the word "Start" at the top of both halves of the paper. Using the scissors, carefully cut the paper in half along the fold line to form two strips.

3. Lightly fold the second sheet of paper into eighths. Then unfold it, leaving creases in the paper. Fold this sheet in half lengthwise.

4. Starting at the fold, draw lines 5.5 cm long on the middle crease and the two creases closest to the ends of the paper.

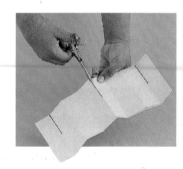

5. Now carefully cut along the lines you drew. Unfold the paper. There should be three slits in the center of the paper.

6. Put the two striped strips of paper together so their Start labels touch one another. Insert the Start ends of the strips up through the center slit and then pull them toward the side slits.

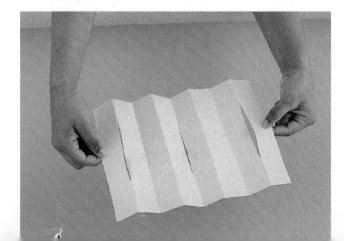

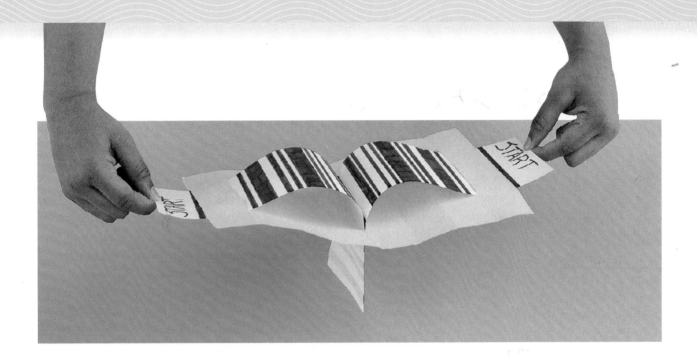

7. Insert the ends of the strips into the side slits. Pull the ends of the strips and watch what happens at the center slit.

8. Practice pulling the strips until you can make the two strips come up through the center and go down through the sides at the same time.

## Analyze and Conclude

1. **Making Models** What feature of the ocean floor does the center slit stand for? What prominent feature of the ocean floor is missing from the model at this point?

2. **Making Models** What do the side slits stand for? What does the space under the paper stand for?

3. **Comparing and Contrasting** As shown by your model, how does the ocean floor close to the center slit differ from the ocean floor near a side slit? How does this difference affect the depth of the ocean?

4. **Making Models** What do the stripes on the strips stand for? Why is it important that your model have an identical pattern of stripes on both sides of the center slit?

5. **Applying Concepts** Explain how differences in density and temperature provide some of the force needed to cause sea-floor spreading and subduction.

6. **Communicating** Use your own words to describe the process of sea-floor spreading. What parts of the process were not shown by your model?

## More to Explore

How could you modify your model to show an island that formed where a large amount of molten rock erupted from the mid-ocean ridge? How could you show what would happen to the island over a long period of time?

# The Theory of Plate Tectonics

## Reading Preview

### Key Concepts
- What is the theory of plate tectonics?
- What are the three types of plate boundaries?

### Key Terms
- plate
- scientific theory
- plate tectonics • fault
- divergent boundary
- rift valley
- convergent boundary
- transform boundary

### 🎯 Target Reading Skill

**Building Vocabulary** A definition states the meaning of a word or phrase by telling about its most important feature or function. After you read the section, reread the paragraphs that contain definitions of Key Terms. Use all the information you have learned to write a definition of each Key Term in your own words.

---

**Lab zone** **Discover Activity**

## How Well Do the Continents Fit Together?

1. Using a world map in an atlas, trace the shape of each continent and Madagascar on a sheet of paper. Also trace the shape of India and the Arabian Peninsula.
2. Carefully cut apart the landmasses, leaving Asia and Europe as one piece. Separate India and the Arabian Peninsula from Asia.
3. Piece together the continents as they may have looked before the breakup of Pangaea. Then attach your reconstruction of Pangaea to a sheet of paper.

**Think It Over**
**Drawing Conclusions** How well did the pieces of your continents fit together? Do your observations support the idea that today's landmasses were once joined together? Explain.

---

Have you ever dropped a hard-boiled egg? If so, you may have noticed that the eggshell cracked in an irregular pattern of pieces. Earth's lithosphere, its solid outer shell, is not one unbroken layer. It is more like that cracked eggshell. It's broken into pieces separated by jagged cracks.

A Canadian scientist, J. Tuzo Wilson, observed that there are cracks in the continents similar to those on the ocean floor. In 1965, Wilson proposed a new way of looking at these cracks. According to Wilson, the lithosphere is broken into separate sections called **plates.** The plates fit together along cracks in the lithosphere. As shown in Figure 22, the plates carry the continents or parts of the ocean floor, or both. Wilson combined what geologists knew about sea-floor spreading, Earth's plates, and continental drift into a single theory. A **scientific theory** is a well-tested concept that explains a wide range of observations.

**FIGURE 21**
**A Cracked Eggshell**
Earth's lithosphere is broken into plates like the cracked shell of a hard-boiled egg.

# How Plates Move

The theory of **plate tectonics** (tek TAHN iks) states that pieces of Earth's lithosphere are in slow, constant motion, driven by convection currents in the mantle. **The theory of plate tectonics explains the formation, movement, and subduction of Earth's plates.**

How can Earth's plates move? What force is great enough to move the heavy continents? Geologists think that movement of convection currents in the mantle is the major force that causes plate motion. During subduction, gravity pulls one edge of a plate down into the mantle. The rest of the plate also moves. This slow movement is similar to what happens in a pot of soup when gravity causes the cooler, denser soup near the surface to sink.

As the plates move, they collide, pull apart, or grind past each other, producing spectacular changes in Earth's surface. These changes include volcanoes, mountain ranges, and deep-ocean trenches.

**Lab zone** **Skills Activity**

## Predicting

Study the map of Earth's plates in Figure 22. Notice the arrows that show the direction of plate movement. Now find the Nazca plate on the map. Which direction is it moving? Find the South American plate and describe its movement. What do you think will happen as these plates continue to move?

**FIGURE 22**

Plate boundaries divide the lithosphere into large plates.
**Interpreting Maps** *Which plates include only ocean floor? Which plates include both continents and ocean floor?*

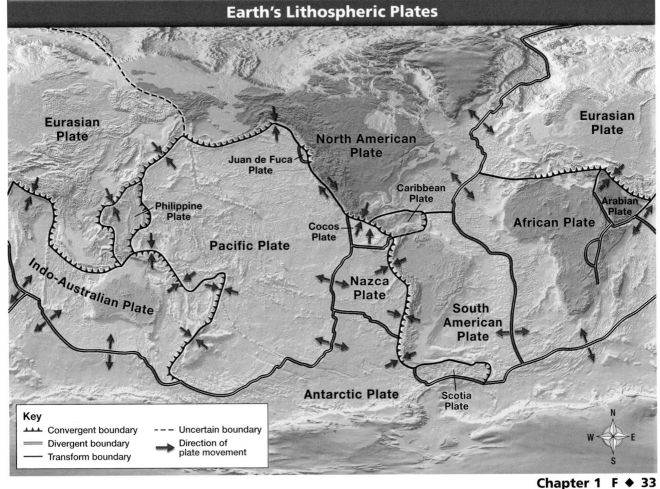

**Earth's Lithospheric Plates**

Eurasian Plate

North American Plate

Juan de Fuca Plate

Philippine Plate

Caribbean Plate

Cocos Plate

Pacific Plate

Indo-Australian Plate

Nazca Plate

Eurasian Plate

Arabian Plate

African Plate

South American Plate

Antarctic Plate

Scotia Plate

**Key**

▲▲▲ Convergent boundary
═══ Divergent boundary
—— Transform boundary
- - - Uncertain boundary
➜ Direction of plate movement

N W E S

# Plate Boundaries

The edges of Earth's plates meet at plate boundaries. Plate boundaries extend deep into the lithosphere. **Faults**—breaks in Earth's crust where rocks have slipped past each other—form along these boundaries. **As shown in Figure 23, there are three kinds of plate boundaries: divergent boundaries, convergent boundaries, and transform boundaries. A different type of plate movement occurs along each type of boundary.**

Scientists have used instruments on satellites to measure plate motion very precisely. The plates move at amazingly slow rates: from about 1 to 24 centimeters per year. The North American and Eurasian plates are moving apart at a rate of 2.5 centimeters per year. That's about as fast as your fingernails grow. This may not seem like much, but these plates have been moving apart for tens of millions of years.

**Divergent Boundaries**  The place where two plates move apart, or diverge, is called a **divergent boundary** (dy VUR junt). Most divergent boundaries occur along the mid-ocean ridges where sea-floor spreading occurs.

Divergent boundaries also occur on land. When a divergent boundary develops on land, two of Earth's plates slide apart. A deep valley called a **rift valley** forms along the divergent boundary. For example, the Great Rift Valley in East Africa marks a deep crack in the African continent.

FIGURE 23
## Plate Tectonics

Plate movements have built many of the features of Earth's land surfaces and ocean floors.
**Predicting**  *What will eventually happen if a rift valley continues to pull apart?*

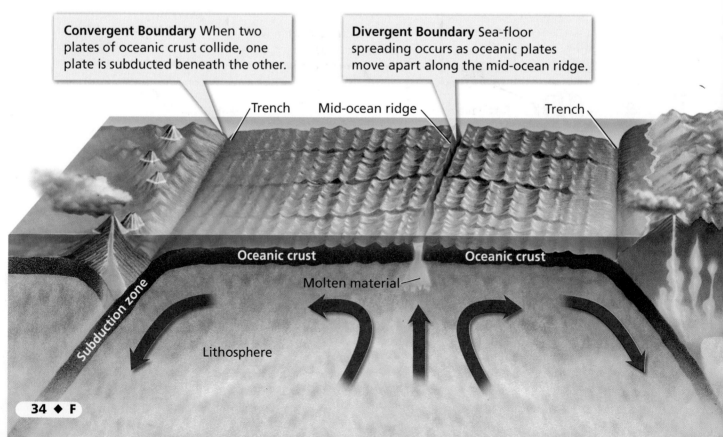

**Convergent Boundary** When two plates of oceanic crust collide, one plate is subducted beneath the other.

**Divergent Boundary** Sea-floor spreading occurs as oceanic plates move apart along the mid-ocean ridge.

Trench    Mid-ocean ridge    Trench

Oceanic crust    Oceanic crust

Molten material

Subduction zone

Lithosphere

**Convergent Boundaries** The place where two plates come together, or converge, is called a **convergent boundary** (kun VUR junt). When two plates converge, the result is called a collision. When two plates collide, the density of the plates determines which one comes out on top.

Oceanic crust becomes cooler and denser as it spreads away from the mid-ocean ridge. Where two plates carrying oceanic crust meet at a trench, the plate that is more dense sinks under the other plate.

Sometimes a plate carrying oceanic crust collides with a plate carrying continental crust. Oceanic crust is more dense than continental crust. The less dense continental crust can't sink under the more dense oceanic crust. Instead, subduction occurs as the oceanic plate sinks beneath the continental plate.

When two plates carrying continental crust collide, subduction does not take place. Neither piece of crust is dense enough to sink very far into the mantle. Instead, the collision squeezes the crust into mighty mountain ranges.

**Transform Boundaries** A **transform boundary** is a place where two plates slip past each other, moving in opposite directions. Earthquakes often occur along transform boundaries, but crust is neither created nor destroyed.

 **Reading Checkpoint** What features form where two continental plates come together?

 **Math Skills**

## Calculating a Rate

To calculate the rate of plate motion, divide the distance the plate moves by the time it takes to move that distance.

$$Rate = \frac{Distance}{Time}$$

For example, a plate takes 2 million years to move 156 km. Calculate its rate of motion.

$$\frac{156 \text{ km}}{2,000,000 \text{ years}} = 7.8 \text{ cm per year}$$

**Practice Problem** The Pacific plate is sliding past the North American plate. It has taken 10 million years for the plate to move 600 km. What is the Pacific plate's rate of motion?

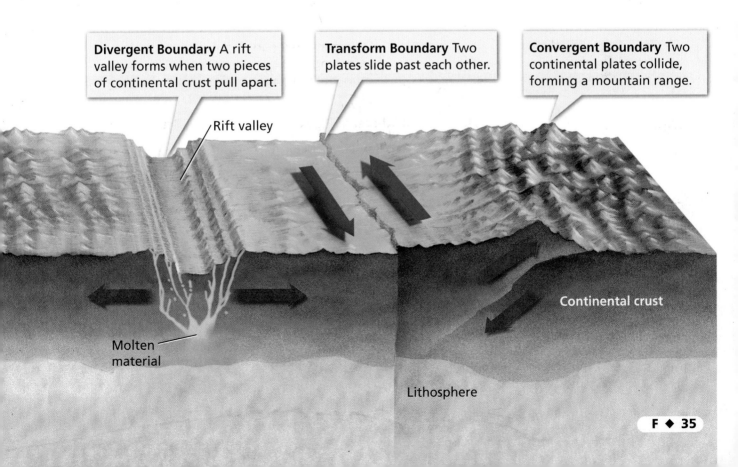

**Divergent Boundary** A rift valley forms when two pieces of continental crust pull apart.

**Transform Boundary** Two plates slide past each other.

**Convergent Boundary** Two continental plates collide, forming a mountain range.

Rift valley

Molten material

Continental crust

Lithosphere

**225 Million Years Ago**

**Plate Motions Over Time** The movement of Earth's plates has greatly changed Earth's surface. Geologists have evidence that, before Pangaea existed, other supercontinents formed and split apart over billions of years. Pangaea itself formed when Earth's landmasses drifted together about 260 million years ago. Then, about 225 million years ago, Pangaea began to break apart. Figure 24 shows how major landmasses have moved since the breakup of Pangaea.

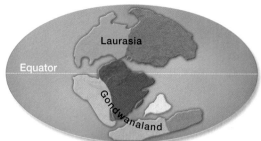

**180–200 Million Years Ago**

**FIGURE 24**
**Continental Drift**
It has taken the continents about 225 million years since the breakup of Pangaea to move to their present locations. **Posing Questions** *What questions would you need to answer in order to predict where the continents will be in 50 million years?*

**135 Million Years Ago**

**Earth Today**

**Go Online**
**active art**

**For:** Continental Drift activity
**Visit:** PHSchool.com
**Web Code:** cfp-1015

---

## Section 5 Assessment

🎯 **Target Reading Skill** **Building Vocabulary** Use your definitions to help answer the questions.

### Reviewing Key Concepts

**1. a. Defining** What are plates?
  **b. Summarizing** In your own words, what is the theory of plate tectonics?
  **c. Relating Cause and Effect** What do scientists think causes the movement of Earth's plates?
**2. a. Listing** What are the three types of plate boundaries?
  **b. Describing** Describe the type of movement that occurs at each type of plate boundary.
  **c. Predicting** What is likely to occur at a plate boundary where oceanic crust collides with continental crust?

**Math** ▶ **Practice**

**3. Calculating a Rate** There are two islands on opposite sides of a mid-ocean ridge in the Atlantic Ocean. During the last 8 million years, the distance between the islands has increased by 200 kilometers. Calculate the rate at which the two plates are diverging.

# Modeling Mantle Convection Currents

## Problem
How might convection in Earth's mantle affect tectonic plates?

## Skills Focus
making models, observing

## Materials
- large plastic bottle • food coloring • small glass jar • aluminum foil or plastic wrap
- rubber band • several paper hole punches or small pieces of paper • tap water

## Procedure
1. Fill the large bottle about half full with cold tap water.
2. Partly fill the small jar with hot tap water and stir in 6 drops of food coloring. Carefully add enough hot water to fill the jar to the brim.
3. Cover the top of the jar with aluminum foil or plastic wrap and secure with a rubber band.
4. Carefully lower the jar into the bottle of tap water.
5. Place the pieces of paper on the surface of the water.
6. Without disturbing the water, use the tip of the pencil to make two small holes about 2–4 mm in diameter in the material covering the jar.
7. Predict what will happen to the colored water and to the pieces of paper floating on the surface.
8. Observe the contents of the jar, as well as the paper pieces on the surface of the water.

## Analyze and Conclude
1. **Observing** Describe what happened to the colored water and to the pieces of paper after the holes were punched in the material covering the jar.
2. **Drawing Conclusions** How did your prediction compare with what actually happened to the colored water and pieces of paper?
3. **Inferring** What type of heat transfer took place in the bottle? Describe how the transfer occurred.
4. **Making Models** Which part of your model represents a tectonic plate? Which part represents Earth's mantle?
5. **Communicating** How well do you think this lab modeled the movement of Earth's plates? What similarities exist between this model and actual plate movement? What factors weren't you able to model in this lab?

## Designing Experiments
Repeat this activity, but develop a plan to measure the temperature of the water inside the large bottle. Is there a difference in temperature between the water's surface and the water near the top of the small jar? Do you observe any change in the convection currents as the water temperature changes? With your teacher's approval, carry out your plan.

# Study Guide

Equator  Pangaea

## 1 Earth's Interior

**Key Concepts**

- Geologists have used two main types of evidence to learn about Earth's interior: direct evidence from rock samples and indirect evidence from seismic waves.

- The three main layers of Earth are the crust, the mantle, and the core. These layers vary greatly in size, composition, temperature, and pressure.

- The crust is a layer of solid rock that includes both dry land and the ocean floor.

- Earth's mantle is made up of rock that is very hot, but solid. Scientists divide the mantle into layers based on physical characteristics.

- The core is made mostly of the metals iron and nickel. It consists of two parts—a liquid outer core and a solid inner core.

**Key Terms**

- seismic waves • pressure • crust • basalt
- granite • mantle • lithosphere
- asthenosphere • outer core • inner core

## 2 Convection and the Mantle

**Key Concepts**

- There are three types of heat transfer: radiation, conduction, and convection.

- Heating and cooling of the fluid, changes in the fluid's density, and the force of gravity combine to set convection currents in motion.

- Heat from the core and the mantle itself causes convection currents in the mantle.

**Key Terms**

- radiation • conduction • convection
- density • convection current

## 3 Drifting Continents

**Key Concepts**

- Wegener's hypothesis was that all the continents had once been joined together in a single landmass and have since drifted apart.

- Wegener gathered evidence from different scientific fields to support his ideas about continental drift. He studied land features, fossils, and evidence of climate change.

- Wegener could not provide a satisfactory explanation for the force that pushes or pulls the continents.

**Key Terms**

- continental drift • Pangaea • fossil

## 4 Sea-Floor Spreading

**Key Concepts**

- In sea-floor spreading, the sea floor spreads apart along both sides of a mid-ocean ridge as new crust is added. As a result, the ocean floors move like conveyor belts, carrying the continents along with them.

- Several types of evidence supported Hess's theory of sea-floor spreading: eruptions of molten material, magnetic stripes in the rock of the ocean floor, and the ages of the rocks.

- In a process taking tens of millions of years, part of the ocean floor sinks back into the mantle at deep-ocean trenches.

**Key Terms**

- mid-ocean ridge • sonar • sea-floor spreading
- deep-ocean trench • subduction

## 5 The Theory of Plate Tectonics

**Key Concepts**

- The theory of plate tectonics explains the formation, movement, and subduction of Earth's plates.

- There are three kinds of plate boundaries: divergent boundaries, convergent boundaries, and transform boundaries. A different type of plate movement occurs along each.

**Key Terms**

- plate • scientific theory • plate tectonics
- fault • divergent boundary • rift valley
- convergent boundary • transform boundary

# Review and Assessment

**Go Online**
PHSchool.com

**For:** Self-Assessment
**Visit:** PHSchool.com
**Web Code:** cfa-1010

## Organizing Information

**Comparing and Contrasting** Fill in the compare-and-contrast table to compare the characteristics of the different types of plate boundaries. Then give it a title.

| Type of Plate Boundary | Type of Motion | Effect on Crust | Feature(s) Formed |
|---|---|---|---|
| a. _____?_____ boundary | Plates slide past each other. | b. _____?_____ | c. _____?_____ |
| d. _____?_____ boundary | e. _____?_____ | Subduction or mountain building | f. _____?_____ |
| g. _____?_____ boundary | h. _____?_____ | i. _____?_____ | Mid-ocean ridge, ocean floor |

## Reviewing Key Terms

**Choose the letter of the best answer.**

1. The relatively soft layer of the upper mantle is the
   a. asthenosphere.
   b. lithosphere.
   c. inner core.
   d. continental crust.

2. The transfer of heat by the direct contact of particles of matter is
   a. pressure.
   b. radiation.
   c. conduction.
   d. convection.

3. Subduction of the ocean floor takes place at
   a. the lower mantle.
   b. mid-ocean ridges.
   c. rift valleys.
   d. trenches.

4. The process that powers plate tectonics is
   a. radiation.
   b. convection.
   c. conduction.
   d. subduction.

5. Two plates collide with each other at
   a. a divergent boundary.
   b. a convergent boundary.
   c. the boundary between the mantle and the crust.
   d. a transform boundary.

**If the statement is true, write *true*. If it is false, change the underlined word or words to make the statement true.**

6. Continental <u>crust</u> is made of rocks such as granite.

7. Slow movements of mantle rock called <u>radiation</u> transfer heat in the mantle.

8. The single landmass that broke apart 250 million years ago was <u>Pangaea</u>.

9. <u>Mid-ocean ridges</u> are places where oceanic crust sinks back to the mantle.

10. When two continental plates diverge, a <u>transform boundary</u> forms.

## Writing in Science

**Prediction** Now that you have learned about the theory of plate tectonics, write a paragraph predicting what the shape and positions of Earth's continents will be 50 million years in the future. Include what would happen to the oceans if continental landmasses became connected in new ways or drifted from their present locations.

**Discovery** CHANNEL SCHOOL™

*Plate Tectonics*

Video Preview
Video Field Trip
▶ Video Assessment

# Review and Assessment

## Checking Concepts

**11.** What kinds of indirect evidence do geologists use to study the structure of Earth?

**12.** How do temperature and pressure change as you go deeper into Earth?

**13.** What happens in Earth's interior to produce Earth's magnetic field? Describe the layer where the magnetic field is produced.

**14.** Why are there convection currents in the mantle?

**15.** Why are the oldest parts of the ocean floor no older than about 200 million years old?

**16.** How do magnetic stripes form on the ocean floor? Why are these stripes significant?

## Thinking Critically

**17. Comparing and Contrasting** How are oceanic and continental crust alike? How do they differ?

**18. Sequencing** Place these terms in correct order so they begin at Earth's surface and move toward the center: inner core, asthenosphere, lower mantle, lithosphere, outer core.

**19. Predicting** In the diagram below, a plate of oceanic crust is colliding with a plate of continental crust. What will happen? Why?

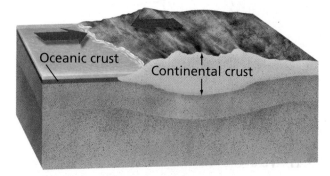

**20. Relating Cause and Effect** What do many geologists think is the driving force of plate tectonics? Explain.

**21. Making Judgments** Scientists refer to plate tectonics as a *theory*. What is a theory? How is plate tectonics a theory? Why isn't continental drift considered a theory? (*Hint*: Refer to the Skills Handbook for more on theories.)

## Math Practice

**22. Calculating a Rate** It takes 100,000 years for a plate to move about 14 kilometers. Calculate the rate of plate motion.

## Applying Skills

**Use the map to answer Questions 23–25.**

*Geologists think that a new plate boundary is forming in the Indian Ocean. The part of the plate carrying Australia is twisting away from the part of the plate carrying India.*

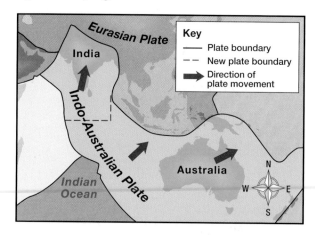

**23. Interpreting Maps** In what direction is the part of the plate carrying Australia moving? In what direction is the part carrying India moving?

**24. Predicting** As India and Australia move in different directions, what type of plate boundary will form between them?

**25. Inferring** What features could occur where the northern part of the Indo-Australian plate is colliding with the Eurasian plate?

## Lab zone Chapter **Project**

**Performance Assessment** Present your model to the class. Point out the types of plate boundaries on your model. Discuss the plate motions and landforms that result in these areas.

# Standardized Test Prep

**Choose the letter that best answers the question or completes the statement.**

1. Which of the following is evidence for sea-floor spreading?
   **A** matching patterns of magnetic stripes in the ocean floor
   **B** volcanic eruptions along mid-ocean ridges
   **C** older rock found farther from mid-ocean ridges
   **D** all of the above

2. Wegener thought the continents moved because fossils of the same organisms are found on widely separated continents. Wegener's use of fossil evidence is an example of a(n)
   **F** prediction.
   **G** observation.
   **H** inference.
   **J** controlled experiment.

3. The table below shows the movement of rock away from a mid-ocean ridge, and the time in years it takes sea-floor spreading to move the rock that distance.

| Distance (meters) | Time (years) |
|-------------------|--------------|
| 50                | 4,000        |
| 100               | 8,000        |
| 150               | 12,000       |

What is the speed of the rock?

  **F** 0.0125 m per year      **G** 12.5 m per year
  **H** 80 m per year         **J** 200,000 m per year

4. Which of the following best describes the process in the diagram below?
   **A** Converging plates form a transform boundary.
   **B** Converging plates form volcanoes.
   **C** Diverging plates form a mid-ocean ridge.
   **D** Diverging plates form a rift valley.

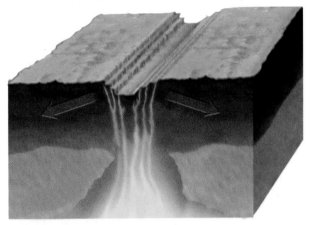

**Constructed Response**

5. Today, the Mediterranean Sea lies between Europe and Africa. But the African plate is moving toward the Eurasian plate at a rate of a few centimeters per year. Predict how this area will change in 100 million years. In your answer, first explain how the Mediterranean Sea will change. Then explain what will happen on land.

# Chapter

# 2

# Earthquakes

## Chapter Preview

interactive Textbook

An earthquake destroyed this freeway in Oakland, California, in 1989. ▶

## Lab zone™ Chapter Project

### Design and Build an Earthquake-Safe House

Earthquakes like the ones that caused the damage in this picture are proof that our planet is subject to great forces from within. Earthquakes remind us that we live on the moving pieces of Earth's crust. In this Chapter Project you will design a structure that can withstand earthquakes.

**Your Goal** To design, build, and test a model structure that is earthquake resistant

Your structure must

- be made of materials that have been approved by your teacher
- be built to specifications agreed on by your class
- be able to withstand several "earthquakes" of increasing intensity
- be built following the safety guidelines in Appendix A

**Plan It!** Before you design your model, find out how earthquakes damage structures such as homes, office buildings, and highways. Preview the chapter to find out how engineers design structures to withstand earthquakes. Then choose materials for your structure and sketch your design. When your teacher has approved your design, build and test your structure.

# Forces in Earth's Crust

## Reading Preview

### Key Concepts
- How does stress in the crust change Earth's surface?
- Where are faults usually found, and why do they form?
- What land features result from the forces of plate movement?

### Key Terms
- stress • tension
- compression • shearing
- normal fault • hanging wall
- footwall • reverse fault
- strike-slip fault • anticline
- syncline • plateau

### Target Reading Skill
**Building Vocabulary**
A definition states the meaning of a word or phrase. As you read, write a definition of each Key Term in your own words.

Lab zone Discover **Activity**

### How Does Stress Affect Earth's Crust?

1. Put on your goggles.
2. Holding a popsicle stick at both ends, slowly bend it into an arch.
3. Release the pressure on the popsicle stick and observe what happens.
4. Repeat Steps 1 and 2. This time, however, keep bending the ends of the popsicle stick toward each other. What happens to the wood?

**Think It Over**
**Predicting** Think of the popsicle stick as a model for part of Earth's crust. What do you think might eventually happen as the forces of plate movement bend the crust?

The movement of Earth's plates creates enormous forces that squeeze or pull the rock in the crust as if it were a candy bar. These forces are examples of **stress,** a force that acts on rock to change its shape or volume. (A rock's volume is the amount of space the rock takes up.) Because stress is a force, it adds energy to the rock. The energy is stored in the rock until the rock changes shape or breaks.

If you try to break a caramel candy bar in two, it may only bend and stretch at first. Like a candy bar, many types of rock can bend or fold. But beyond a certain limit, even these rocks will break.

**FIGURE 1**
**Effects of Stress**
Powerful forces in Earth's crust caused the ground beneath this athletic field in Taiwan to change its shape.

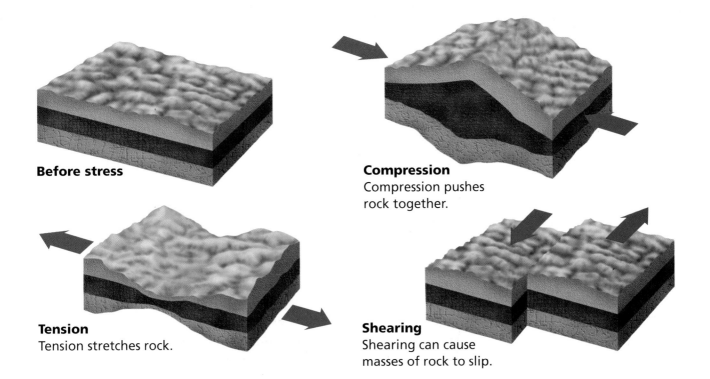

**Before stress**

**Compression**
Compression pushes
rock together.

**Tension**
Tension stretches rock.

**Shearing**
Shearing can cause
masses of rock to slip.

## Types of Stress

Three different kinds of stress can occur in the crust—tension, compression, and shearing. **Tension, compression, and shearing work over millions of years to change the shape and volume of rock.** These forces cause some rocks to become brittle and snap. Other rocks bend slowly, like road tar softened by the sun. Figure 2 shows how stress affects the crust.

Most changes in the crust occur so slowly that they cannot be observed directly. But if you could speed up time so a billion years passed by in minutes, you could see the crust bend, stretch, break, tilt, fold, and slide. The slow shift of Earth's plates causes these changes.

**Tension** The stress force called **tension** pulls on the crust, stretching rock so that it becomes thinner in the middle. The effect of tension on rock is somewhat like pulling apart a piece of warm bubble gum. Tension occurs where two plates are moving apart.

**Compression** The stress force called **compression** squeezes rock until it folds or breaks. One plate pushing against another can compress rock like a giant trash compactor.

**Shearing** Stress that pushes a mass of rock in two opposite directions is called **shearing.** Shearing can cause rock to break and slip apart or to change its shape.

 **Reading Checkpoint** How does shearing affect rock in Earth's crust?

FIGURE 2
**Stress in Earth's Crust**
Stress forces push, pull, or twist the rocks in Earth's crust.
**Relating Cause and Effect** *Which type of stress tends to shorten part of the crust?*

# Kinds of Faults

When enough stress builds up in rock, the rock breaks, creating a fault. Recall that a fault is a break in the rock of the crust where rock surfaces slip past each other. The rocks on both sides of a fault can move up or down or sideways. **Most faults occur along plate boundaries, where the forces of plate motion push or pull the crust so much that the crust breaks. There are three main types of faults: normal faults, reverse faults, and strike-slip faults.**

**Normal Faults** Tension in Earth's crust pulls rock apart, causing **normal faults.** In a normal fault, the fault is at an angle, so one block of rock lies above the fault while the other block lies below the fault. The block of rock that lies above is called the **hanging wall.** The rock that lies below is called the **footwall.** Look at Figure 3 to see how the hanging wall lies above the footwall. When movement occurs along a normal fault, the hanging wall slips downward. Normal faults occur where plates diverge, or pull apart. For example, normal faults are found along the Rio Grande rift valley in New Mexico, where two pieces of Earth's crust are under tension.

FIGURE 3
## Kinds of Faults

There are three main kinds of faults: normal faults, reverse faults, and strike-slip faults. **Inferring** *Which half of a normal fault would you expect to form the floor of a valley? Why?*

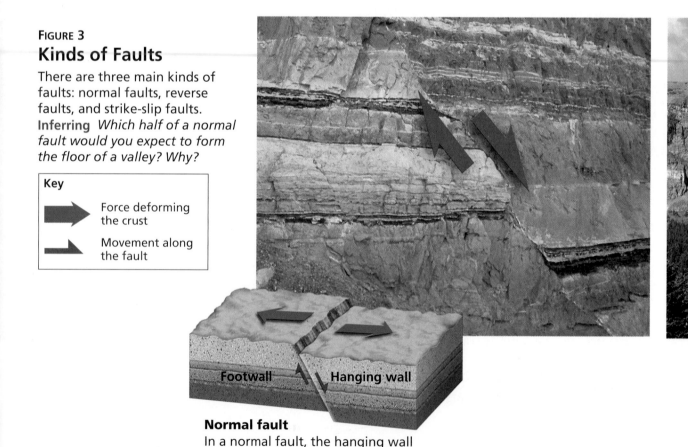

Key

→ Force deforming the crust

▶ Movement along the fault

**Footwall**   **Hanging wall**

**Normal fault**
In a normal fault, the hanging wall slips down relative to the footwall.

**Reverse Faults** In places where the rock of the crust is pushed together, compression causes reverse faults to form. A **reverse fault** has the same structure as a normal fault, but the blocks move in the opposite direction. Look at Figure 3 to see how the rocks along a reverse fault move. As in a normal fault, one side of a reverse fault lies at an angle above the other side. The rock forming the hanging wall of a reverse fault slides up and over the footwall. Movement along reverse faults produced part of the northern Rocky Mountains in the western United States and Canada.

**Strike-Slip Faults** In places where plates move past each other, shearing creates strike-slip faults. In a **strike-slip fault,** the rocks on either side of the fault slip past each other sideways, with little up or down motion. A strike-slip fault that forms the boundary between two plates is called a transform boundary. The San Andreas fault in California is an example of a strike-slip fault that is a transform boundary.

**Go Online**
SciLINKS
NSTA

**For:** Links on faults
**Visit:** www.SciLinks.org
**Web Code:** scn-1021

✓ Reading Checkpoint ) **What is the difference between a hanging wall and a footwall?**

**Reverse fault**
In a reverse fault, the hanging wall moves up relative to the footwall.

**Strike-slip fault**
Rocks on either side of a strike-slip fault slip past each other.

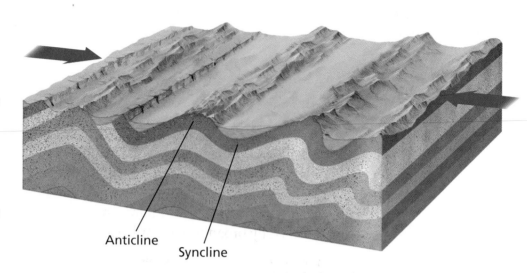

**FIGURE 4**
**Effects of Folding**
Compression and folding of the crust produce anticlines, which arch upward, and synclines, which dip downward. Over millions of years, folding can push up high mountain ranges.
**Predicting** *If the folding in the diagram continued, what kind of fault might form?*

Anticline       Syncline

**Lab zone** Try This **Activity**

**Modeling Stress**

You can model the stresses that create faults.

1. Knead a piece of plastic putty until it is soft.
2. Push the ends of the putty toward the middle.
3. Pull the ends apart.
4. Push half of the putty one way and the other half in the opposite direction.

**Classifying** Which step in this activity models the type of stress that would produce anticlines and synclines?

# Changing Earth's Surface

The forces produced by the movement of Earth's plates can fold, stretch, and uplift the crust. **Over millions of years, the forces of plate movement can change a flat plain into landforms such as anticlines and synclines, folded mountains, fault-block mountains, and plateaus.**

**Folding Earth's Crust** Sometimes plate movement causes the crust to fold. Have you ever skidded on a rug that wrinkled up as your feet pushed it across the floor? Much as the rug wrinkles, rock stressed by compression may bend without breaking. Folds are bends in rock that form when compression shortens and thickens part of Earth's crust. A fold can be only a few centimeters across or hundreds of kilometers wide. You can often see small folds in the rock exposed where a highway has been cut through a hillside.

Geologists use the terms anticline and syncline to describe upward and downward folds in rock. A fold in rock that bends upward into an arch is an **anticline,** shown in Figure 4. A fold in rock that bends downward to form a valley is a **syncline.** Anticlines and synclines are found in many places where compression forces have folded the crust. The central Appalachian Mountains in Pennsylvania are folded mountains made up of parallel ridges (anticlines) and valleys (synclines).

The collision of two plates can cause compression and folding of the crust over a wide area. Folding produced some of the world's largest mountain ranges. The Himalayas in Asia and the Alps in Europe formed when pieces of the crust folded during the collision of two plates.

**Stretching Earth's Crust** When two normal faults cut through a block of rock, a fault-block mountain forms. You can see a diagram of this process in Figure 5. How does this process begin? Where two plates move away from each other, tension forces create many normal faults. When two of these normal faults form parallel to each other, a block of rock is left lying between them. As the hanging wall of each normal fault slips downward, the block in between moves upward, forming a fault-block mountain.

If you traveled by car from Salt Lake City to Los Angeles, you would cross the Great Basin. This region contains many ranges of fault-block mountains separated by broad valleys, or basins.

 **Reading Checkpoint** **What type of plate movement causes fault-block mountains to form?**

**FIGURE 5**
**Fault-Block Mountains**
As tension forces pull the crust apart, two parallel normal faults can form a range of fault-block mountains, like this mountain range in Idaho.

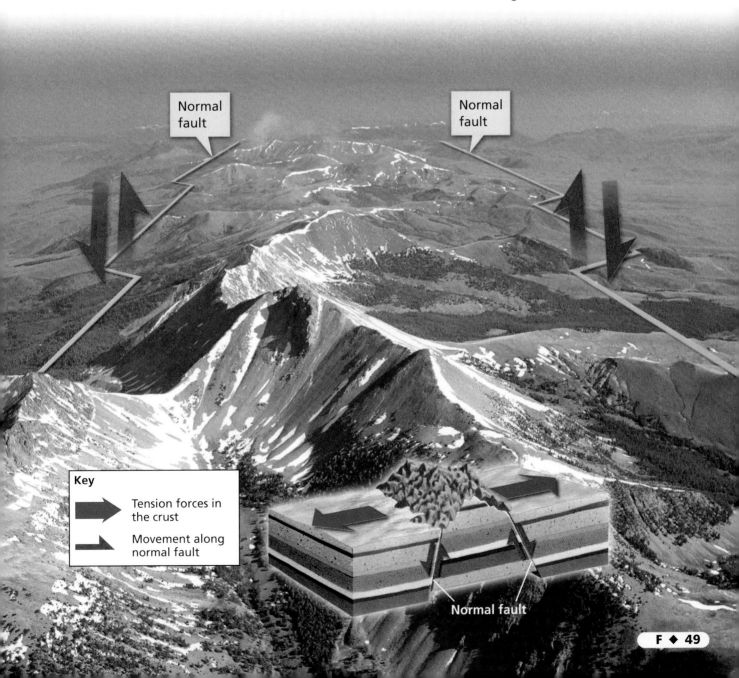

Normal fault

Normal fault

**Key**

Tension forces in the crust

Movement along normal fault

Normal fault

FIGURE 6
**The Kaibab Plateau**
The flat land on the horizon is the Kaibab Plateau, which forms the North Rim of the Grand Canyon in Arizona. The Kaibab Plateau is part of the Colorado Plateau.

**Uplifting Earth's Crust** The forces that raise mountains can also uplift, or raise, plateaus. A **plateau** is a large area of flat land elevated high above sea level. Some plateaus form when forces in Earth's crust push up a large, flat block of rock. Like a fancy sandwich, a plateau consists of many different flat layers, and is wider than it is tall.

Forces deforming the crust uplifted the Colorado Plateau in the "Four Corners" region of Arizona, Utah, Colorado, and New Mexico. Much of the Colorado Plateau lies more than 1,500 meters above sea level. Figure 6 shows one part of that plateau in northern Arizona.

## Section 1 Assessment

**Target Reading Skill** Building Vocabulary
Refer to your definitions of the Key Terms to help you answer the following questions.

**Reviewing Key Concepts**

1. a. **Reviewing** What are the three main types of stress in rock?
   b. **Relating Cause and Effect** How does tension change the shape of Earth's crust?
   c. **Comparing and Contrasting** Compare the way that compression affects the crust to the way that tension affects the crust.
2. a. **Describing** What is a fault?
   b. **Explaining** Why do faults often occur along plate boundaries?
   c. **Relating Cause and Effect** What type of fault is formed when plates diverge, or pull apart? What type of fault is formed when plates are pushed together?

3. a. **Listing** Name five kinds of landforms caused by plate movement.
   b. **Relating Cause and Effect** What are three landforms produced by compression in the crust? What landform is produced by tension?

**Lab zone** At-Home **Activity**

**Modeling Faults** To model Earth's crust, roll modeling clay into layers and then press the layers together to form a rectangular block. Use a plastic knife to slice through the block at an angle, forming a fault. Explain which parts of your model represent the land surface, the hanging wall, and the footwall. Then show the three ways in which the sides of the fault can move.

# Earthquakes and Seismic Waves

## Reading Preview

### Key Concepts
- How does the energy of an earthquake travel through Earth?
- What are the scales used to measure the strength of an earthquake?
- How do scientists locate the epicenter of an earthquake?

### Key Terms
- earthquake • focus
- epicenter • P wave
- S wave • surface wave
- Mercalli scale • magnitude
- Richter scale • seismograph
- moment magnitude scale

### Target Reading Skill

**Identifying Main Ideas** As you read Types of Seismic Waves, write the main idea in a graphic organizer like the one below. Then write three supporting details. The supporting details further explain the main idea.

**Main Idea**

Seismic waves carry the energy of an earthquake.

| Detail | Detail | Detail |
|--------|--------|--------|

## Lab zone Discover **Activity**

### How Do Seismic Waves Travel Through Earth?

1. Stretch a spring toy across the floor while a classmate holds the other end. Do not overstretch the toy.
2. Gather together about four coils of the spring toy and release them. In what direction do the coils move?
3. Once the spring toy has stopped moving, jerk one end of the toy from side to side once. Be certain your classmate has a secure grip on the other end. In what direction do the coils move?

**Think It Over**

**Observing** Describe the two types of wave motion that you observed in the spring toy.

Earth is never still. Every day, worldwide, there are several thousand earthquakes. An **earthquake** is the shaking and trembling that results from the movement of rock beneath Earth's surface. Most earthquakes are too small to notice. But a large earthquake can produce dramatic changes in Earth's surface and cause great damage.

The forces of plate movement cause earthquakes. Plate movements produce stress in Earth's crust, adding energy to rock and forming faults. Stress increases along a fault until the rock breaks. An earthquake begins. In seconds, the earthquake releases an enormous amount of stored energy.

Most earthquakes begin in the lithosphere within about 100 kilometers of Earth's surface. The **focus** (FOH kus) is the area beneath Earth's surface where rock that is under stress breaks, triggering an earthquake. The point on the surface directly above the focus is called the **epicenter** (EP uh sen tur).

## Types of Seismic Waves

Like a pebble thrown into a pond, an earthquake produces vibrations called waves. These waves carry energy as they travel outward. During an earthquake, seismic waves race out from the focus in all directions. Seismic waves are vibrations that travel through Earth carrying the energy released during an earthquake. The seismic waves move like ripples in a pond. **Seismic waves carry energy from an earthquake away from the focus, through Earth's interior, and across the surface.** That's what happened in 2002, when a powerful earthquake ruptured the Denali fault in Alaska, shown in Figure 7.

There are three main categories of seismic waves: P waves, S waves, and surface waves. An earthquake sends out two types of waves from its focus: P waves and S waves. When these waves reach Earth's surface at the epicenter, surface waves develop.

FIGURE 7
### Seismic Waves

This diagram shows an earthquake along the Denali fault. An earthquake occurs when rocks fracture deep in the crust. The seismic waves move out in all directions from the focus.
**Interpreting Diagrams** *At what point do seismic waves first reach the surface?*

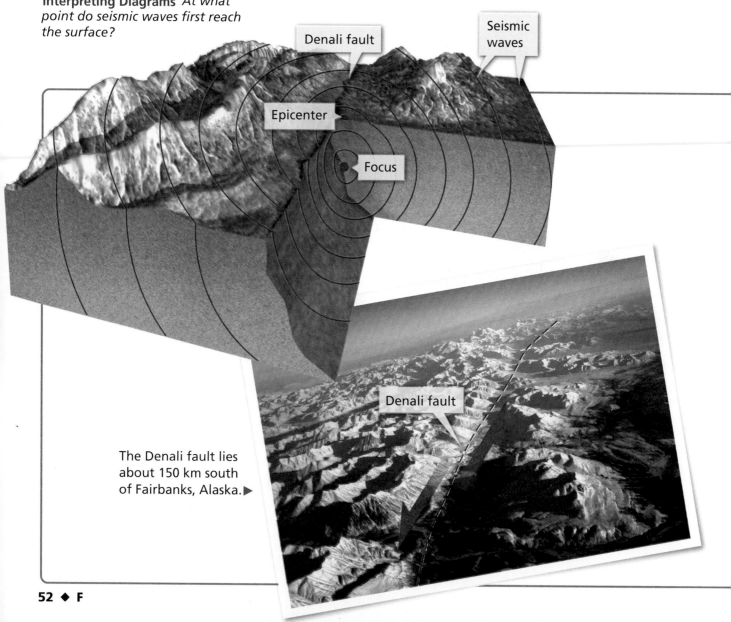

Denali fault

Seismic waves

Epicenter

Focus

The Denali fault lies about 150 km south of Fairbanks, Alaska. ▶

Denali fault

**P Waves** The first waves to arrive are primary waves, or P waves. **P waves** are seismic waves that compress and expand the ground like an accordion. Like the other types of seismic waves, P waves can damage buildings. Look at Figure 7 to see how P waves move.

**S Waves** After P waves come secondary waves, or S waves. **S waves** are seismic waves that vibrate from side to side as well as up and down. They shake the ground back and forth. When S waves reach the surface, they shake structures violently. Unlike P waves, which travel through both solids and liquids, S waves cannot move through liquids.

**Surface Waves** When P waves and S waves reach the surface, some of them become surface waves. **Surface waves** move more slowly than P waves and S waves, but they can produce severe ground movements. Some surface waves make the ground roll like ocean waves. Other surface waves shake buildings from side to side.

**Reading Checkpoint** Which type of seismic wave causes the ground to roll like ocean waves?

Go Online
*active art*

For: Seismic Waves activity
Visit: PHSchool.com
Web Code: cfp-1022

**P waves ▼**
The crust vibrates forward and back along the path of the wave.

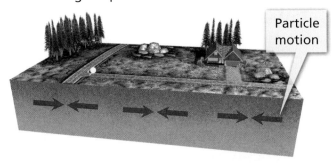

Particle motion

Direction of waves ⟶

**S waves ▼**
The crust vibrates from side to side and up and down.

Particle motion

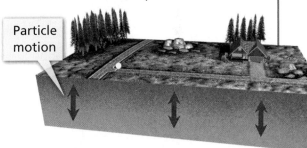

Direction of waves ⟶

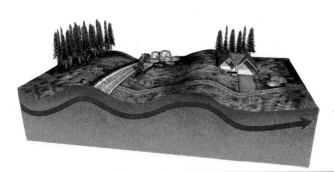

◀ **Surface waves**
The ground surface rolls with a wavelike motion.

# Measuring Earthquakes

When an earthquake occurs, people want to know "How big was the quake?" and "Where was it centered?" When geologists want to know the size of an earthquake, they must consider many factors. As a result, there are at least 20 different measures for rating earthquakes, each with its strengths and shortcomings. **Three commonly used methods of measuring earthquakes are the Mercalli scale, the Richter scale, and the moment magnitude scale.**

**The Mercalli Scale** The **Mercalli scale** was developed to rate earthquakes according to the level of damage at a given place. The 12 steps of the Mercalli scale, shown in Figure 9, describe an earthquake's effects. The same earthquake can have different Mercalli ratings because it causes different amounts of ground motion at different locations.

**The Richter Scale** An earthquake's **magnitude** is a number that geologists assign to an earthquake based on the earthquake's size. Geologists determine magnitude by measuring the seismic waves and fault movement that occur during an earthquake. The **Richter scale** is a rating of an earthquake's magnitude based on the size of the earthquake's seismic waves. The seismic waves are measured by a **seismograph.** A seismograph is an instrument that records and measures seismic waves. The Richter scale provides accurate measurements for small, nearby earthquakes. But it does not work well for large or distant earthquakes.

Slight Damage

Moderate Damage

Great Destruction

**FIGURE 8**
**Levels of Earthquake Damage**
The level of damage caused by an earthquake varies depending on the magnitude of the earthquake and the distance from the epicenter.

**FIGURE 9**
**The Mercalli Scale**
The Mercalli scale uses Roman numerals to rank earthquakes by how much damage they cause.
**Applying Concepts** *How would you rate the three examples of earthquake damage in Figure 8?*

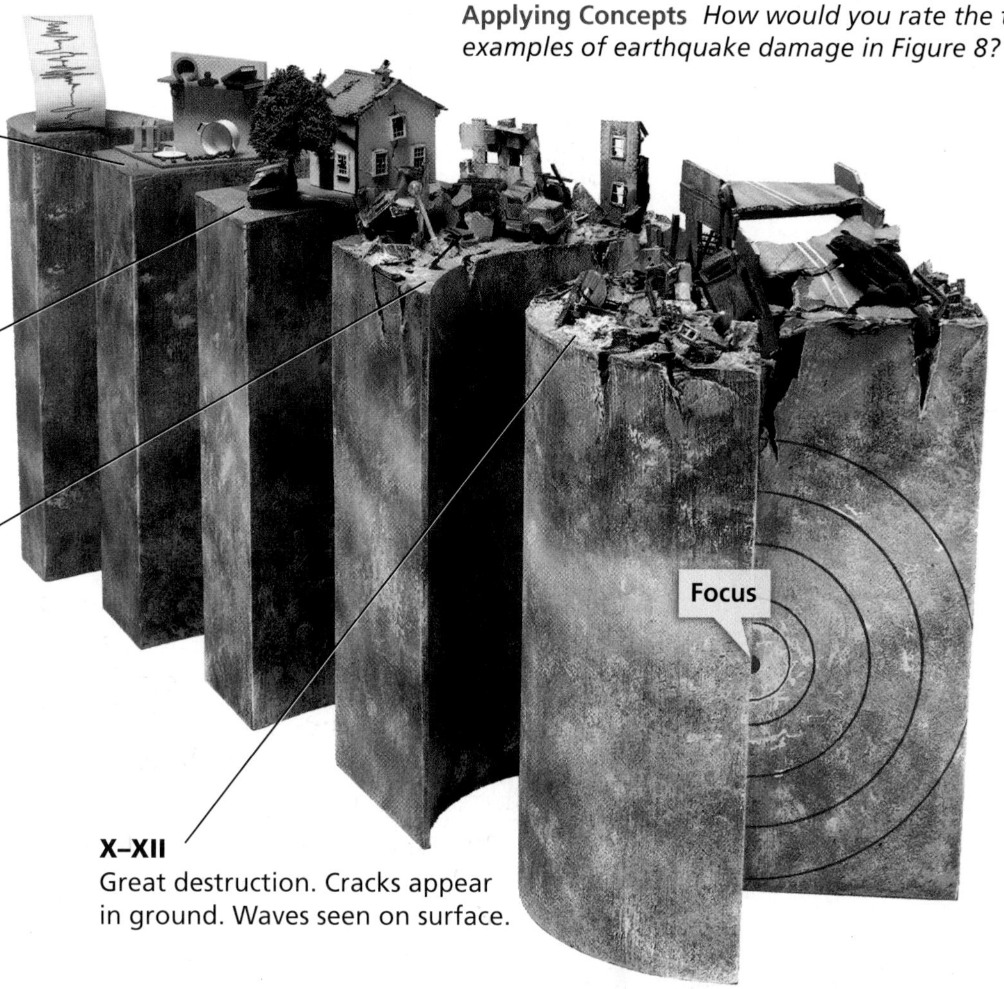

**I–III**
People notice vibrations like those from a passing truck. Unstable objects disturbed.

**IV–VI**
Slight damage. People run outdoors.

**VII–IX**
Moderate to heavy damage. Buildings jolted off foundations or destroyed.

**X–XII**
Great destruction. Cracks appear in ground. Waves seen on surface.

Focus

**The Moment Magnitude Scale** Geologists today often use the **moment magnitude scale,** a rating system that estimates the total energy released by an earthquake. The moment magnitude scale can be used to rate earthquakes of all sizes, near or far. You may hear news reports that mention the Richter scale. But the number they quote is almost always the moment magnitude for that earthquake.

To rate an earthquake on the moment magnitude scale, geologists first study data from seismographs. The data show what kinds of seismic waves the earthquake produced and how strong they were. The data also help geologists infer how much movement occurred along the fault and the strength of the rocks that broke when the fault slipped. Geologists use all this information to rate the quake on the moment magnitude scale.

 **Reading Checkpoint** What evidence do geologists use to rate an earthquake on the moment magnitude scale?

**Lab zone** Skills **Activity**

**Classifying**

Classify the earthquake damage at these locations using the Mercalli scale.

1. Many buildings are destroyed; cracks form in the ground.
2. Several old brick buildings and a bridge collapse.
3. Canned goods fall off shelves; walls crack; people go outside to see what's happening.

**Comparing Magnitudes** An earthquake's magnitude tells geologists how much energy was released by the earthquake. Each one-point increase in magnitude represents the release of roughly 32 times more energy. For example, a magnitude 6 quake releases 32 times as much energy as a magnitude 5 quake, and about 1,000 times as much as a magnitude 4 quake.

The effects of an earthquake increase with magnitude. People scarcely notice earthquakes with magnitudes below 3. Earthquakes with a magnitude below 5 are small and cause little damage. Those with a magnitude between 5 and 6 can cause moderate damage. Earthquakes with a magnitude above 6 can cause great damage. Fortunately, the most powerful earthquakes, with a magnitude of 8 or above, are rare. During the twentieth century, only two earthquakes measured above 9 on the moment magnitude scale. These earthquakes occurred in Chile in 1960 and in Alaska in 1964.

**FIGURE 10**
**Collecting Seismic Data**
This geologist is checking data collected after an earthquake. These data can be used to pinpoint the epicenter of an earthquake.

# Locating the Epicenter

**Geologists use seismic waves to locate an earthquake's epicenter.** Seismic waves travel at different speeds. P waves arrive at a seismograph first, with S waves following close behind. To tell how far the epicenter is from the seismograph, scientists measure the difference between the arrival times of the P waves and S waves. The farther away an earthquake is, the greater the time between the arrival of the P waves and the S waves.

## Math ▸ Analyzing Data

### Seismic Wave Speeds

Seismographs at five observation stations recorded the arrival times of the P and S waves produced by an earthquake. These data are shown in the graph.

1. **Reading Graphs** What variable is shown on the *x*-axis of the graph? The *y*-axis?

2. **Reading Graphs** How long did it take the S waves to travel 2,000 km?

3. **Estimating** How long did it take the P waves to travel 2,000 km?

4. **Calculating** What is the difference in the arrival times of the P waves and the S waves at 2,000 km? At 4,000 km?

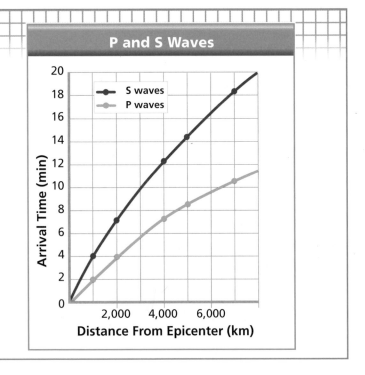

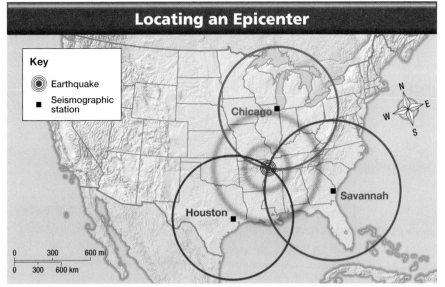

**Locating an Epicenter**

**Key**
◎ Earthquake
■ Seismographic station

Chicago

Houston

Savannah

0   300   600 mi
0  300  600 km

FIGURE 11
The map shows how to find the epicenter of an earthquake using data from three seismographic stations. **Measuring** *Use the map scale to determine the distances from Savannah and Houston to the epicenter. Which is closer?*

Geologists then draw at least three circles using data from different seismographs set up at stations all over the world. The center of each circle is a particular seismograph's location. The radius of each circle is the distance from that seismograph to the epicenter. As you can see in Figure 11, the point where the three circles intersect is the location of the epicenter.

 **Reading Checkpoint** **What do geologists measure to determine the distance from a seismograph to an epicenter?**

# Section 2 Assessment

## Target Reading Skill

**Identifying Main Ideas** Use your graphic organizer to help you answer Question 1 below.

## Reviewing Key Concepts

**1. a. Reviewing** How does energy from an earthquake reach Earth's surface?
   **b. Describing** What kind of movement is produced by each of the three types of seismic waves?
   **c. Sequencing** When do P waves arrive at the surface in relation to S waves and surface waves?

**2. a. Defining** What is an earthquake's magnitude?
   **b. Describing** How is magnitude measured using the Richter scale?
   **c. Applying Concepts** What are the advantages of using the moment magnitude scale to measure an earthquake?

**3. a. Explaining** What type of data do geologists use to locate an earthquake's epicenter?
   **b. Interpreting Maps** Study the map in Figure 11 above. Then describe the method that scientists use to determine the epicenter of an earthquake.

## Writing in Science

**News Report** As a television news reporter, you are covering an earthquake rated between IV and V on the Mercalli scale. Write a short news story describing the earthquake's effects. Your lead paragraph should tell *who, what, where, when,* and *how.* (*Hint:* Refer to Figure 9 for examples of earthquake damage.)

# Finding the Epicenter

## Problem

How can you locate an earthquake's epicenter?

## Skills Focus

interpreting data, drawing conclusions

## Materials

- drawing compass with pencil
- outline map of the United States

| Data Table | | |
| --- | --- | --- |
| City | Difference in P and S Wave Arrival Times | Distance to Epicenter |
| Denver, Colorado | 2 min 40 s | |
| Houston, Texas | 1 min 50 s | |
| Chicago, Illinois | 1 min 10 s | |

## Procedure

1. Make a copy of the data table showing differences in earthquake arrival times.

2. The graph shows how the difference in arrival time between P waves and S waves depends on the distance from the epicenter of the earthquake. Find the difference in arrival time for Denver on the *y*-axis of the graph. Follow this line across to the point at which it crosses the curve. To find the distance to the epicenter, read down from this point to the *x*-axis of the graph. Enter this distance in the data table.

3. Repeat Step 2 for Houston and Chicago.

4. Set your compass at a radius equal to the distance from Denver to the earthquake epicenter that you previously recorded in your data table.

5. Draw a circle with the radius determined in Step 4, using Denver as the center. Draw the circle on your copy of the map. (*Hint:* Draw your circles carefully. You may need to draw some parts of the circles off the map.)

6. Repeat Steps 4 and 5 for Houston and Chicago.

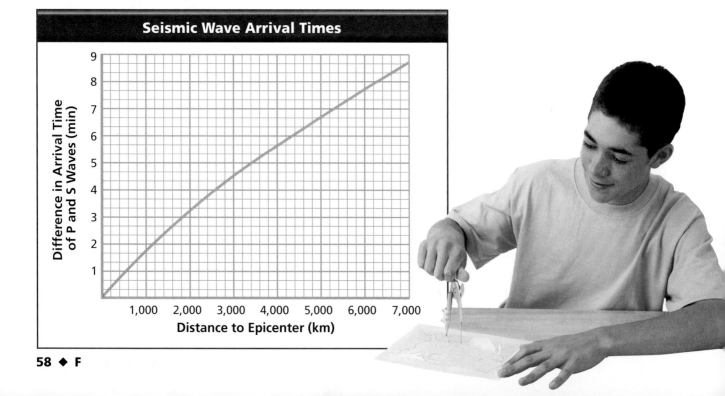

**Seismic Wave Arrival Times**

Difference in Arrival Time of P and S Waves (min)

Distance to Epicenter (km)

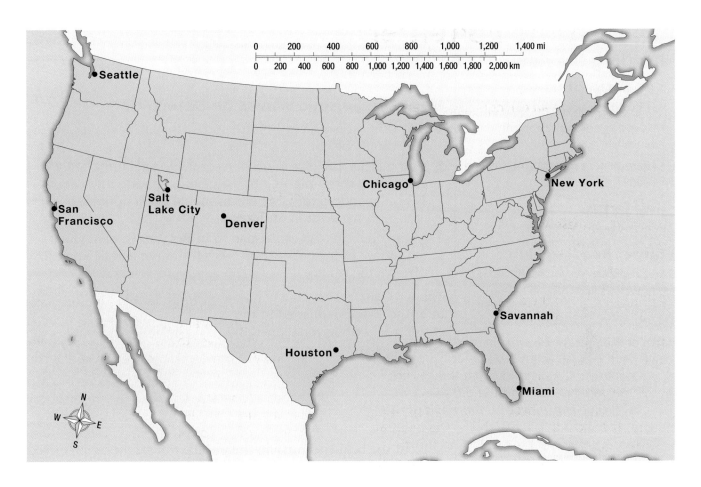

## Analyze and Conclude

1. **Drawing Conclusions** Observe the three circles you have drawn. Where is the earthquake's epicenter?

2. **Measuring** Which city on the map is closest to the earthquake epicenter? How far, in kilometers, is this city from the epicenter?

3. **Inferring** In which of the three cities listed in the data table would seismographs detect the earthquake first? Last?

4. **Estimating** About how far from San Francisco is the epicenter that you found? What would be the difference in arrival times of the P waves and S waves for a recording station in San Francisco?

5. **Interpreting Data** What happens to the difference in arrival times between P waves and S waves as the distance from the earthquake increases?

6. **Communicating** Review the procedure you followed in this lab and then answer the following question. When you are trying to locate an epicenter, why is it necessary to know the distance from the epicenter for at least three recording stations?

## More to Explore

You have just located an earthquake's epicenter. Find this earthquake's location on the map of Earthquake Risk in the United States (Figure 18). What is the risk of earthquakes in the area of this quake?

Now look at the map of Earth's Lithospheric Plates (Figure 22 in the chapter "Plate Tectonics"). What conclusions can you draw from this map about the cause of earthquakes in this area?

# Monitoring Earthquakes

## Reading Preview

### Key Concepts
- How do seismographs work?
- How do geologists monitor faults?
- How are seismographic data used?

### Key Terms
- seismogram  • friction

### 🎯 Target Reading Skill

**Sequencing** As you read, make a flowchart like the one below that shows how a seismograph produces a seismogram. Write each step of the process in a separate box in the order in which it occurs.

**How a Seismograph Works**

| Incoming seismic waves |
| --- |

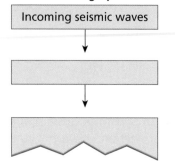

---

### How Can Seismic Waves Be Detected?

1. ✂ Using scissors, cut 4 plastic stirrers in half. Each piece should be about 5 cm long.

2. Your teacher will give you a pan containing gelatin. Gently insert the 8 stirrer pieces into the gelatin, spacing them about 2–3 cm apart in a row. The pieces should stand upright, but not touch the bottom of the pan.

3. At the opposite end of the pan from the stirrers, gently tap the surface of the gelatin once with the eraser end of a pencil. Observe the results.

**Think It Over**

**Inferring** What happened to the stirrer pieces when you tapped the gelatin? What was responsible for this effect?

---

Look at the beautiful vase in the photo. You might be surprised to learn that the vase is actually a scientific instrument. Can you guess what it was designed to do? Zhang Heng, an astronomer, designed and built this earthquake detection device in China nearly 2,000 years ago. It is said to have detected an earthquake centered several hundred kilometers away.

Earthquakes are dangerous, so people want to monitor them. To *monitor* means to "watch closely." Like the ancient Chinese, many societies have used technology to determine when and where earthquakes have occurred. During the late 1800s, scientists developed seismographs that were much more sensitive and accurate than any earlier devices.

**FIGURE 12**
**Earthquake Detector**
Nearly 2,000 years ago, a Chinese scientist invented this instrument to detect earthquakes.

# The Seismograph

A simple seismograph can consist of a heavy weight attached to a frame by a spring or wire. A pen connected to the weight rests its point on a drum that can rotate. As the drum rotates slowly, the pen draws a straight line on paper wrapped tightly around the drum. **Seismic waves cause the seismograph's drum to vibrate. But the suspended weight with the pen attached moves very little. Therefore, the pen stays in place and records the drum's vibrations.**

**Measuring Seismic Waves** When you write a sentence, the paper stays in one place while your hand moves the pen. But in a seismograph, it's the pen that remains stationary while the paper moves. Why is this? All seismographs make use of a basic principle of physics: Whether it is moving or at rest, every object resists any change to its motion. A seismograph's heavy weight resists motion during a quake. But the rest of the seismograph is anchored to the ground and vibrates when seismic waves arrive.

**Reading a Seismogram** You have probably seen a zigzag pattern of lines used to represent an earthquake. The pattern of lines, called a **seismogram,** is the record of an earthquake's seismic waves produced by a seismograph. Study the seismogram in Figure 13 and notice when the P waves, S waves, and surface waves arrive. The height of the jagged lines drawn on the seismograph's drum is greater for a more severe earthquake or for an earthquake close to the seismograph.

✓ **Reading Checkpoint** What is a seismogram?

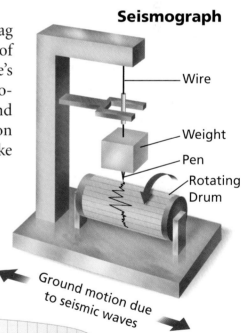

**FIGURE 13**
**Recording Seismic Waves**
A seismograph records seismic waves, producing a seismogram. Today, electronic seismographs contain sensors instead of pens. **Interpreting Diagrams** *What is the function of the weight in the seismograph?*

**Seismograph**

Wire

Weight

Pen

Rotating Drum

Ground motion due to seismic waves

**Seismogram**

Earlier

Later

**P waves** travel fastest and arrive first.

**S waves** arrive shortly after P waves.

**Surface waves** produce the largest disturbance on the seismogram.

# Instruments That Monitor Faults

Along a fault, scientists may detect a slight rise or fall in the elevation and tilt of the land. Geologists hypothesize that such changes signal a buildup of stress in rock. Increasing stress could eventually lead to an earthquake. **To monitor faults, geologists have developed instruments to measure changes in elevation, tilting of the land surface, and ground movements along faults.** Some of the instruments that geologists use to monitor these movements include tiltmeters, creep meters, laser-ranging devices, and satellites.

**Tiltmeters** A tiltmeter measures tilting or raising of the ground. If you have ever used a carpenter's level, you have used a type of tiltmeter. The tiltmeters used by geologists consist of two bulbs that are filled with a liquid and connected by a hollow stem. Notice that if the land rises or falls slightly, the liquid will flow from one bulb to the other. Each bulb contains a measuring scale to measure the depth of the liquid in that bulb. Geologists read the scales to measure the amount of tilt occurring along the fault.

**Creep Meters** A creep meter uses a wire stretched across a fault to measure horizontal movement of the ground. On one side of the fault, the wire is anchored to a post. On the other side, the wire is attached to a weight that can slide if the fault moves. Geologists determine how much the fault has moved by measuring how much the weight has moved against a scale.

**Laser-Ranging Devices** A laser-ranging device uses a laser beam to detect horizontal fault movements. The device times a laser beam as it travels to a reflector and back. Thus, the device can detect any change in distance to the reflector.

**GPS Satellites** Scientists can monitor changes in elevation as well as horizontal movement along faults using a network of Earth-orbiting satellites called GPS. GPS, the Global Positioning System, was developed to help ships and planes find their routes. As shown in Figure 14, GPS can also be used to locate points on Earth's surface with great precision. Using GPS, scientists measure tiny movements of markers set up on the opposite sides of a fault.

 **How does a creep meter work?**

FIGURE 14

# Motion Detectors

To detect slight motions along faults, geologists use several types of devices.
**Comparing and Contrasting** *Which of these devices measure horizontal movement? Which ones measure vertical movement?*

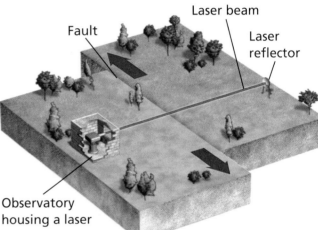

**Tiltmeter**
A tiltmeter measures vertical movement.

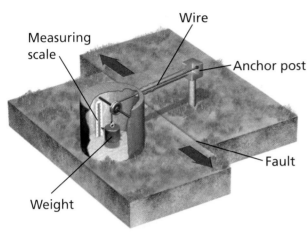

**Creep Meter**
A creep meter measures horizontal movement.

**Laser-Ranging Device**
A laser-ranging device measures horizontal movement.

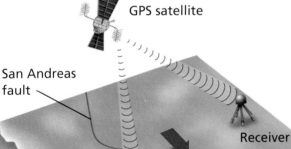

**GPS Satellites**
Ground-based receivers use the GPS satellite system to measure changes in elevation and tilt of the land as well as horizontal movement along a fault.

### Measuring Friction

You can measure the force of friction.

1. Place a small weight on a smooth, flat tabletop. Use a spring scale to pull the weight across the surface. How much force is shown on the spring scale? (*Hint:* The unit of force is newtons.)
2. Tape a piece of sandpaper to the tabletop. Repeat Step 1, pulling the weight across the sandpaper.

Is the force of friction greater for a smooth surface or for a rough surface?

# Using Seismographic Data

Scientists collect and use seismographic data in a variety of ways. **Seismographs and fault-monitoring devices provide data used to map faults and detect changes along faults. Geologists are also trying to use these data to develop a method of predicting earthquakes.**

**Mapping Faults** Faults are often hidden by a thick layer of rock or soil. How can geologists map a hidden fault?

When seismic waves encounter a fault, the waves are reflected off the fault. Seismographs can detect these reflected seismic waves. Geologists then use these data to map the fault's length and depth. Knowing the location of hidden faults helps scientists determine the earthquake risk for the area.

**Monitoring Changes Along Faults** Geologists study the types of movement that occur along faults. How rocks move along a fault depends on how much friction there is between the sides of the fault. **Friction** is the force that opposes the motion of one surface as it moves across another surface. Friction exists because surfaces are not perfectly smooth.

Where friction along a fault is low, the rocks on both sides of the fault slide by each other without much sticking. Therefore stress does not build up, and big earthquakes are unlikely. Where friction is moderate, the sides of the fault jam together. Then from time to time they jerk free, producing small earthquakes. Where friction is high, the rocks lock together and do not move. In this case, stress increases until it is strong enough to overcome the friction force. For example, in most places along the San Andreas fault in California, friction is high and the plates lock. Stress builds up until an earthquake occurs.

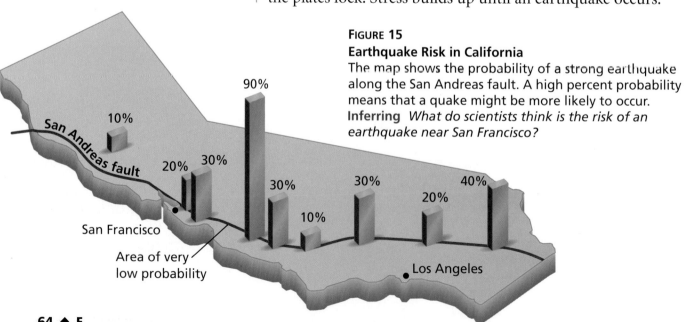

**FIGURE 15**
**Earthquake Risk in California**
The map shows the probability of a strong earthquake along the San Andreas fault. A high percent probability means that a quake might be more likely to occur.
**Inferring** *What do scientists think is the risk of an earthquake near San Francisco?*

Figure 15 shows how geologists in California have used data about how the San Andreas fault moves. They have tried to estimate the earthquake risk along different parts of the fault. Unfortunately, this attempt at forecasting earthquakes has not worked yet.

**Trying to Predict Earthquakes** Even with data from many sources, geologists can't predict when and where a quake will strike. Usually, stress along a fault increases until an earthquake occurs. Yet sometimes stress builds up along a fault, but an earthquake fails to occur. Or, one or more earthquakes may relieve stress along another part of the fault. Exactly what will happen remains uncertain.

The problem of predicting earthquakes is one of many scientific questions that remain unsolved. If you become a scientist, you can work to find answers to these questions. Much remains to be discovered!

 **Reading Checkpoint** Why is it difficult to predict earthquakes?

**FIGURE 16**
**Seismographic Data**
A geologist interprets a seismogram. Understanding changes that precede earthquakes may help in efforts to predict them.

---

## Section 3 Assessment

**Target Reading Skill** Sequencing Refer to your flowchart about seismographs as you answer Question 1.

### Reviewing Key Concepts

1. **a. Defining** What is a seismograph?
   **b. Explaining** How does a seismograph record seismic waves?
   **c. Predicting** A seismograph records a strong earthquake and a weak earthquake. How would the seismograms for the two earthquakes compare?

2. **a. Reviewing** What four instruments are used to monitor faults?
   **b. Describing** What changes does each instrument measure?
   **c. Inferring** A satellite that monitors a fault detects an increasing tilt in the land surface along the fault. What could this change in the land surface indicate?

3. **a. Listing** What are three ways in which geologists use seismographic data?
   **b. Explaining** How do geologists use seismographic data to make maps of faults?
   **c. Making Generalizations** Why do geologists collect data on friction along the sides of faults?

## Writing in Science

**Patent Application** You are an inventor who has created a simple device that can detect an earthquake. To protect your rights to the invention, you apply for a patent. In your patent application, describe your device and how it will indicate the direction and strength of an earthquake. You may include a sketch.

# Technology Lab

# Design a Seismograph

## Problem

Can you design and build a seismograph that can record the movements of simulated earthquakes?

## Skills Focus

designing, evaluating, troubleshooting

## Materials

- large book
- pencil
- pen
- 2 strips of paper
- optional materials provided by your teacher

## Procedure

**PART 1** Research and Investigate

1. With two lab partners, create a model of a seismograph. Begin by placing a large book on a table.

2. Wind a strip of paper about one meter long around a pencil.

3. Hold the pencil with the paper wound around it in one hand. In your other hand, hold a pen against the paper.

4. As you hold the pen steady, have one lab partner slowly pull on the paper so that it slides across the book.

5. After a few seconds, the other lab partner should jiggle the book gently for 10 seconds to model a weak earthquake, and then for 10 seconds to model a strong earthquake.

6. Observe the pen markings on the paper strip. Compare how the seismograph recorded the weak earthquake and the strong earthquake. Record your observations in your notebook.

7. Repeat Steps 1–6 with a new paper strip. Compare the two paper strips to see how consistent your seismograph recordings were. Record your observations.

## PART 2 Design and Build

8. Using what you learned from the seismo-graph model in Part 1, develop your own design for a seismograph. Your seismograph should be able to
   - record vibrations continuously for 30 seconds
   - produce a seismogram that can distinguish between gentle and strong earthquakes
   - record seismic readings consistently from trial to trial

9. Sketch your design on a sheet of paper. Then make a list of the materials you will need. Materials might include a heavy weight, a roll of paper, a pen, wood blocks, wood dowels, and duct tape.

10. Obtain your teacher's approval for your design. Then construct your seismograph.

## PART 3 Evaluate and Redesign

11. Test your seismograph in a series of simu-lated earthquakes of different strengths. Evaluate how well your seismograph func-tions. Does it meet the criteria outlined in Step 8? Make note of any problems.

12. Based on your tests, decide how you could improve the design of your seismograph. Then make any necessary changes to your seismograph and test how it functions.

## Analyze and Conclude

1. **Evaluating** What problems or shortcomings did you encounter with the seismograph you tested in Part 1? Why do you think these problems occurred?

2. **Designing a Solution** How did you incorpo-rate what you learned in Part 1 into your seismograph design in Part 2? For example, what changes did you make to improve con-sistency from trial to trial?

3. **Troubleshooting** As you designed, built, and tested your seismograph, what problems did you encounter? How did you solve these problems?

4. **Working With Design Constraints** What limi-tations did factors such as gravity, materials, costs, time, or other factors place on the design and function of your seismograph? Describe how you adapted your design to work within these limitations.

5. **Evaluating the Impact on Society** Why is it important for scientists around the world to have access to accurate and durable seismo-graphs?

## Communicate

Write an advertisement trying to "sell" your seis-mograph. In your ad, explain how your design and evaluation process helped you improve your seis-mograph. Include a labeled sketch of your design.

## Reading Preview

### Key Concepts
- How do geologists determine earthquake risk?
- What kinds of damage does an earthquake cause?
- What can be done to increase earthquake safety and reduce earthquake damage?

### Key Terms
- liquefaction
- aftershock • tsunami
- base-isolated building

### ⊙ Target Reading Skill
**Asking Questions** Before you read, preview the red headings and ask a *what, how,* or *where* question for each. As you read, write answers to your questions.

**Earthquake Safety**

| Question | Answer |
|----------|--------|
| Where is quake risk highest? | Earthquake risk is highest . . . |
|  |  |

Lab zone **Discover Activity**

### Can Bracing Prevent Building Collapse?

1. Tape four straws together to make a square frame. Hold the frame upright on a flat surface.
2. Hold the bottom straw down with one hand while you push the top straw to the left with the other. Push it as far as it will go without breaking the frame.
3. Tape a fifth straw horizontally across the middle of the frame. Repeat Step 2.

**Think It Over**
**Predicting** What effect did the fifth straw have? What effect would a piece of cardboard taped to the frame have? Based on your observations, how would an earthquake affect the frame of a house?

Imagine being sound asleep in your bed in the middle of the night. Suddenly, you are jolted wide awake as your home begins to rattle and shake. As objects fall off shelves and walls crack, you crouch under a desk for protection. Around the city, large buildings collapse and fires break out. The quake lasts less than a minute, but leaves behind great devastation. That's what happened in September 1999 when a magnitude 7.6 earthquake hit Taipei, Taiwan. The quake killed more than 2,000 people, and injured thousands more.

**FIGURE 17**
**Earthquake Rescue**
After an earthquake in Taipei, emergency crews worked to put out fires and rescue victims in collapsed buildings.

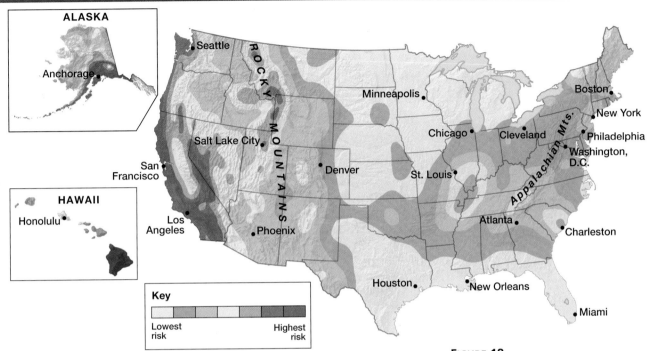

Key

Lowest risk — Highest risk

ALASKA
Anchorage
Seattle
ROCKY MOUNTAINS
Minneapolis
Boston
New York
Chicago
Cleveland
Philadelphia
Washington, D.C.
Salt Lake City
Appalachian Mts.
San Francisco
Denver
St. Louis
HAWAII
Honolulu
Los Angeles
Phoenix
Atlanta
Charleston
Houston
New Orleans
Miami

**FIGURE 18**
The map shows areas where serious earthquakes are likely to occur, based on the locations of previous earthquakes.
**Interpreting Maps** *Where are damaging earthquakes least likely to occur? Most likely to occur?*

# Earthquake Risk

Geologists know that earthquakes are likely wherever plate movement stores energy in the rock along faults. **Geologists can determine earthquake risk by locating where faults are active and where past earthquakes have occurred.**

Look at Figure 18. In the United States, the risk is highest along the Pacific coast in California, Washington, and Alaska. Plates meet along the Pacific coast, causing many active faults. In California, the Pacific plate and North American plate meet along the San Andreas fault. In Washington, earthquakes result from the subduction of the Juan de Fuca plate beneath the North American plate. In Alaska, subduction of the Pacific plate causes many earthquakes.

The eastern United States generally has a low risk of earthquakes because this region lies far from plate boundaries. But, the East has experienced some of the most powerful quakes in the nation's history. Scientists hypothesize that the continental plate forming most of North America is under stress. This stress could disturb faults that lie hidden beneath thick layers of soil and rock.

 **Reading Checkpoint** What area of the United States has the highest earthquake risk?

## Try This Activity

### Stable or Unstable?

1. Make a model of a fault by placing two small, folded towels side by side on a flat surface.
2. Pile a stack of books on the fault by placing the light books on the bottom and the heaviest ones on top.
3. Gently pull the towels in opposite directions until the pile topples.
4. Repeat the process, but this time with the heavier books on the bottom.

**Relating Cause and Effect** Which one of your structures was more stable than the other? Why?

# How Earthquakes Cause Damage

When a major earthquake strikes, it can cause great damage. **Causes of earthquake damage include shaking, liquefaction, aftershocks, and tsunamis.**

**Shaking** The shaking produced by seismic waves can trigger landslides or avalanches. Shaking can also damage or destroy buildings and bridges, topple utility poles, and fracture gas and water mains. S waves and surface waves, with their side-to-side and up-and-down movement, can cause severe damage near the epicenter. As the seismic waves sweep through the ground, they can put enough stress on buildings to tear them apart.

The types of rock and soil determine where and how much the ground shakes. The most violent shaking may occur kilometers away from the epicenter. Loose soil shakes more violently than solid rock. This means a house built on sandy soil will shake more than a house built on solid rock.

**Liquefaction** In 1964, when a powerful earthquake roared through Anchorage, Alaska, cracks opened in the ground. Some of the cracks were 9 meters wide. The cracks were created by liquefaction. **Liquefaction** (lik wih FAK shun) occurs when an earthquake's violent shaking suddenly turns loose, soft soil into liquid mud. Liquefaction is likely where the soil is full of moisture. As the ground gives way, buildings sink and pull apart.

**Aftershocks** Sometimes, buildings weakened by an earthquake collapse during an aftershock. An **aftershock** is an earthquake that occurs after a larger earthquake in the same area. Aftershocks may strike hours, days, or even months later.

**FIGURE 19**
**Liquefaction Damage**
An earthquake caused the soil beneath this building to liquefy. Liquefaction can change soil to liquid mud.
**Posing Questions** *What are some questions people might ask before building in a quake-prone area?*

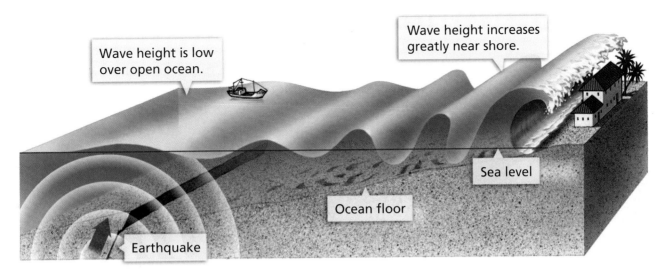

Wave height is low over open ocean.

Wave height increases greatly near shore.

Sea level

Ocean floor

Earthquake

**Tsunamis** When an earthquake jolts the ocean floor, plate movement causes the ocean floor to rise slightly and push water out of its way. The water displaced by the earthquake may form a large wave called a **tsunami** (tsoo NAH mee), shown in Figure 20. A tsunami spreads out from an earthquake's epicenter and speeds across the ocean. In the open ocean, the height of the wave is low. As a tsunami approaches shallow water, the wave grows into a mountain of water.

## Steps to Earthquake Safety

What should you do if an earthquake strikes? The main danger is from falling objects and flying glass. **The best way to protect yourself is to drop, cover, and hold.**

If you are indoors when a quake strikes, crouch beneath a sturdy table or desk and hold on to it. If no desk or table is available, crouch against an inner wall, away from the outside of a building, and cover your head and neck with your arms. Avoid windows, mirrors, wall hangings, and furniture that might topple.

If you are outdoors, move to an open area such as a playground. Avoid vehicles, power lines, trees, and buildings. Sit down to avoid being thrown down.

After a quake, water and power supplies may fail, food stores may be closed, and travel may be difficult. People may have to wait days for these services to be restored. To prepare, an earthquake kit containing canned food, water, and first aid supplies should be stored where it is easy to reach.

**FIGURE 20**
**How a Tsunami Forms**
A tsunami begins as a low wave, but turns into a huge wave as it nears the shore. In 2004, a powerful earthquake in the Indian Ocean triggered several tsunamis. The tsunamis caused great loss of life and destruction to coastal areas around the Indian Ocean.

 **Reading Checkpoint** How can furniture be dangerous during a quake? How can it protect you?

# Designing Safer Buildings

Most earthquake-related deaths and injuries result from damage to buildings or other structures. **To reduce earthquake damage, new buildings must be made stronger and more flexible. Older buildings may be modified to withstand stronger quakes.** People can protect their homes from the dangers of earthquakes. Figure 21 shows some of the steps that can make houses earthquake-safe. Some steps strengthen the house itself. Others may help to keep objects from tipping or falling and causing injury.

FIGURE 21

## An Earthquake-Safe House

People can take a variety of steps to make their homes safer in an earthquake.
**Predicting** *During a quake, what might happen to a house that was not bolted to its foundation?*

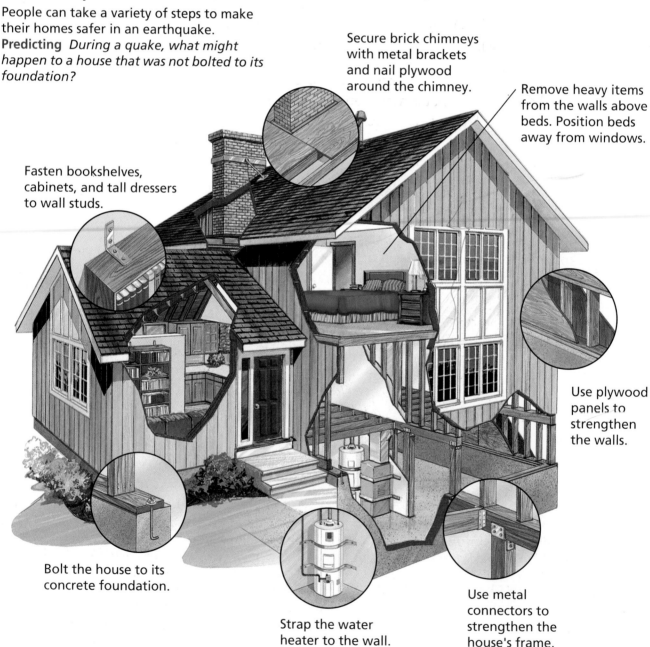

Secure brick chimneys with metal brackets and nail plywood around the chimney.

Remove heavy items from the walls above beds. Position beds away from windows.

Fasten bookshelves, cabinets, and tall dressers to wall studs.

Use plywood panels to strengthen the walls.

Bolt the house to its concrete foundation.

Strap the water heater to the wall.

Use metal connectors to strengthen the house's frame.

**Protecting Structures** The way in which a building is constructed determines whether it can withstand an earthquake. During an earthquake, brick buildings and some wood-frame buildings may collapse if their walls have not been reinforced, or strengthened. To combat damage caused by liquefaction, new homes built on soft ground should be anchored to solid rock below the soil. Bridges and highway overpasses can be built on supports that go through soft soil to firmer ground. To find out more about how buildings can withstand earthquakes, look at *Seismic-Safe Buildings* on the following pages.

A **base-isolated building** is designed to reduce the amount of energy that reaches the building during an earthquake. A base-isolated building rests on shock-absorbing rubber pads or springs. Like the suspension of a car, the pads and springs smooth out a bumpy ride. During a quake, the building moves gently back and forth without any violent shaking.

**Making Utilities Safer** Earthquakes can cause fire and flooding when gas pipes and water mains break. Flexible joints can be installed in gas and water lines to keep them from breaking. Automatic shut-off valves also can be installed on these lines to cut off gas and water flow.

For: More on earthquake risk
Visit: PHSchool.com
Web Code: cfd-1024

 **Reading Checkpoint** How can utilities be protected from earthquake damage?

---

## Section 4 Assessment

**Target Reading Skill** **Asking Questions** Work with a partner to check the answers in your graphic organizer.

### Reviewing Key Concepts

**1. a. Identifying** What factors help geologists determine earthquake risk for a region?
   **b. Comparing and Contrasting** Why does the risk of quakes vary across the United States?

**2. a. Listing** What are four ways that earthquakes cause damage?
   **b. Relating Cause and Effect** How does liquefaction cause damage during an earthquake?
   **c. Developing Hypotheses** How might heavy rain before an earthquake affect the danger of liquefaction?

**3. a. Reviewing** How can you protect yourself during an earthquake?
   **b. Describing** What will happen to a base-isolated building when seismic waves strike the building during an earthquake?

**Lab zone** **At-Home Activity**

**Quake Safety Plan** Work with an adult family member to develop an earthquake safety plan. The plan should tell family members what to do during an earthquake. It should list items your family would need if a quake cut electrical power and water lines. It should also explain where to shut off the gas if your home has a natural gas line. Share your earthquake safety plan with the rest of your family.

# Seismic-Safe Buildings

Breaking one thin twig doesn't require much force. Breaking a bundle of thin twigs does. Like one thin twig, the walls, beams, and other supporting parts of a building can snap as seismic energy travels through the structure. Reinforcing a building's parts makes them more like the bundle of twigs—stronger and less likely to snap when a quake occurs.

### What Are Seismic-Safe Buildings?

Seismic-safe buildings have features that reduce earthquake damage. Some of these features strengthen a building. Others allow the building to move, or shield the building from the energy of seismic waves. In earthquake-prone areas, most tall, steel-frame buildings may have one or more of the seismic-safe features shown here.

**Shear Walls** A shear wall transfers some of a quake's energy from roofs and floors to the building's foundation.

**Tension Ties** These devices firmly "tie" the floors and ceilings of a building to the walls. Tension ties absorb and scatter earthquake energy and thus reduce damage.

**Base Isolators** These pads separate, or isolate, a building from its foundation and prevent some of an earthquake's energy from entering the building.

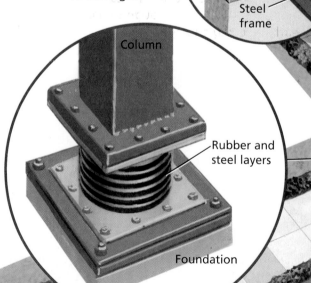

Tension tie

Steel frame

Column

Rubber and steel layers

Foundation

## Seismic-Safe, But at What Cost?

Seismic-safe buildings save lives and reduce damage. Despite these benefits, the technologies have drawbacks. Seismic-safe features, such as cross braces, may reduce the amount of usable space in a building. It is also expensive to add seismic-safe features to an existing building. Communities must make trade-offs between the benefits and the costs of seismic-safe buildings.

**Even steel-frame buildings need seismic-safe design features.**

**Cross Braces** Steel cross braces are placed between stories to stiffen a building's frame and absorb energy during an earthquake.

**Dampers**
Dampers work like the shock absorbers in a car to absorb some of the energy of seismic waves.

Piston

Damper

Brace

**Flexible Pipes** Water and gas pipes have flexible joints. Flexible pipes bend as energy passes through them, greatly reducing damage.

## Weigh the Impact

**1. Identify the Need**
Your city has hired you to decide which buildings or other structures most need to be able to withstand an earthquake. List three types of structures that you think need to be seismic-safe.

**2. Research**
Research how the structures on your list can be made safe. Choose one structure from your list and make notes on how it can be made safe.

**3. Write**
Using your notes, write a report that explains how your structure can be designed or modified to withstand earthquakes.

**For:** More on seismic-safe buildings
**Visit:** PHSchool.com
**Web Code:** cfh-1020

# Chapter 2

# Study Guide

## 1 Forces in Earth's Crust

### Key Concepts

- Tension, compression, and shearing work over millions of years to change the shape and volume of rock.

- Faults usually occur along plate boundaries, where the forces of plate motion push or pull the crust so much that the crust breaks. There are three main types of faults: normal faults, reverse faults, and strike-slip faults.

- Over millions of years, the forces of plate movement can change a flat plain into landforms such as anticlines and synclines, folded mountains, fault-block mountains, and plateaus.

### Key Terms

| | |
|---|---|
| stress | footwall |
| tension | reverse fault |
| compression | strike-slip fault |
| shearing | anticline |
| normal fault | syncline |
| hanging wall | plateau |

## 2 Earthquakes and Seismic Waves

### Key Concepts

- Seismic waves carry energy from an earthquake away from the focus, through Earth's interior, and across the surface.

- Three commonly used ways of measuring earthquakes are the Mercalli scale, the Richter scale, and the moment magnitude scale.

- Geologists use seismic waves to locate an earthquake's epicenter.

### Key Terms

| | |
|---|---|
| earthquake | Mercalli scale |
| focus | magnitude |
| epicenter | Richter scale |
| P wave | seismograph |
| S wave | moment magnitude scale |
| surface wave | |

## 3 Monitoring Earthquakes

### Key Concepts

- During an earthquake, seismic waves cause the seismograph's drum to vibrate. But the suspended weight with the pen attached moves very little. Therefore, the pen stays in place and records the drum's vibrations.

- To monitor faults, geologists have developed instruments to measure changes in elevation, tilting of the land surface, and ground movements along faults.

- Seismographs and fault-monitoring devices provide data used to map faults and detect changes along faults. Geologists are also trying to use these data to develop a method of predicting earthquakes.

### Key Terms

| | |
|---|---|
| seismogram | friction |

## 4 Earthquake Safety

### Key Concepts

- Geologists can determine earthquake risk by locating where faults are active and where past earthquakes have occurred.

- Causes of earthquake damage include shaking, liquefaction, aftershocks, and tsunamis.

- The best way to protect yourself is to drop, cover, and hold.

- To reduce earthquake damage, new buildings must be made stronger and more flexible. Older buildings may be modified to withstand stronger quakes.

### Key Terms

| | |
|---|---|
| liquefaction | tsunami |
| aftershock | base-isolated building |

# Review and Assessment

## Organizing Information

**Relating Cause and Effect** Fill in the cause-and-effect graphic organizer to show how different stress forces produce different kinds of faults.

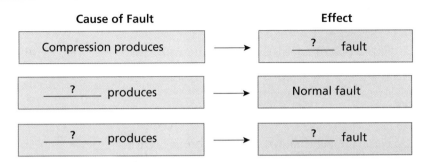

Cause of Fault → Effect

| Compression produces | → | ____?____ fault |
| ____?____ produces | → | Normal fault |
| ____?____ produces | → | ____?____ fault |

## Reviewing Key Terms

**Choose the letter of the best answer.**

1. The force that causes part of the crust to become shorter and thicker is
   a. tension.
   b. compression.
   c. shearing.
   d. normal force.

2. When the hanging wall of a fault slips down with respect to the footwall, the result is a
   a. reverse fault.
   b. syncline.
   c. normal fault.
   d. strike-slip fault.

3. Which of the following is a rating of earthquake damage at a particular location?
   a. moment magnitude scale
   b. focus scale
   c. Mercalli scale
   d. Richter scale

4. The largest waves on a seismogram are
   a. P waves.
   b. S waves.
   c. surface waves.
   d. tsunamis.

5. In the hours after an earthquake, people should not go inside a building, even if it appears undamaged, because of
   a. aftershocks.
   b. liquefaction.
   c. tsunamis.
   d. deformation.

**If the statement is true, write _true._ If it is false, change the underlined word or words to make the statement true.**

6. <u>Liquefaction</u> forces squeeze or pull the rock in Earth's crust.

7. Rock uplifted by <u>normal faults</u> creates fault-block mountains.

8. An earthquake's <u>epicenter</u> is located deep underground.

9. As <u>S waves</u> move through the ground, they cause it to compress and then expand.

10. <u>Tsunamis</u> are triggered by earthquakes originating beneath the ocean floor.

## Writing in Science

**Cause-and-Effect Paragraph** Now that you have learned about the awesome power of earthquakes, write a paragraph about how earthquakes cause damage. Discuss both the natural and human-made factors that contribute to an earthquake's destructive power.

**Discovery CHANNEL SCHOOL**

*Earthquakes*
Video Preview
Video Field Trip
▶ Video Assessment

# Review and Assessment

## Checking Concepts

11. What process causes stress in Earth's crust?

12. Explain how a fault-block mountain forms.

13. What type of stress in the crust results in the formation of folded mountains? Explain.

14. What are plateaus and how do they form?

15. Describe what happens along a fault beneath Earth's surface when an earthquake occurs.

16. How is the amount of energy released by an earthquake related to its magnitude?

17. What does the height of the jagged lines on a seismogram indicate?

18. How can homes and other structures be protected from liquefaction?

## Thinking Critically

19. **Classifying** Look at the diagram of a fault below. Describe how the hanging wall moves in relation to the footwall. What kind of fault is this?

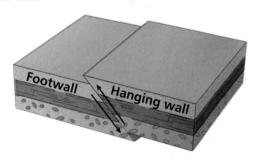

20. **Analyzing Data** A geologist has data about an earthquake from two seismographic stations. Is this enough information to determine the location of the epicenter? Why or why not?

21. **Predicting** A community has just built a street across a strike-slip fault that has frequent earthquakes. How will movement along the fault affect the street?

22. **Making Generalizations** How can filled land and loose, soft soil affect the amount of damage caused by an earthquake? Explain.

## Applying Skills

**Use the graph to answer Questions 23–26.**

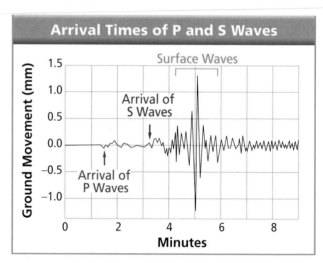

23. **Interpreting Diagrams** In what order did the seismic waves arrive at the seismograph station?

24. **Interpreting Diagrams** Which type of seismic wave produced the largest ground movement?

25. **Analyzing Data** What was the difference in arrival times for the P waves and S waves?

26. **Predicting** What would the seismogram look like several hours after this earthquake? How would it change if an aftershock occurred?

## Lab zone Chapter **Project**

**Performance Assessment** Before testing how your model withstands an earthquake, explain to your classmates how and why you changed your model. When your model is tested, observe how it withstands the earthquake. How would a real earthquake compare with the method used to test your model? If it were a real building, could your structure withstand an earthquake? How could you improve your model?

# Standardized Test Prep

**Choose the letter that best answers the question or completes the statement.**

1. Stress will build until an earthquake occurs if friction along a fault is
  **A** decreasing.
  **B** high.
  **C** low.
  **D** changed to heat.

2. To estimate the total energy released by an earthquake, a geologist should use the
  **F** Mercalli scale.
  **G** Richter scale.
  **H** epicenter scale.
  **J** moment magnitude scale.

*Use the information below and your knowledge of science to answer Questions 3 through 5.*

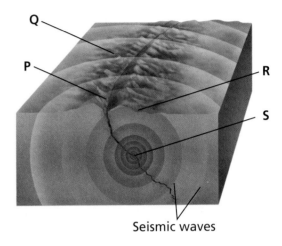

Seismic waves

3. In the diagram, the epicenter is located at point
  **A** Q.
  **B** P.
  **C** R.
  **D** S.

4. When an earthquake occurs, seismic waves travel
  **F** from P in all directions.
  **G** from R to S.
  **H** from S in all directions.
  **J** from Q to P.

5. At point R, seismic waves from an earthquake would be
  **A** weaker than at P.
  **B** likely to cause little damage.
  **C** weaker than at Q.
  **D** likely to cause the most damage.

## Constructed Response

6. Explain the process that forms a strike-slip fault and leads to an earthquake along the fault. In your answer, discuss the force that causes stress in Earth's crust, the type of stress that produces a strike-slip fault, the characteristics of a strike-slip fault, and what happens before and during the earthquake.

# Chapter

# 3

# Volcanoes

Red-hot lava from Mount Kilauea, a volcano in Hawaii, cools to form solid rock.

Lab zone™ Chapter **Project**

## Volcanoes and People

The eruptions of a volcano can be dangerous. Yet volcanoes and people have been closely connected throughout history. People often live near volcanoes because of the benefits they offer, from rich soil, to minerals, to hot springs. In this chapter project, you will investigate how volcanoes have affected the people living in a volcanic region.

**Your Goal** To make a documentary about life in a volcanic region

Your documentary must

- describe the type of volcano you chose and give its history
- focus on one topic, such as how people have benefited from living near the volcano or how people show the volcano in their art and stories
- use a variety of media

**Plan It!** Brainstorm with a group of other students which geographic area you would like to learn about. Your teacher may suggest some volcanic regions for you to check out. Decide what research resources you will need and what media you want to use. For media, you might consider video, computer art, overhead transparencies, a skit, or a mural. Be creative! When your documentary is finished, rehearse your presentation. Then present your documentary to your class.

# Volcanoes and Plate Tectonics

## Reading Preview

### Key Concepts
- Where are most of Earth's volcanoes found?
- How do hot spot volcanoes form?

### Key Terms
- volcano  • magma  • lava
- Ring of Fire  • island arc
- hot spot

### Target Reading Skill
**Asking Questions** Before you read, preview the red headings. In a graphic organizer like the one below, ask a *where, what,* or *how* question for each heading. As you read, write the answers to your questions.

**Volcanoes and Plate Tectonics**

| Question | Answer |
|----------|--------|
| Where are volcanoes found? | Most volcanoes are found along plate boundaries. |
| | |

Lab zone Discover **Activity**

### Where Are Volcanoes Found on Earth's Surface?

1. Look at the map of Earth's Active Volcanoes in Figure 2. What symbols are used to represent volcanoes? What other symbols are shown on the map?

2. Do the locations of the volcanoes form a pattern? Do the volcanoes seem related to any other features on Earth's surface?

**Think About It**

**Developing Hypotheses** Develop a hypothesis to explain where Earth's volcanoes are located.

In 2002, Mount Etna erupted in glowing fountains and rivers of molten rock. Located on the island of Sicily in the Mediterranean Sea, Mount Etna is Europe's largest volcano. Over the last 2,500 years, it has erupted often. The ancient Greeks believed that Mount Etna was one home of Hephaestus, the Greek god of fire. Beneath the volcano was the forge where Hephaestus made beautiful metal objects for the other Greek gods.

The eruption of a volcano is among the most awe-inspiring events on Earth. A **volcano** is a weak spot in the crust where molten material, or magma, comes to the surface. **Magma** is a molten mixture of rock-forming substances, gases, and water from the mantle. When magma reaches the surface, it is called **lava.** After lava has cooled, it forms solid rock. Lava released during volcanic activity builds up Earth's surface.

**FIGURE 1**
**Lava Flow on Mount Etna**
A lava flow from Mount Etna in Sicily almost buried this small building.

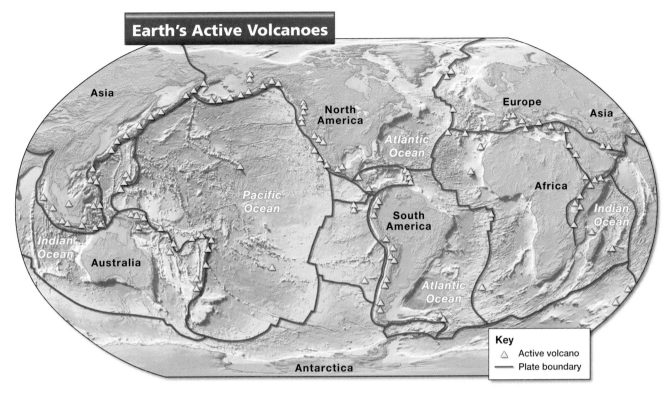

**Earth's Active Volcanoes**

Asia

North America

Europe

Asia

Atlantic Ocean

Africa

Pacific Ocean

South America

Indian Ocean

Indian Ocean

Australia

Atlantic Ocean

Antarctica

**Key**
△ Active volcano
— Plate boundary

# Volcanoes and Plate Boundaries

There are about 600 active volcanoes on land. Many more lie beneath the sea, where it is difficult for scientists to observe and map them. Figure 2 shows the location of some of Earth's major volcanoes. Notice how volcanoes occur in belts that extend across continents and oceans. One major volcanic belt is the **Ring of Fire,** formed by the many volcanoes that rim the Pacific Ocean.

**Volcanic belts form along the boundaries of Earth's plates.** At plate boundaries, huge pieces of the crust diverge (pull apart) or converge (push together). As a result, the crust often fractures, allowing magma to reach the surface. Most volcanoes form along diverging plate boundaries such as mid-ocean ridges and along converging plate boundaries where subduction takes place. For example, Mount Etna formed near the boundary of the Eurasian and African plates.

**Diverging Boundaries** Volcanoes form along the mid-ocean ridges, which mark diverging plate boundaries. Recall that ridges are long, underwater mountain ranges that sometimes have a rift valley down their center. Along the rift valley, lava pours out of cracks in the ocean floor, gradually building new mountains. Volcanoes also form along diverging plate boundaries on land. For example, there are several large volcanoes along the Great Rift Valley in East Africa.

**FIGURE 2**
Many of Earth's volcanoes are located along the boundaries of tectonic plates. The Ring of Fire is a belt of volcanoes that circles the Pacific Ocean. **Observing** *What other regions have a large number of volcanoes?*

Go Online
PLANET DIARY

For: More on volcanoes
Visit: PHSchool.com
Web Code: cfd-1031

**Converging Boundaries** Many volcanoes form near converging plate boundaries where oceanic plates return to the mantle. Volcanoes may form where two oceanic plates collide or where an oceanic plate collides with a continental plate. Figure 3 shows how converging plates produce volcanoes.

Many volcanoes occur near boundaries where two oceanic plates collide. Through subduction, the older, denser plate sinks beneath a deep-ocean trench into the mantle. Some of the rock above the subducting plate melts and forms magma. Because the magma is less dense than the surrounding rock, it rises toward the surface. Eventually, the magma breaks through the ocean floor, creating volcanoes.

The resulting volcanoes create a string of islands called an **island arc.** The curve of an island arc echoes the curve of its deep-ocean trench. Major island arcs include Japan, New Zealand, Indonesia, the Philippines, the Aleutians, and the Caribbean islands.

Volcanoes also occur where an oceanic plate is subducted beneath a continental plate. Collisions of this type produced the volcanoes of the Andes Mountains in South America and the volcanoes of the Pacific Northwest in the United States.

**Reading Checkpoint** How did the volcanoes in the Andes Mountains form?

FIGURE 3
**Volcanoes at Converging Boundaries**
Volcanoes often form where two oceanic plates collide or where an oceanic plate collides with a continental plate. In both situations, an oceanic plate sinks beneath a trench. Rock above the plate melts to form magma, which then erupts to the surface as lava.

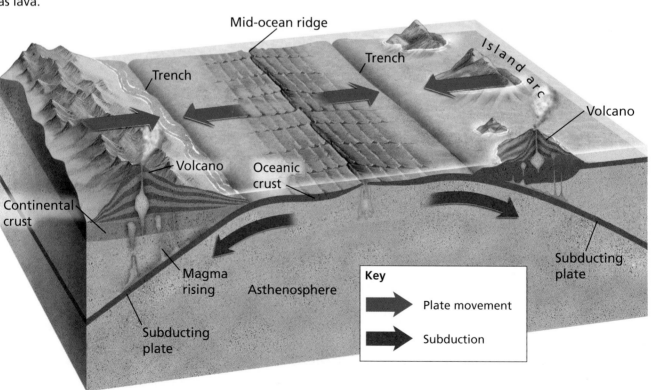

Mid-ocean ridge

Trench

Island arc

Trench

Volcano

Volcano

Oceanic crust

Continental crust

Magma rising

Asthenosphere

Subducting plate

Subducting plate

**Key**

→ Plate movement

→ Subduction

**FIGURE 4**
**Hot Spot Volcanoes**
Eventually, the Pacific plate's movement will carry the island of Hawaii away from the hot spot.
*Inferring* *Which island on the map formed first?*

# Hot Spot Volcanoes

Some volcanoes result from "hot spots" in Earth's mantle. A **hot spot** is an area where material from deep within the mantle rises and then melts, forming magma. **A volcano forms above a hot spot when magma erupts through the crust and reaches the surface.** Some hot spot volcanoes lie in the middle of plates far from any plate boundaries. Other hot spots occur on or near plate boundaries.

A hot spot in the ocean floor can gradually form a series of volcanic mountains. For example, the Hawaiian Islands formed one by one over millions of years as the Pacific plate drifted over a hot spot. Hot spots can also form under the continents. Yellowstone National Park in Wyoming marks a hot spot under the North American plate.

# Section 1 Assessment

🔄 **Target Reading Skill** Asking Questions Work with a partner to check the answers in your graphic organizer.

## Reviewing Key Concepts

1. a. **Defining** What is a volcano?
   b. **Reviewing** Where are most volcanoes located?
   c. **Relating Cause and Effect** What causes volcanoes to form at a diverging plate boundary?
2. a. **Defining** What is a hot spot?
   b. **Summarizing** How does a hot spot volcano form?
   c. **Predicting** What features form as an oceanic plate moves across a hot spot?

**Writing** in Science

**Travel Brochure** As a travel agent, you are planning a Pacific Ocean cruise that will visit volcanoes in the Ring of Fire and Hawaii. Write a travel brochure describing the types of volcanoes the group will see and explaining why the volcanoes formed where they did.

# Mapping Earthquakes and Volcanoes

## Problem

Is there a pattern in the locations of earthquakes and volcanoes?

## Skills Focus

interpreting data

## Materials

- outline world map showing longitude and latitude
- 4 pencils of different colors

## Procedure

1. Use the information in the table to mark the location of each earthquake on the world map. Use a colored pencil to draw a letter E inside a circle at each earthquake location.

2. Use a pencil of a second color to mark the volcanoes on the world map. Indicate each volcano with the letter V inside a circle.

3. Use a third pencil to lightly shade the areas in which earthquakes are found.

4. Use a fourth colored pencil to lightly shade the areas in which volcanoes are found.

## Analyze and Conclude

1. **Interpreting Data** How are earthquakes distributed on the map? Are they scattered evenly or concentrated in zones?

2. **Interpreting Data** How are volcanoes distributed? Are they scattered evenly or concentrated in zones?

3. **Inferring** From your data, what can you infer about the relationship between earthquakes and volcanoes?

4. **Communicating** Suppose you added the locations of additional earthquakes and volcanoes to your map. Would the overall pattern of earthquakes and volcanoes change? Explain in writing why you think the pattern would or would not change.

| Earthquakes and Volcanoes | | | |
|---|---|---|---|
| Earthquakes | | Volcanoes | |
| Longitude | Latitude | Longitude | Latitude |
| 120° W | 40° N | 150° W | 60° N |
| 110° E | 5° S | 70° W | 35° S |
| 77° W | 4° S | 120° W | 45° N |
| 88° E | 23° N | 61° W | 15° N |
| 121° E | 14° S | 105° W | 20° N |
| 34° E | 7° N | 75° W | 0° |
| 74° W | 44° N | 122° W | 40° N |
| 70° W | 30° S | 30° E | 40° N |
| 10° E | 45° N | 60° E | 30° N |
| 85° W | 13° N | 160° E | 55° N |
| 125° E | 23° N | 37° E | 3° S |
| 30° E | 35° N | 145° E | 40° N |
| 140° E | 35° N | 120° E | 10° S |
| 12° E | 46° N | 14° E | 41° N |
| 75° E | 28° N | 105° E | 5° S |
| 150° W | 61° N | 35° E | 15° N |
| 68° W | 47° S | 70° W | 30° S |
| 175° E | 41° S | 175° E | 39° S |
| 121° E | 17° N | 123° E | 38° N |

## More to Explore

On a map of the United States, locate active volcanoes and areas of earthquake activity. Determine the distance from your home to the nearest active volcano.

# Properties of Magma

## Reading Preview

### Key Concepts
- Why is it helpful to know the physical and chemical properties of a substance?
- What causes some liquids to flow more easily than others?
- What factors determine the viscosity of magma?

### Key Terms
- element
- compound
- physical property
- chemical property
- viscosity
- silica
- pahoehoe
- aa

### Target Reading Skill
**Identifying Main Ideas**
As you read Viscosity of Magma, write the main idea in a graphic organizer like the one below. Then write three supporting details that further explain the main idea.

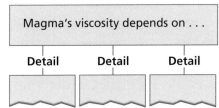

**Main Idea**

Magma's viscosity depends on . . .

| Detail | Detail | Detail |
|--------|--------|--------|

### Lab zone · Discover **Activity**

#### How Fast Do Liquids Flow?

1. Fill one third of a small plastic cup with honey. Fill one third of another cup with cooking oil.
2. Hold the cup containing honey over a third cup and tip it until the liquid begins to flow out of the cup. Time how long it takes from the time the cup was tipped until all the liquid drains out of the cup. Record the time.
3. Repeat Step 2 with the cup filled with oil.

**Think About It**
Forming Operational Definitions The tendency of a fluid to resist flowing is called viscosity. How did you measure the viscosity of honey and cooking oil? Which had a greater viscosity?

Measured from the bottom of the Pacific Ocean, the Big Island of Hawaii is the largest mountain on Earth. The island is made up of massive volcanoes. One of these volcanoes, Mount Kilauea (kee loo AY uh) erupts frequently and produces huge amounts of lava.

At a temperature of around 1,000°C, lava from Mount Kilauea is very dangerous. Yet most of the time, the lava moves slower than a person can walk—about 1 kilometer per hour. Some types of lava move much more slowly—less than the length of a football field in an entire day. How fast lava flows depends on the properties of the magma from which it formed.

## Physical and Chemical Properties

Like all substances, magma and lava are made up of elements and compounds. An **element** is a substance that cannot be broken down into other substances. Carbon, hydrogen, and oxygen are examples of elements. A **compound** is a substance made of two or more elements that have been chemically combined. Water, carbon dioxide, and table salt are familiar compounds. **Each substance has a particular set of physical and chemical properties. These properties can be used to identify a substance or to predict how it will behave.**

**FIGURE 5**
**Pouring Honey**
A liquid with high viscosity, such as honey, pours slowly from its container.
**Predicting** *If you poured water out of a similar container, how would its behavior differ from the honey? Explain your answer.*

**Physical Properties** A **physical property** is any characteristic of a substance that can be observed or measured without changing the composition of the substance. Examples of physical properties include density, hardness, melting point, boiling point, and whether a substance is magnetic. A substance always has the same physical properties under particular conditions. Under normal conditions at sea level, for example, water's freezing point is 0°C and its boiling point is 100°C. Between its freezing and boiling points, water is a liquid.

**Chemical Properties** A **chemical property** is any property that produces a change in the composition of matter. Examples of chemical properties include a substance's ability to burn and its ability to combine, or react, with other substances. You can often tell that one substance has reacted with another if it changes color, produces a gas, or forms a new, solid substance. For example, a piece of silver jewelry darkens when exposed to air. This change indicates that silver has reacted with oxygen to form tarnish. The ability to react with oxygen is a chemical property of silver.

 **Reading Checkpoint** **Is the boiling point of a substance a physical property or a chemical property?**

## What Is Viscosity?

When you pour yourself a glass of milk, you are making use of a familiar physical property of liquids. Because particles in a liquid are free to move around one another, a liquid can flow from place to place. The physical property of liquids called **viscosity** (vis KAHS uh tee) is the resistance of a liquid to flowing. **Because liquids differ in viscosity, some liquids flow more easily than others.**

The greater the viscosity of a liquid, the slower it flows. For example, honey is a thick, sticky liquid with high viscosity. Honey flows slowly. The lower the viscosity, the more easily a liquid flows. Water, rubbing alcohol, and vinegar are thin, runny liquids with low viscosities.

Why do different liquids have different viscosities? The answer lies in the movement of the particles that make up each type of liquid. In some liquids, there is a greater degree of friction among the liquid's particles. These liquids have higher viscosity.

 **Reading Checkpoint** **Why do liquids differ in viscosity?**

**Go Online**
SciLINKS NSTA

**For:** Links on volcanic eruptions
**Visit:** www.SciLinks.org
**Web Code:** scn-1032

## Magma Composition

Magma varies in composition and is classified according to the amount of silica it contains. The graphs show the average composition of two types of magma. Use the graphs to answer the questions.

1. **Reading Graphs** Study both graphs. What materials make up both types of magma?

2. **Reading Graphs** Which type of magma has more silica? About how much silica does this type of magma contain?

3. **Estimating** A third type of magma has a silica content that is halfway between that of the other two types. About how much silica does this magma contain?

4. **Predicting** What type of magma would have a higher viscosity? Explain.

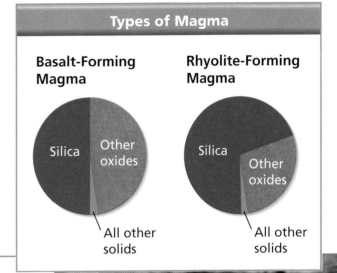

**Types of Magma**

**Basalt-Forming Magma**

Silica · Other oxides · All other solids

**Rhyolite-Forming Magma**

Silica · Other oxides · All other solids

# Viscosity of Magma

At the extremely high temperatures and pressures inside Earth, mantle rock sometimes melts to form magma. Surprisingly, the properties of magma can vary. For example, not all types of magma have the same viscosity. **The viscosity of magma depends upon its silica content and temperature.**

**Silica Content** Magma is a complex mixture, but its major ingredient is silica. The compound **silica** is made up of particles of the elements oxygen and silicon. Silica is one of the most abundant materials in Earth's crust. The silica content of magma ranges from about 50 percent to 70 percent.

The amount of silica in magma helps to determine its viscosity. The more silica magma contains, the higher its viscosity. Magma that is high in silica produces light-colored lava that is too sticky to flow very far. When this type of lava cools, it forms the rock rhyolite, which has the same composition as granite.

The less silica magma contains, the lower its viscosity. Low-silica magma flows readily and produces dark-colored lava. When this kind of lava cools, it forms rocks like basalt.

**FIGURE 6**
**Sampling Magma**
A geologist samples magma from a lava flow in Hawaii.

Pahoehoe

Aa

**FIGURE 7**
**Pahoehoe and Aa**
Both pahoehoe and aa can come from the same volcano. Pahoehoe flows easily and hardens into a rippled surface. Aa hardens into rough chunks. **Inferring** *Which type of lava has lower viscosity?*

**Temperature** How does temperature affect viscosity? Viscosity increases as temperature decreases. On a hot day, honey pours easily. But if you put the honey in the refrigerator, its viscosity increases. The cold honey flows very slowly.

The temperature of magma and lava can range from about 750°C to 1,175°C. The hotter the magma is, the lower its viscosity and the more rapidly it flows. Cooler types of magma have high viscosity and flow very slowly.

In Figure 7, you can see how temperature differences produce two different types of lava: pahoehoe and aa. **Pahoehoe** (pah HOH ee hoh ee) is fast-moving, hot lava that has low viscosity. The surface of a lava flow formed from pahoehoe looks like a solid mass of wrinkles, billows, and ropelike coils. Lava that is cooler and slower-moving is called **aa** (AH ah). Aa has higher viscosity than pahoehoe. When aa hardens, it forms a rough surface consisting of jagged lava chunks.

**Reading Checkpoint** How hot are magma and lava?

## Section 2 Assessment

**Target Reading Skill** **Identifying Main Ideas**
Use your graphic organizer to help you answer Question 3 below.

**Reviewing Key Concepts**

1. a. **Defining** What is a physical property?
   b. **Defining** What is a chemical property?
   c. **Classifying** Magma is a hot, liquid mixture that changes to solid rock when it cools and hardens. Which of these characteristics are physical properties?
2. a. **Identifying** What is viscosity?
   b. **Applying Concepts** Which has a higher viscosity, a fast-flowing liquid or a slow-flowing liquid?
   c. **Inferring** What can you infer about the amount of friction among the particles of a liquid that has low viscosity?

3. a. **Reviewing** What two main factors affect magma's viscosity?
   b. **Predicting** A lava flow cools as it moves away from the vent. How would this affect the surface appearance of the lava flow?

**Lab zone** **At-Home Activity**

**Cooling Lava** Place cold water in one cup and hot tap water in another. Ask members of your family to predict what will happen when melted candle wax drops into each cup of water. Have an adult family member drip melted wax from a candle into each cup. **CAUTION:** *Handle the lit candle carefully.* Explain how this models what happens when lava cools quickly or slowly.

# Volcanic Eruptions

## Reading Preview

### Key Concepts
- What happens when a volcano erupts?
- What are the two types of volcanic eruptions?
- What are a volcano's stages of activity?

### Key Terms
- magma chamber • pipe
- vent • lava flow • crater
- pyroclastic flow • dormant
- extinct

### Target Reading Skill

**Using Prior Knowledge** Before you read, look at the section headings to see what the section is about. Then write what you know about how a volcano erupts in a graphic organizer like the one below. As you read, write what you learn.

| What You Know |
| --- |
| 1. Lava flows out of a volcano. |
| 2. |

| What You Learned |
| --- |
| 1. |
| 2. |

---

Discover **Activity**

### What Are Volcanic Rocks Like?

Volcanoes produce lava, which hardens into rock. Two of these rocks are pumice and obsidian.

1. Observe samples of pumice and obsidian with a hand lens.
2. How would you describe the texture of the pumice? What could have caused this texture?
3. Observe the surface of the obsidian. How does the surface of the obsidian differ from pumice?

**Think It Over**
**Developing Hypotheses** What could have produced the difference in texture between the two rocks? Explain your answer.

Pumice

Obsidian

---

In Hawaii, there are many myths about Pele (PAY lay), the fire goddess of volcanoes. Pele lives in the depths of Hawaii's erupting volcanoes. According to legend, when Pele is angry, she causes a volcanic eruption. One result of an eruption is "Pele's hair," a fine, threadlike rock formed by lava. Pele's hair forms when lava sprays out of the ground like water from a fountain. As it cools, the lava stretches and hardens into thin strands, as shown in Figure 8.

Where does this lava come from? Lava begins as magma, which usually forms in the asthenosphere. The materials of the asthenosphere are under great pressure. Liquid magma is less dense than the solid material around it. Therefore, magma flows upward into any cracks in the rock above. As magma rises, it sometimes becomes trapped beneath layers of rock. But if an opening in weak rock allows the magma to reach the surface, a volcano forms.

**FIGURE 8**
**Pele's Hair**
Pele's hair is a type of rock formed from lava. Each strand is as fine as spun glass.

# Magma Reaches Earth's Surface

A volcano is more than a large, cone-shaped mountain. Inside a volcano is a system of passageways through which magma moves.

**Inside a Volcano** All volcanoes have a pocket of magma beneath the surface and one or more cracks through which the magma forces its way. Beneath a volcano, magma collects in a pocket called a **magma chamber.** The magma moves upward through a **pipe,** a long tube in the ground that connects the magma chamber to Earth's surface. You can see these features in Figure 10.

Molten rock and gas leave the volcano through an opening called a **vent.** Often, there is one central vent at the top of a volcano. However, many volcanoes also have other vents that open on the volcano's sides. A **lava flow** is the area covered by lava as it pours out of a vent. A **crater** is a bowl-shaped area that may form at the top of a volcano around the central vent.

**A Volcanic Eruption** What pushes magma to the surface? The explosion of a volcano is similar to the soda water bubbling out of a warm bottle of soda pop. You cannot see the carbon dioxide gas in a bottle of soda pop because it is dissolved in the liquid. But when you open the bottle, the pressure is released. The carbon dioxide expands and forms bubbles, which rush to the surface. Like the carbon dioxide in soda pop, dissolved gases are trapped in magma. These dissolved gases are under tremendous pressure.

**FIGURE 9**
**Lava Burp**
During an eruption on Mount Kilauea, the force of a bursting gas bubble pushes up a sheet of red-hot lava.

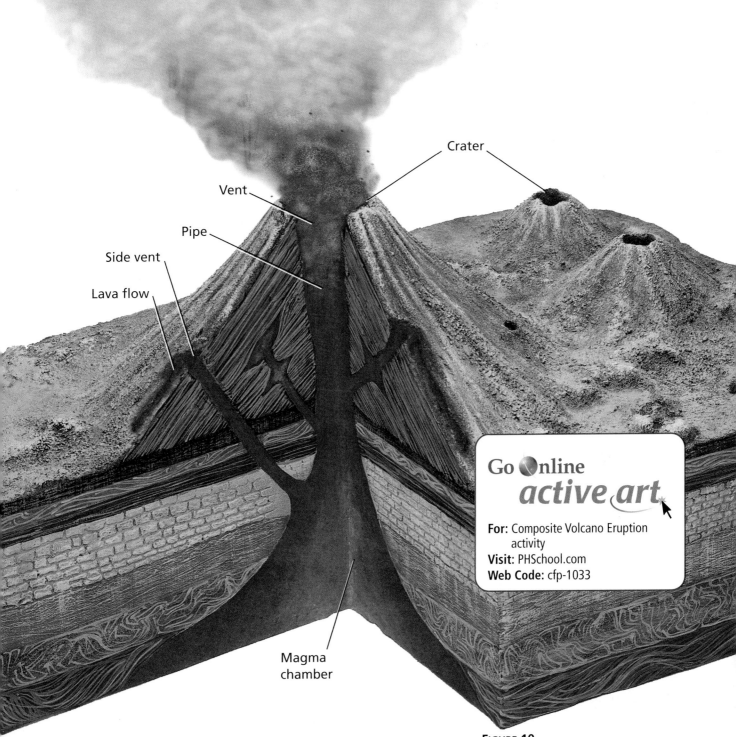

Vent

Pipe

Side vent

Lava flow

Crater

Magma
chamber

**Go Online**
*active art*

**For:** Composite Volcano Eruption
activity
**Visit:** PHSchool.com
**Web Code:** cfp-1033

**FIGURE 10**
**A Volcano Erupts**
A volcano forms where magma
breaks through Earth's crust and
lava flows over the surface.
**Interpreting Diagrams** *What part
of a volcano connects the vent
with the magma chamber?*

As magma rises toward the surface, the pressure of the surrounding rock on the magma decreases. The dissolved gases
begin to expand, forming bubbles. As pressure falls within the
magma, the size of the gas bubbles increases greatly. These
expanding gases exert an enormous force. **When a volcano
erupts, the force of the expanding gases pushes magma from
the magma chamber through the pipe until it flows or
explodes out of the vent.** Once magma escapes from the volcano and becomes lava, the remaining gases bubble out.

 **Reading
Checkpoint** **What happens to the pressure in magma as the
magma rises toward the surface?**

## Gases in Magma

This activity models the gas bubbles in a volcanic eruption.

1. In a 1- or 2-liter plastic bottle, mix 10 g of baking soda into 65 mL of water.
2. Put about six raisins in the water.
3. While swirling the water and raisins, add 65 mL of vinegar and stir vigorously.
4. Once the liquid stops moving, observe the raisins.

**Making Models** What happens after you add the vinegar? What do the raisins and bubbles represent? How is this model similar to the way magma behaves in a volcano?

# Kinds of Volcanic Eruptions

Some volcanic eruptions occur gradually. Others are dramatic explosions. **Geologists classify volcanic eruptions as quiet or explosive.** The physical properties of its magma determine how a volcano erupts. Whether an eruption is quiet or explosive depends on the magma's silica content and viscosity.

**Quiet Eruptions** A volcano erupts quietly if its magma is low in silica. Low-silica magma has low viscosity and flows easily. The gases in the magma bubble out gently. Lava with low viscosity oozes quietly from the vent and can flow for many kilometers. Quiet eruptions can produce both pahoehoe and aa.

The Hawaiian Islands were formed from quiet eruptions. On the Big Island of Hawaii, lava pours out of the crater near the top of Mount Kilauea. But lava also flows out of long cracks on the volcano's sides. Quiet eruptions have built up the Big Island over hundreds of thousands of years.

**Explosive Eruptions** A volcano erupts explosively if its magma is high in silica. High-silica magma has high viscosity, making it thick and sticky. The high-viscosity magma does not always flow out of the crater. Instead, it builds up in the volcano's pipe, plugging it like a cork in a bottle. Dissolved gases, including water vapor, cannot escape from the thick magma. The trapped gases build up pressure until they explode. The erupting gases and steam push the magma out of the volcano with incredible force. That's what happened during the eruption of Mount St. Helens, shown in Figure 11.

Before Eruption

During Eruption

An explosive eruption breaks lava into fragments that quickly cool and harden into pieces of different sizes. The smallest pieces are volcanic ash—fine, rocky particles as small as a speck of dust. Pebble-sized particles are called cinders. Larger pieces, called bombs, may range from the size of a base-ball to the size of a car. A **pyroclastic flow** (py roh KLAS tik) occurs when an explosive eruption hurls out a mixture of hot gases, ash, cinders, and bombs.

Pumice and obsidian, which you observed if you did the Discover Activity, form from high-silica lava. Obsidian forms when lava cools very quickly, giving it a smooth, glossy surface like glass. Pumice forms when gas bubbles are trapped in fast-cooling lava, leaving spaces in the rock.

 **Reading Checkpoint** ) **What is a pyroclastic flow?**

**FIGURE 11**
**An Explosive Eruption**
Mount St. Helens in Washington State erupted at 8:30 A.M. on May 18, 1980. The explosion blew off the top of the mountain, leaving a huge crater and causing great destruction.

After Eruption

**Volcano Hazards** Although quiet eruptions and explosive eruptions produce different hazards, both types of eruption can cause damage far from the crater's rim.

During a quiet eruption, lava flows from vents, setting fire to, and then burying, everything in its path. A quiet eruption can cover large areas with a thick layer of lava.

During an explosive eruption, a volcano can belch out hot clouds of deadly gases as well as ash, cinders, and bombs. Volcanic ash can bury entire towns. If it becomes wet, the heavy ash can cause roofs to collapse. If a jet plane sucks ash into its engine, the engine may stall. Eruptions can cause landslides and avalanches of mud, melted snow, and rock. The Science and History timeline shows the effects of several explosive eruptions.

✓ **Reading Checkpoint** How does volcanic ash cause damage?

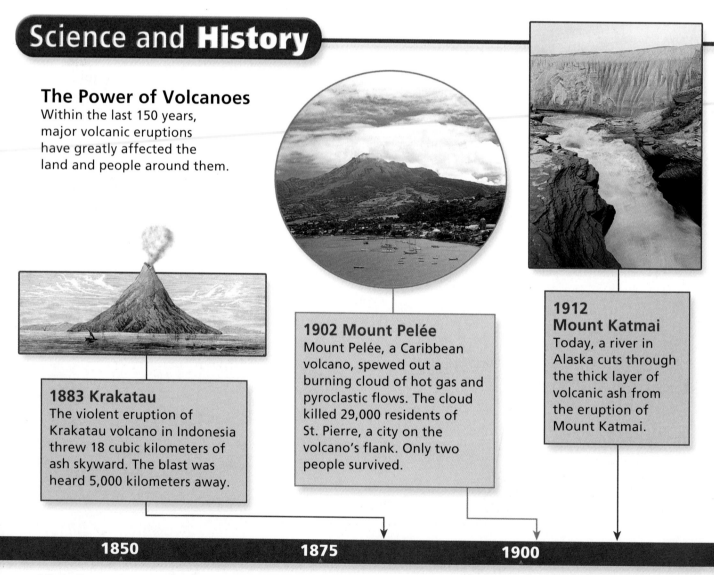

# Science and **History**

## The Power of Volcanoes
Within the last 150 years, major volcanic eruptions have greatly affected the land and people around them.

**1883 Krakatau**
The violent eruption of Krakatau volcano in Indonesia threw 18 cubic kilometers of ash skyward. The blast was heard 5,000 kilometers away.

**1902 Mount Pelée**
Mount Pelée, a Caribbean volcano, spewed out a burning cloud of hot gas and pyroclastic flows. The cloud killed 29,000 residents of St. Pierre, a city on the volcano's flank. Only two people survived.

**1912 Mount Katmai**
Today, a river in Alaska cuts through the thick layer of volcanic ash from the eruption of Mount Katmai.

1850　　　　1875　　　　1900

# Stages of Volcanic Activity

The activity of a volcano may last from less than a decade to more than 10 million years. Most long-lived volcanoes, however, do not erupt continuously. Geologists try to determine a volcano's past and whether the volcano will erupt again.

**Life Cycle of a Volcano** Geologists often use the terms *active, dormant,* or *extinct* to describe a volcano's stage of activity. An active, or live, volcano is one that is erupting or has shown signs that it may erupt in the near future. A dormant, or sleeping, volcano is like a sleeping bear. Scientists expect a **dormant** volcano to awaken in the future and become active. An **extinct,** or dead, volcano is unlikely to erupt again.

The time between volcanic eruptions may span hundreds to many thousands of years. People living near a dormant volcano may be unaware of the danger. But a dormant volcano can become active at any time.

## Writing in Science

**Research and Write** People have written eyewitness accounts of famous volcanic eruptions. Research one of the eruptions in the timeline. Then write a letter describing what someone observing the eruption might have seen.

**1991 Mount Pinatubo**
Pinatubo in the Philippines spewed out huge quantities of ash that rose high into the atmosphere and buried nearby areas.

**2002 Mount Etna**
Bulldozers constructed a wall against a scalding river of lava creeping down the slopes of Mount Etna in Sicily.

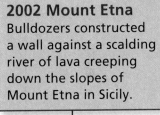

**1980 Mount St. Helens**
When Mount St. Helens in Washington exploded, it blasted one cubic kilometer of volcanic material skyward.

| 1950 | 1975 | 2000 |

FIGURE 12
**Volcano Watch**
Near Mount Kilauea in Hawaii, these geologists are testing instruments to monitor temperatures in and around a crater.

**Monitoring Volcanoes** Geologists have been more successful in predicting volcanic eruptions than in predicting earthquakes. Geologists use instruments to detect changes in and around a volcano. These changes may give warning a short time before a volcano erupts. But geologists cannot be certain about the type of eruption or how powerful it will be.

Geologists use tiltmeters and other instruments to detect slight surface changes in elevation and tilt caused by magma moving underground. They monitor any gases escaping from the volcano. A temperature increase in underground water may be a sign that magma is nearing the surface. Geologists also monitor the many small earthquakes that occur around a volcano before an eruption. The upward movement of magma triggers these quakes.

 **How do geologists monitor volcanoes?**

# Section 3 Assessment

**Target Reading Skill** Using Prior Knowledge Review your graphic organizer and revise it based on what you just learned in the section.

## Reviewing Key Concepts

1. **a. Listing** What are the main parts of a volcano?
   **b. Sequencing** Describe the order of parts through which magma travels as it moves to the surface.
   **c. Relating Cause and Effect** As a volcano erupts, what force pushes magma out of a volcano onto the surface?
2. **a. Identifying** What are the two main kinds of volcanic eruptions?
   **b. Explaining** What properties of magma help to determine the type of eruption?
   **c. Inferring** What do lava flows made of pahoehoe and aa indicate about the type of volcanic eruption that occurred?

3. **a. Naming** What are the three stages of volcanic activity?
   **b. Predicting** Which is more likely to be dangerous—a volcano that erupts frequently or a volcano that has been inactive for a hundred years? Why?

## Writing in Science

**Interview** You are a television news reporter who will be interviewing a geologist. The geologist has just returned from studying a nearby volcano that may soon erupt. Write the questions that you would ask. Be sure to ask about the evidence that an eruption is coming, the type of eruption expected, and any hazards that will result. Write an answer for each question.

## Reading Preview

### Key Concepts
- What landforms do lava and ash create?
- How does magma that hardens beneath the surface create landforms?
- What other distinctive features occur in volcanic areas?

### Key Terms
- shield volcano • cinder cone
- composite volcano • caldera
- volcanic neck • dike
- sill • batholith
- geothermal activity • geyser

### Target Reading Skill

**Outlining** As you read, make an outline about volcanic landforms that you can use for review. Use the red headings for main topics and the blue headings for subtopics.

| Volcanic Landforms |
|---|
| I. Landforms From Lava and Ash |
|   A. Shield Volcanoes |
|   B. |
|   C. |
|   D. |
|   E. |
| II. Landforms From Magma |

**Lab zone Discover Activity**

### How Can Volcanic Activity Change Earth's Surface?

1. Use tape to secure the neck of a balloon over one end of a straw.
2. Place the balloon in the center of a box with the straw protruding.
3. Partially inflate the balloon.
4. Put damp sand on top of the balloon until it is covered.
5. Slowly inflate the balloon more. Observe what happens to the surface of the sand.

**Think It Over**
**Making Models** This activity models one of the ways in which volcanic activity can cause a mountain to form. What do you think the sand represents? What does the balloon represent?

Volcanoes have created some of Earth's most spectacular landforms. The perfect cone of Mount Fuji in Japan, shown in Figure 13, is famous around the world.

For much of Earth's history, volcanic activity on and beneath the surface has built up Earth's land areas. Volcanic activity also formed the rock of the ocean floor. Some volcanic landforms arise when lava flows build up mountains and plateaus on Earth's surface. Other volcanic landforms are the result of the buildup of magma beneath the surface.

**FIGURE 13**
**Mount Fuji**
The almost perfect volcanic cone of Mount Fuji in Japan has long been a favorite subject for artists.

# Landforms From Lava and Ash

Volcanic eruptions create landforms made of lava, ash, and other materials. These landforms include shield volcanoes, cinder cone volcanoes, composite volcanoes, and lava plateaus. Look at Figure 14 to see these features. Another landform results from the collapse of a volcanic mountain.

**Shield Volcanoes** At some places on Earth's surface, thin layers of lava pour out of a vent and harden on top of previous layers. Such lava flows gradually build a wide, gently sloping mountain called a **shield volcano.** Shield volcanoes rising from a hot spot on the ocean floor created the Hawaiian Islands.

**Cinder Cone Volcanoes** If a volcano's lava has high viscosity, it may produce ash, cinders, and bombs. These materials build up around the vent in a steep, cone-shaped hill or small mountain called a **cinder cone.** For example, Paricutín in Mexico erupted in 1943 in a farmer's cornfield. The volcano built up a cinder cone about 400 meters high.

FIGURE 14
## Volcanic Mountains

Volcanic activity is responsible for building up much of Earth's surface. Lava from volcanoes cools and hardens into three types of mountains. It can also form lava plateaus. **Classifying** *What type of volcano is formed from thin, low-silica lava?*

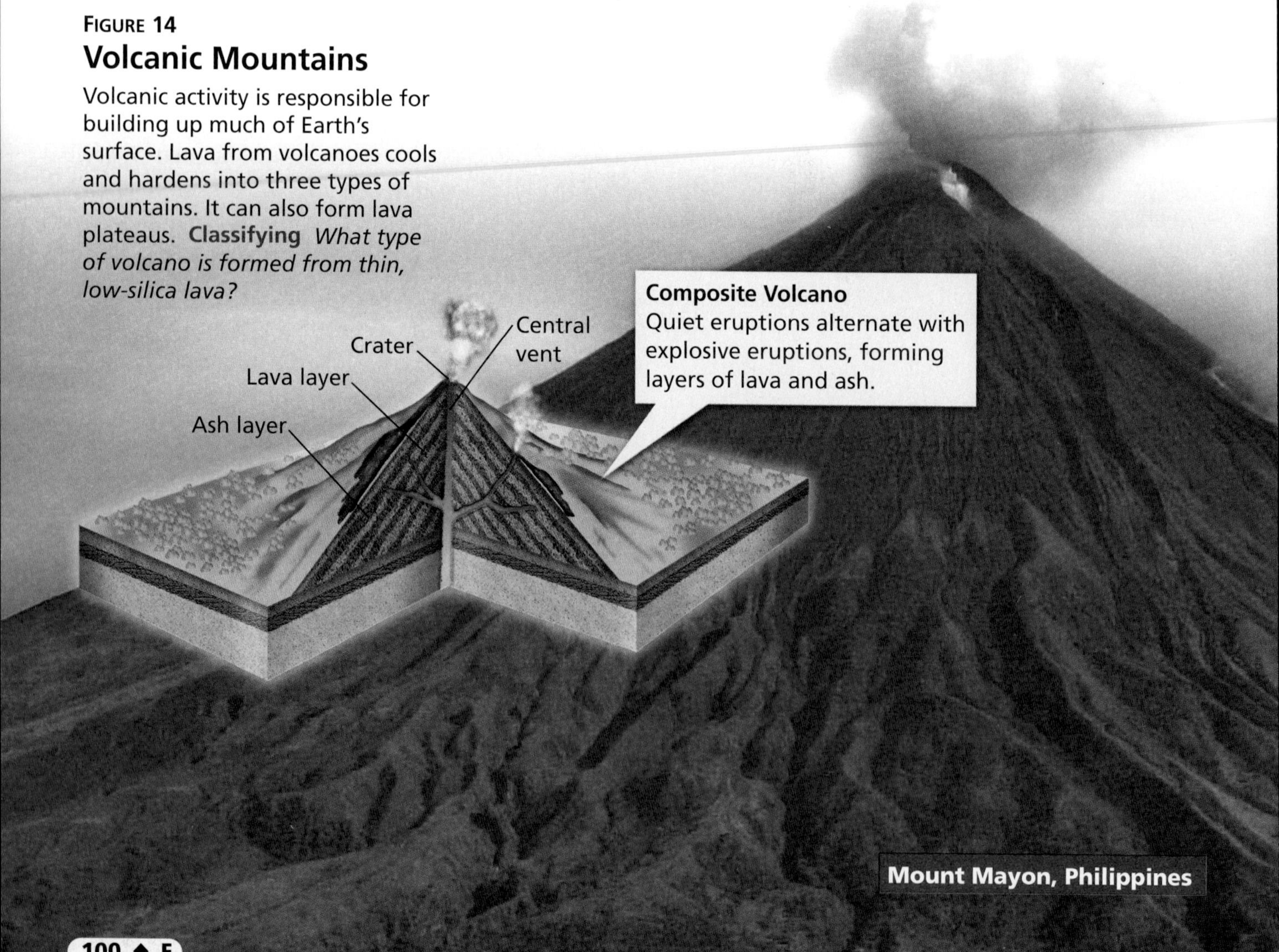

Crater

Lava layer

Ash layer

Central vent

**Composite Volcano**
Quiet eruptions alternate with explosive eruptions, forming layers of lava and ash.

**Mount Mayon, Philippines**

**Composite Volcanoes** Sometimes, lava flows alternate with explosive eruptions of ash, cinder, and bombs. The result is a composite volcano. **Composite volcanoes** are tall, cone-shaped mountains in which layers of lava alternate with layers of ash. Examples of composite volcanoes include Mount Fuji in Japan and Mount St. Helens in Washington State.

**Lava Plateaus** Instead of forming mountains, some eruptions of lava form high, level areas called lava plateaus. First, lava flows out of several long cracks in an area. The thin, runny lava travels far before cooling and solidifying. Again and again, floods of lava flow on top of earlier floods. After millions of years, these layers of lava can form high plateaus. One example is the Columbia Plateau, which covers parts of the states of Washington, Oregon, and Idaho.

**DISCOVERY**
CHANNEL
**SCHOOL**

*Volcanoes*

Video Preview
▶ Video Field Trip
Video Assessment

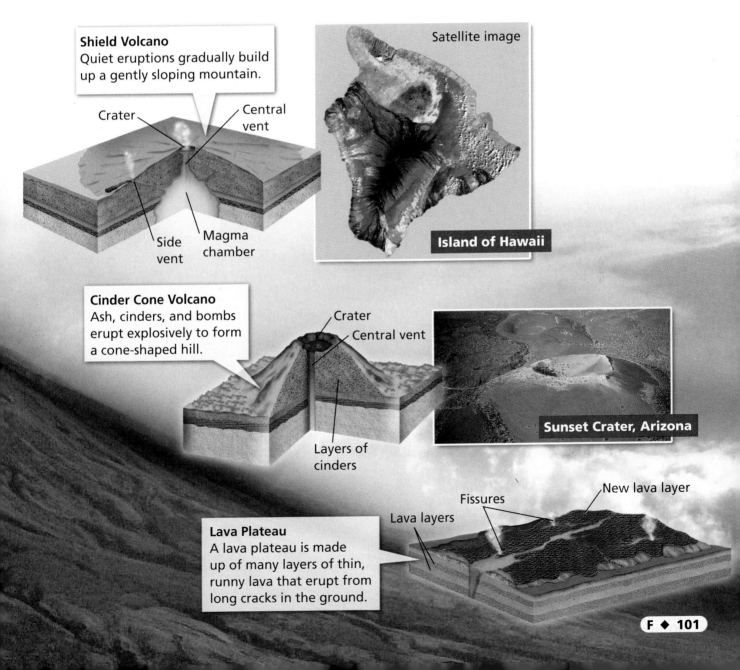

**Shield Volcano**
Quiet eruptions gradually build up a gently sloping mountain.

Crater

Central vent

Side vent

Magma chamber

Satellite image

**Island of Hawaii**

**Cinder Cone Volcano**
Ash, cinders, and bombs erupt explosively to form a cone-shaped hill.

Crater

Central vent

Layers of cinders

**Sunset Crater, Arizona**

Fissures

New lava layer

Lava layers

**Lava Plateau**
A lava plateau is made up of many layers of thin, runny lava that erupt from long cracks in the ground.

FIGURE 15

**How a Caldera Forms**
Today, Crater Lake (right) fills an almost circular caldera. A caldera forms when a volcano's magma chamber empties and the roof of the chamber collapses.

Crater Lake

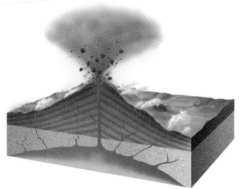

**1** The top of a composite volcano explodes. Lava flows partially empty the magma chamber.

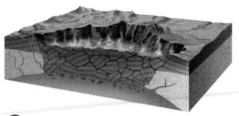

**2** The roof of the magma chamber collapses, forming a caldera.

**3** Later, a small cinder cone forms in the caldera, which partly fills with water.

**Calderas** The huge hole left by the collapse of a volcanic mountain is called a **caldera** (kal DAIR uh). The hole is filled with the pieces of the volcano that have fallen inward, as well as some lava and ash.

How does a caldera form? Enormous eruptions may empty the main vent and the magma chamber beneath a volcano. The mountain becomes a hollow shell. With nothing to support it, the top of the mountain collapses inward, forming a caldera.

In Figure 15 you can see steps in the formation of Crater Lake, a caldera in Oregon. Crater Lake formed about 7,700 years ago when a huge explosive eruption partly emptied the magma chamber of a volcano called Mount Mazama. When the volcano exploded, the top of the mountain was blasted into the atmosphere. The caldera that formed eventually filled with water from rain and snow. Wizard Island in Crater Lake is a small cinder cone that formed during a later eruption inside the caldera.

**Soils From Lava and Ash** Why would anyone live near an active volcano? People often settle close to volcanoes to take advantage of the fertile volcanic soil. The lava, ash, and cinders that erupt from a volcano are initially barren. Over time, however, the hard surface of the lava breaks down to form soil. When volcanic ash breaks down, it releases potassium, phosphorus, and other substances that plants need. As soil develops, plants are able to grow. Some volcanic soils are among the richest soils in the world. Saying that soil is rich means that it's fertile, or able to support plant growth.

✓ Reading Checkpoint  How are volcanic soils important?

# Landforms From Magma

Sometimes magma forces its way through cracks in the upper crust, but fails to reach the surface. There the magma cools and hardens into rock. Over time, the forces that wear away Earth's surface—such as flowing water, ice, or wind—may strip away the layers above the hardened magma and finally expose it. **Features formed by magma include volcanic necks, dikes, and sills, as well as batholiths and dome mountains.**

**Volcanic Necks** A volcanic neck looks like a giant tooth stuck in the ground. A **volcanic neck** forms when magma hardens in a volcano's pipe. The softer rock around the pipe wears away, exposing the hard rock of the volcanic neck. Ship Rock in New Mexico, shown in Figure 16, is a volcanic neck formed from a volcano that erupted about 30 million years ago.

**Dikes and Sills** Magma that forces itself across rock layers hardens into a **dike.** Sometimes, a dike can be seen slanting through bedrock along a highway cut.

When magma squeezes between horizontal layers of rock, it forms a **sill.** One famous example of a sill is the Palisades in New York State and New Jersey. The Palisades form a series of long, dark cliffs. These cliffs stretch for about 30 kilometers along the west bank of the Hudson River.

**Go Online**
*SciLINKS* NSTA

**For:** Links on volcanic effects
**Visit:** www.SciLinks.org
**Web Code:** scn-1034

FIGURE 16
**Volcanic Necks, Dikes, and Sills**
Magma that hardens beneath the surface may form volcanic necks, dikes, and sills. A dike extends outward from Ship Rock, a volcanic neck in New Mexico.
**Comparing and Contrasting** *What is the difference between a dike and a sill?*

Volcanic neck

Dike

Sill

**Batholiths** Large rock masses called batholiths form the core of many mountain ranges. A **batholith** (BATH uh lith) is a mass of rock formed when a large body of magma cools inside the crust. The map in Figure 17 shows just how big batholiths really are. The photograph shows how a batholith looks when the layers of rock above it have worn away.

**Dome Mountains** Other, smaller bodies of hardened magma can create dome mountains. A dome mountain forms when uplift pushes a batholith or smaller body of hardened magma toward the surface. The hardened magma forces the layers of rock to bend upward into a dome shape. Eventually, the rock above the dome mountain wears away, leaving it exposed. This process formed the Black Hills in South Dakota.

# Geothermal Activity

The word *geothermal* comes from the Greek *geo* meaning "Earth" and *therme* meaning "heat." In **geothermal activity,** magma a few kilometers beneath Earth's surface heats underground water. A variety of geothermal features occur in volcanic areas. **Hot springs and geysers are types of geothermal activity that are often found in areas of present or past volcanic activity.**

**Hot Springs** A hot spring forms when groundwater is heated by a nearby body of magma or by hot rock deep underground. The hot water rises to the surface and collects in a natural pool. (Groundwater is water that has seeped into the spaces among rocks deep beneath Earth's surface.) Water from hot springs may contain dissolved gases and other substances from deep within Earth.

**Geysers** Sometimes, rising hot water and steam become trapped underground in a narrow crack. Pressure builds until the mixture suddenly sprays above the surface as a geyser. A **geyser** (GY zur) is a fountain of water and steam that erupts from the ground. Figure 18 shows one of Earth's most famous geysers.

**Geothermal Energy** In some volcanic areas, water heated by magma can provide an energy source called geothermal energy. The people of Reykjavik, Iceland, pipe this hot water into homes for warmth. Geothermal energy can also be used as a source of electricity. Steam from underground is piped into turbines. Inside a turbine, the steam spins a wheel in the same way that blowing on a pinwheel makes the pinwheel turn. The moving wheel in the turbine turns a generator that changes the energy of motion into electrical energy. Geothermal energy provides some electrical power in California and New Zealand.

 **Reading Checkpoint** **How can geothermal energy be used to generate electricity?**

FIGURE 18
**A Geyser Erupts**
Old Faithful, a geyser in Yellowstone National Park, erupts about every 33 to 93 minutes. That's how long it takes for the pressure to build up again after each eruption.

## Section 4 Assessment

🎯 **Target Reading Skill** **Outlining** Use the information in your outline about volcanic landforms to help you answer the questions below.

### Reviewing Key Concepts

1. a. **Identifying** What are the three main types of volcanoes?
   b. **Comparing and Contrasting** Compare the three types of volcanic mountains in terms of shape, type of eruption, and the materials that make up the volcano.
2. a. **Listing** What features form as a result of magma hardening beneath Earth's surface?
   b. **Explaining** What are two ways in which mountains can form as a result of magma hardening beneath Earth's surface?
   c. **Predicting** After millions of years, what landform forms from hardened magma in the pipe of an extinct volcano?

3. a. **Listing** What are some features found in areas of geothermal activity?
   b. **Relating Cause and Effect** What causes a geyser to erupt?

## Writing in Science

**Explaining a Process** Write an explanation of the process that formed Crater Lake. In your answer, include the type of volcanic mountain and eruption involved, as well as the steps in the process. (*Hint:* Look at the diagram in Figure 15 before you write.)

# Gelatin Volcanoes

## Problem

How does magma move inside a volcano?

## Skills Focus

developing hypotheses, making models, observing

## Materials

- plastic cup
- tray or shallow pan
- aluminum pizza pan with holes punched at 2.5-cm intervals
- plastic knife
- unflavored gelatin mold in bowl
- red food coloring and water
- plastic syringe, 10 cc
- rubber gloves
- unlined paper
- 3 small cardboard oatmeal boxes

## Procedure

1. Before magma erupts as lava, how does it travel up from underground magma chambers? Record your hypothesis.

2. Remove the gelatin from the refrigerator. Loosen the gelatin from its container by briefly placing the container of gelatin in a larger bowl of hot water.

3. Place the pizza pan over the gelatin so the mold is near the center of the pizza pan. While holding the pizza pan against the top of the mold, carefully turn the mold and the pizza pan upside down.

4. Carefully lift the bowl off the gelatin mold to create a gelatin volcano.

5. Place the pizza pan with the gelatin mold on top of the oatmeal boxes as shown below.

6. Mix the red food coloring and water in the plastic cup. Then fill the syringe with "magma" (the red water). Remove air bubbles from the syringe by holding it upright and squirting out a small amount of water.

7. Insert the tip of the syringe through a hole in the pizza pan near the center of the gelatin volcano. Inject the magma into the gelatin very slowly. Observe what happens to the magma.

8. Repeat steps 6 and 7 as many times as possible. Observe the movement of the magma each time. Note any differences in the direction the magma takes when the syringe is inserted into different parts of the gelatin volcano. Record your observations.

| Data Table | | | |
|---|---|---|---|
| Test | Initial Location of Magma | Position and Shape of Magma Bodies | Other Observations |
| 1. | | | |
| 2. | | | |
| 3. | | | |
| 4. | | | |

9. Look down on your gelatin volcano from above. Make a sketch of the positions and shapes of the magma bodies. Label your drawing "Top View."

10. Carefully use a knife to cut your volcano in half. Separate the pieces and examine the cut surfaces for traces of the magma bodies.

11. Sketch the positions and shapes of the magma bodies on one of the cut faces. Label your drawing "Cross Section."

## Analyze and Conclude

1. **Observing** Describe how the magma moved through your model. Did the magma move straight up through the center of your model volcano or did it branch off in places? Explain why you think the magma moved in this way.

2. **Developing Hypotheses** What knowledge or experience did you use to develop your hypothesis? How did the actual movement compare with your hypothesis?

3. **Inferring** How would you explain any differences in the direction the magma flowed when the syringe was inserted in different parts of the gelatin volcano?

4. **Making Models** How does what you observed in your model compare to the way magma moves through real volcanoes? How could you change your model to be more like a real volcano?

5. **Communicating** Prepare your model as a display to teach other students about volcanoes. Make a list of the volcanic features in your model. For each feature, write a description of how the feature would form in a real volcano.

## More to Explore

Plan to repeat the investigation using a mold made of two layers of gelatin. Before injecting the magma, predict what effect the layering will have on the movement of magma. Record your observations to determine if your hypothesis was correct. What volcanic feature is produced by this version of the model? Can you think of other volcanic features that you could model using gelatin layers? *Obtain your teacher's permission before carrying out your investigation.*

An eruption of
Mount Kilauea, Hawaii

# Chapter 3

# Study Guide

## 1 Volcanoes and Plate Tectonics

**Key Concepts**

- Volcanic belts form along the boundaries of Earth's plates.
- A volcano forms above a hot spot when magma erupts through the crust and reaches the surface.

**Key Terms**

volcano
magma
lava
Ring of Fire
island arc
hot spot

## 2 Properties of Magma

**Key Concepts**

- Each substance has a particular set of physical and chemical properties. These properties can be used to identify a substance or to predict how it will behave.
- Because liquids differ in viscosity, some liquids flow more easily than others.
- The viscosity of magma depends upon its silica content and temperature.

**Key Terms**

| | |
|---|---|
| element | viscosity |
| compound | silica |
| physical property | pahoehoe |
| chemical property | aa |

## 3 Volcanic Eruptions

**Key Concepts**

- When a volcano erupts, the force of the expanding gases pushes magma from the magma chamber through the pipe until it flows or explodes out of the vent.
- Geologists classify volcanic eruptions as quiet or explosive.
- Geologists often use the terms *active*, *dormant*, or *extinct* to describe a volcano's stage of activity.

**Key Terms**

magma chamber
pipe
vent
lava flow
crater
pyroclastic flow
dormant
extinct

## 4 Volcanic Landforms

**Key Concepts**

- Volcanic eruptions create landforms made of lava, ash, and other materials. These landforms include shield volcanoes, cinder cone volcanoes, composite volcanoes, and lava plateaus.
- Features formed by magma include volcanic necks, dikes, and sills, as well as batholiths and dome mountains.
- Hot springs and geysers are types of geothermal activity that are often found in areas of present or past volcanic activity.

**Key Terms**

shield volcano
cinder cone
composite volcano
caldera
volcanic neck
dike
sill
batholith
geothermal activity
geyser

# Review and Assessment

## Organizing Information

**Concept Map** Fill in the concept map to show the characteristics of the different types of volcanic mountains.

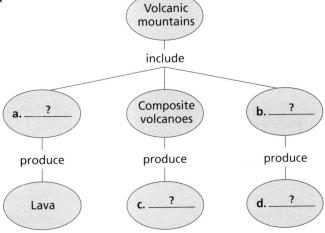

## Reviewing Key Terms

**Choose the letter of the best answer.**

1. Volcanoes found where two oceanic plates collide form a(n)
   **a.** cinder cone.  **b.** island arc.
   **c.** hot spot.  **d.** Ring of Fire.

2. Magma becomes lava when it reaches a volcano's
   **a.** geyser.  **b.** magma chamber.
   **c.** pipe.  **d.** vent.

3. Lava that forms smooth, ropelike coils when it hardens is called
   **a.** aa.  **b.** silica.
   **c.** pahoehoe.  **d.** pyroclastic flow.

4. A volcanic mountain made up of volcanic ash, cinders, and bombs is called a
   **a.** shield volcano.
   **b.** cinder cone.
   **c.** composite volcano.
   **d.** caldera.

5. The collapse of a volcano's magma chamber may produce a(n)
   **a.** crater.
   **b.** island arc.
   **c.** caldera.
   **d.** batholith.

6. Lava that cuts across rock layers hardens to form a feature called a
   **a.** dike.  **b.** caldera.
   **c.** volcanic neck.  **d.** sill.

7. When magma heats underground water, the result may be a
   **a.** lava flow.
   **b.** vent.
   **c.** hot spot.
   **d.** hot spring.

## Writing in Science

**Comparison** Write a comparison of the three different kinds of volcanoes. Discuss the ways in which all three are similar and the ways in which they are different. Use the correct terms to describe each type of volcano.

**Discovery** CHANNEL **SCHOOL**™

**Volcanoes**
Video Preview
Video Field Trip
▶ Video Assessment

# Review and Assessment

## Checking Concepts

8. What is the Ring of Fire?

9. What process causes volcanoes to form along the mid-ocean ridge?

10. What are two ways volcanoes can form near converging plate boundaries?

11. What effect does temperature have on the characteristics of magma?

12. How does a shield volcano form?

13. Describe the three stages in the "life cycle" of a volcano.

14. Why can earthquakes be a warning sign that an eruption is about to happen?

15. How do hot springs form?

## Thinking Critically

16. **Predicting** Is a volcanic eruption likely to occur on the East Coast of the United States? Explain your answer.

17. **Comparing and Contrasting** Compare the way in which an island arc forms with the way in which a hot spot volcano forms.

18. **Making Generalizations** How might a volcanic eruption affect the area around a volcano, including its plant and animal life?

19. **Relating Cause and Effect** Look at the diagram of a lava plateau below. Why doesn't the type of eruption that produces a lava plateau produce a volcanic mountain instead?

Lava plateau

Magma

20. **Predicting** In a particular volcanic region, many small faults fracture the rocks of the crust. What features are likely to form beneath the surface? Explain your answer.

## Applying Skills

**Refer to the diagram to answer Questions 21–24.**

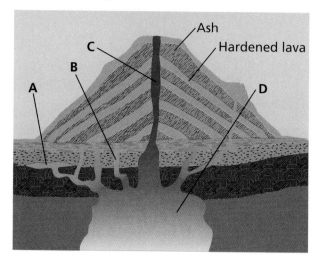

Ash
Hardened lava
C
B
A
D

21. **Classifying** What is this volcano made of? How do geologists classify a volcano made of these materials?

22. **Developing Hypotheses** What is the feature labeled A in the diagram? What is the feature labeled B? How do these features form?

23. **Predicting** What is the feature labeled C in the diagram? If this feature becomes plugged with hardened magma, what could happen to the volcano? Explain.

24. **Inferring** What is the feature labeled D in the diagram? What can you infer about this feature if the volcano becomes dormant?

## Lab zone Chapter **Project**

**Performance Assessment** Present your documentary about a volcanic region to your class. Evaluate how well your documentary presented the information you collected. As you watched the other documentaries, did you see any similarities between how people in different regions live with volcanoes?

# Standardized Test Prep

**Choose the letter that best answers the question or completes the statement.**

**1.** A composite volcano is most likely to form
  A above a hot spot.
  B where an oceanic plate collides with a continental plate.
  C along the mid-ocean ridge.
  D along a rift valley.

**2.** As the temperature of magma increases, its viscosity
  F affects the magma's silica content.
  G increases.
  H stays the same.
  J decreases.

**3.** Which step in a volcanic eruption occurs just before the volcano erupts?
  A Magma collects in the magma chamber.
  B Lava hardens to form volcanic rock.
  C Expanding gases push magma through the pipe.
  D The roof of the empty magma chamber collapses.

**4.** Magma that hardens between layers of rock forms a
  F volcanic neck.
  G dike.
  H batholith.
  J sill.

**5.** The diagram below shows the formation of what volcanic feature?
  A caldera
  B island arc volcano
  C hot spot
  D mid-ocean ridge

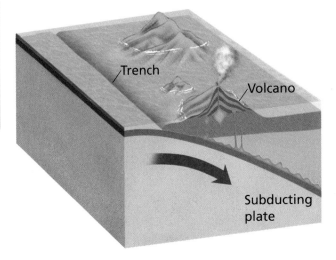

## Constructed Response

**6.** A geologist was observing the area around a dormant volcano. She decided that this volcano must have had an explosive eruption. Describe the evidence geologists would use to make this decision. In your answer, discuss the properties of the magma and the types of rock that would result from an explosive eruption.

# Chapter

# 4

# Minerals

**ınteractive Textbook**

This cave sparkles with thousands of ▶ calcite crystals.

**Lab zone™ Chapter Project**

## Growing a Crystal Garden

Minerals occur in an amazing variety of colors and shapes—from clear, tiny cubes of halite (table salt), to the masses of calcite crystals in the photograph, to precious rubies and sapphires. In this project, you will grow crystals to see how different types of chemicals form different crystal shapes.

**Your Goal** To design and grow a crystal garden

To complete this project successfully, you must

- create a three-dimensional garden scene as a base on which to grow crystals
- prepare at least two different crystal-growth solutions
- observe and record the shapes and growth rates of your crystals
- follow the safety guidelines in Appendix A

**Plan It!** Begin by deciding what materials you will use to create your garden scene. Your teacher will suggest a variety of materials and also describe the types of crystal-growth solutions that you can use. Then, design and build a setting for your crystal garden and add the solutions. Observe and record the growth of the crystals. Finally, display your finished crystal garden to your class. Be prepared to describe your procedure, observations, and conclusions.

# Properties of Minerals

## Reading Focus

### Key Concepts
- What is a mineral?
- How are minerals identified?

### Key Terms
- mineral
- inorganic
- crystal
- streak
- luster
- Mohs hardness scale
- cleavage
- fracture

### ⊙ Target Reading Skill

**Outlining** An outline shows the relationship between major ideas and supporting ideas. As you read, make an outline about the properties of minerals. Use the red headings for the main topics and the blue headings for the subtopics.

| Properties of Minerals |
| --- |
| I. What is a mineral? |
|   A. Naturally occurring |
|   B. Inorganic |
|   C. |
|   D. |
|   E. |
| II. Identifying minerals |

Look at the two different substances in Figure 1. On the left are beautiful quartz crystals. On the right is a handful of coal. Both are solid materials that form beneath Earth's surface. But only one is a mineral. To determine which of the two is a mineral, you need to become familiar with the characteristics of minerals. Then you can decide what's a mineral and what's not!

## What Is a Mineral?

**A mineral is a naturally occurring, inorganic solid that has a crystal structure and a definite chemical composition.** For a substance to be a **mineral,** it must have all five of these characteristics.

**Naturally Occurring** To be classified as a mineral, a substance must be formed by processes that occur in the natural world. The mineral quartz forms naturally as magma cools and hardens deep beneath Earth's surface. Materials made by people, such as plastic, brick, glass, and steel, are not minerals.

**Inorganic** A mineral must also be **inorganic.** This means that the mineral cannot form from materials that were once part of a living thing. For example, coal forms naturally in the crust. But geologists do not classify coal as a mineral because it comes from the remains of plants that lived millions of years ago.

**Solid** A mineral is always a solid, with a definite volume and shape. The particles that make up a solid are packed together very tightly, so they cannot move like the particles that make up a liquid.

**Crystal Structure** The particles of a mineral line up in a pattern that repeats over and over again. The repeating pattern of a mineral's particles forms a solid called a **crystal.** A crystal has flat sides, called faces, that meet at sharp edges and corners. The quartz in Figure 1 has a crystal structure. In contrast, most coal lacks a crystal structure.

**Definite Chemical Composition** A mineral has a definite chemical composition or range of compositions. This means that a mineral always contains certain elements in definite proportions.

Almost all minerals are compounds. For example, a crystal of the mineral quartz has one atom of silicon for every two atoms of oxygen. Each compound has its own properties, or characteristics, which usually differ greatly from the properties of the elements that form it.

Some elements occur in nature in a pure form, and not as part of a compound with other elements. Elements such as copper, silver, and gold are also minerals. Almost all pure, solid elements are metals.

**FIGURE 1**
**Quartz and Coal**
Quartz (below) has all the characteristics of a mineral. But coal (above) is formed from the remains of plants, lacks a crystal structure, and has no definite chemical composition.

✓ **Reading Checkpoint** What does the phrase "definite chemical composition" mean?

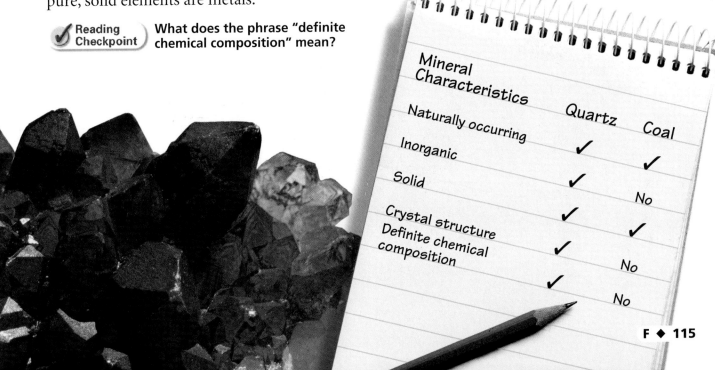

| Mineral Characteristics | Quartz | Coal |
|---|---|---|
| Naturally occurring | ✓ | ✓ |
| Inorganic | ✓ | No |
| Solid | ✓ | ✓ |
| Crystal structure | ✓ | No |
| Definite chemical composition | ✓ | No |

# Identifying Minerals

Geologists have identified about 3,800 minerals. Because there are so many different kinds of minerals, telling them apart can often be a challenge. **Each mineral has characteristic properties that can be used to identify it.** When you have learned to recognize the properties of minerals, you will be able to identify many common minerals around you.

You can see some of the properties of a mineral just by looking at a sample. To observe other properties, however, you need to conduct tests on that sample. As you read about the properties of minerals, think about how you could use them to identify a mineral.

**Color** The color of a mineral is an easily observed physical property. But the color of a mineral alone often provides too little information to make an identification. All three minerals in Figure 2 are the color gold, yet only one is the real thing. Color can be used to identify only those few minerals that always have their own characteristic color. The mineral malachite is always green. The mineral azurite is always blue. No other minerals look quite the same as these.

**FIGURE 2**
**Color of Minerals**
These women in India are searching for bits of gold in river sand. Just because a mineral is gold in color doesn't mean it really is gold. Chalcopyrite and pyrite, also known as "fool's gold," are similar in color to real gold.

Gold          Pyrite          Chalcopyrite

**FIGURE 3**
**Streak**
A mineral's streak can be the same as or quite different from its color.
**Observing** *How do the streaks of these minerals compare with their colors?*

Malachite ▶

Hematite ▶

▲ Galena

**Streak** A streak test can provide a clue to a mineral's identity. The **streak** of a mineral is the color of its powder. You can observe a streak by rubbing a mineral against a piece of unglazed porcelain tile, as shown in Figure 3. Even though the color of the mineral may vary, its streak does not. Surprisingly, the streak color and the mineral color are often different. For example, although pyrite has a gold color, it always produces a greenish black streak. Real gold, on the other hand, produces a golden yellow streak.

**Luster** Another simple test to identify a mineral is to check its luster. **Luster** is the term used to describe how light is reflected from a mineral's surface. Minerals containing metals are often shiny. For example, galena is an ore of lead that has a bright, metallic luster. Quartz has a glassy luster. Some of the other terms used to describe luster include earthy, waxy, and pearly. Figure 4 shows the luster of several minerals.

 **Reading Checkpoint** What characteristic of minerals does the term *luster* describe?

**FIGURE 4**
Geologists use many different terms to describe the luster of minerals.
**Interpreting Tables** *Which mineral has an earthy luster?*

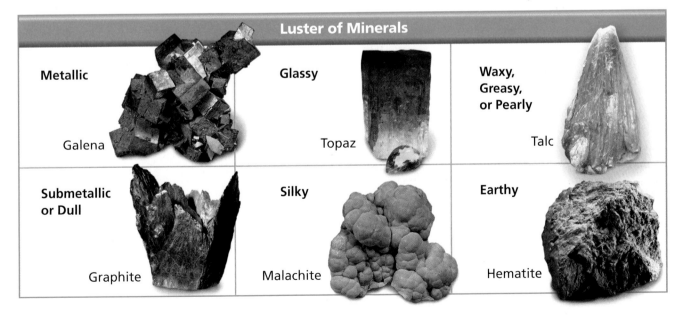

**Luster of Minerals**

| Metallic | Glassy | Waxy, Greasy, or Pearly |
|---|---|---|
| Galena | Topaz | Talc |
| Submetallic or Dull | Silky | Earthy |
| Graphite | Malachite | Hematite |

## Calculating Density

To calculate the density of a mineral, divide the mass of the mineral sample by its volume.

$$\text{Density} = \frac{\text{Mass}}{\text{Volume}}$$

For example, if a sample of olivine has a mass of 237 g and a volume of 72 cm³, then the density is

$$\frac{237 \text{ g}}{72 \text{ cm}^3} = 3.3 \text{ g/cm}^3$$

**Practice Problem**   A sample of calcite has a mass of 324 g and a volume of 120 cm³. What is its density?

**Density**   Each mineral has a characteristic density. Recall that density is the mass in a given space, or mass per unit volume. No matter what the size of a mineral sample, the density of that mineral always remains the same.

You can compare the density of two mineral samples of about the same size. Just pick them up and heft them, or feel their weight, in your hands. You may be able to feel the difference between low-density quartz and high-density galena. If the two samples are the same size, the galena will be almost three times as heavy as the quartz.

But heft provides only a rough measure of density. When geologists measure density, they use a balance to determine the precise mass of a mineral sample. Then they place the mineral in water to determine how much water the sample displaces. The volume of the displaced water equals the volume of the sample. Dividing the sample's mass by its volume gives the density of the mineral:

$$\text{Density} = \frac{\text{Mass}}{\text{Volume}}$$

**Hardness**   When you identify a mineral, one of the best clues you can use is the mineral's hardness. In 1812, Friedrich Mohs, an Austrian mineral expert, invented a test to describe the hardness of minerals. Called the **Mohs hardness scale,** this scale ranks ten minerals from softest to hardest. Look at Figure 5 to see which mineral is the softest and which is the hardest.

FIGURE 5

## Mohs Hardness Scale

Geologists determine a mineral's hardness by comparing it to the hardness of the minerals on the Mohs scale.

**Talc**
The softest known mineral, talc flakes when scratched by a fingernail.

**Gypsum**
A fingernail can easily scratch it.

**Calcite**
A fingernail cannot scratch it, but a copper penny can.

**Fluorite**
A steel knife can easily scratch it.

**Apatite**
A steel knife can scratch it.

1     2     3     4     5

# Math ▶ Analyzing Data

## Mineral Density

Use the line graph of the mass and volume of pyrite samples to answer the questions.

1. **Reading Graphs** What is the mass of Sample B? What is the volume of Sample B?

2. **Calculating** What is the density of Sample B?

3. **Reading Graphs** What is the mass of Sample C? What is the volume of Sample C?

4. **Calculating** What is the density of Sample C?

5. **Comparing and Contrasting** Compare the density of Sample B to that of Sample C.

6. **Predicting** A piece of pyrite has a volume of 40 cm³. What is its mass?

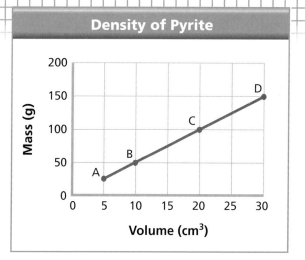

**Density of Pyrite**

7. **Drawing Conclusions** Does the density of a mineral depend on the size of the mineral sample? Explain.

Hardness can be determined by a scratch test. A mineral can scratch any mineral softer than itself, but can be scratched by any mineral that is harder. To determine the hardness of azurite, a mineral not on the Mohs scale, you could try to scratch it with talc, gypsum, or calcite. But none of these minerals scratch azurite. Apatite, rated 5 on the scale, does scratch azurite. Therefore, azurite's hardness is about 4.

**Feldspar**
It can't be scratched by a steel knife, but it can scratch window glass.

**Quartz**
It can scratch steel and hard glass easily.

**Topaz**
It can scratch quartz.

**Corundum**
It can scratch topaz.

**Diamond**
The hardest known mineral, diamond can scratch all other substances.

6  7  8  9  10

## Classifying

1. Use your fingernail to try to scratch talc, calcite, and quartz. Record which minerals you were able to scratch.

2. Now try to scratch the minerals with a penny. Were your results different? Explain.

3. Were there any minerals you were unable to scratch with either your fingernail or the penny?

4. In order of increasing hardness, how would you classify the three minerals?

**Crystal Systems** The crystals of each mineral grow atom by atom to form that mineral's crystal structure. Geologists classify these structures into six groups based on the number and angle of the crystal faces. These groups are called crystal systems. For example, all halite crystals are cubic. Halite crystals have six square faces that meet at right angles, forming a perfect cube.

Sometimes, the crystal structure is obvious from the mineral's appearance. Crystals that grow in an open space can be almost perfectly formed. But crystals that grow in a tight space are often incompletely formed. In other minerals, the crystal structure is visible only under a microscope. A few minerals, such as opal, are considered minerals even though their particles are not arranged in a crystal structure. Figure 6 shows minerals that belong to each of the six crystal systems.

**Cleavage and Fracture** The way a mineral breaks apart can help to identify it. A mineral that splits easily along flat surfaces has the property called **cleavage.** Whether a mineral has cleavage depends on how the atoms in its crystals are arranged. The arrangement of atoms in the mineral causes it to break apart more easily in one direction than another. Look at the photo of mica in Figure 7. Mica separates easily in only one direction, forming flat sheets. Therefore, mica has cleavage. Feldspar is another common mineral that has cleavage.

FIGURE 6
**Properties of Minerals**
All crystals of the same mineral have the same crystal structure. Each mineral also has other characteristic properties.
**Interpreting Data** *Which mineral has the lowest density?*

**Magnetite**
**Crystal System:** Cubic
**Color:** Black
**Streak:** Black
**Luster:** Metallic
**Hardness:** 6
**Density (g/cm³):** 5.2
**Special Property:** Magnetic

**Quartz**
**Crystal System:** Hexagonal
**Color:** Transparent, various colors
**Streak:** Colorless
**Luster:** Glassy
**Hardness:** 7
**Density (g/cm³):** 2.6
**Special Property:** Fractures like broken glass

**Rutile**
**Crystal System:** Tetragonal
**Color:** Black or reddish brown
**Streak:** Light brown
**Luster:** Metallic or gemlike
**Hardness:** 6–6.5
**Density (g/cm³):** 4.2–4.3
**Special Property:** Not easily melted

**Cleavage**

Mica cleaves into thin, flat sheets that are almost transparent.

**Fracture**

When quartz fractures, the break looks like the surface of a seashell.

Most minerals do not split apart evenly. Instead, they have a characteristic type of fracture. **Fracture** describes how a mineral looks when it breaks apart in an irregular way. Geologists use a variety of terms to describe fracture. For example, quartz has a shell-shaped fracture. When quartz breaks, it produces curved, shell-like surfaces that look like chipped glass. Pure metals, like copper and iron, have a hackly fracture—they form jagged points. Some soft minerals that crumble easily like clay have an earthy fracture. Minerals that form rough, irregular surfaces when broken have an uneven fracture.

**FIGURE 7**
**Cleavage and Fracture**
How a mineral breaks apart can help to identify it.
**Applying Concepts** *How would you test a mineral to determine whether it has cleavage or fracture?*

✓ **Reading Checkpoint** Compare the fracture of quartz to the fracture of a pure metal, such as iron.

Go **Online**
*active art*

**For:** Crystal Systems activity
**Visit:** PHSchool.com
**Web Code:** cfp-1041

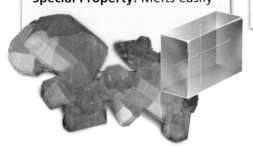

**Sulfur**
**Crystal System:** Orthorhombic
**Color:** Lemon yellow to yellowish brown
**Streak:** White
**Luster:** Greasy
**Hardness:** 2
**Density (g/cm³):** 2.0–2.1
**Special Property:** Melts easily

**Azurite**
**Crystal System:** Monoclinic
**Color:** Blue
**Streak:** Pale blue
**Luster:** Glassy to dull or earthy
**Hardness:** 3.5–4
**Density (g/cm³):** 3.8
**Special Property:** Reacts to acid

**Microcline Feldspar**
**Crystal System:** Triclinic
**Color:** Pink, white, red-brown, or green
**Streak:** Colorless
**Luster:** Glassy
**Hardness:** 6
**Density (g/cm³):** 2.6
**Special Property:** Cleaves well in two directions

## FIGURE 8
**Special Properties**
The special properties of minerals include fluorescence, magnetism, radioactivity, and reaction to acids. Other minerals have useful optical or electrical properties.

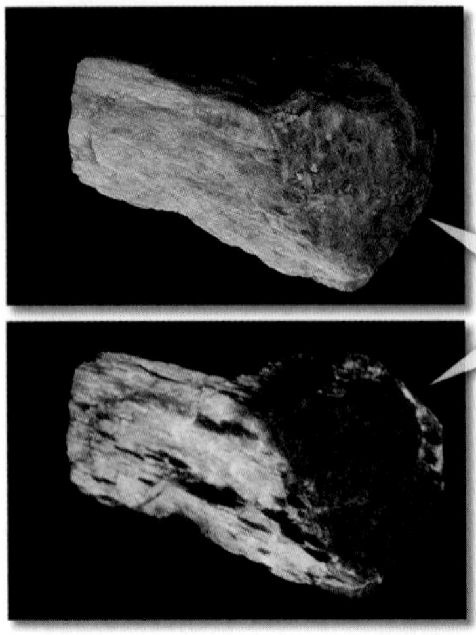

**Fluorescence**
Scheelite glows in ultraviolet light.

**Optical Properties**
Calcite bends light to produce a double image.

**Reactivity**
Aragonite reacts chemically to acids.

**Magnetism**
Magnetite attracts these iron staples.

**Special Properties** Some minerals can be identified by special physical properties. For example, magnetism occurs naturally in a few minerals. Minerals that glow under ultraviolet light have a property known as fluorescence (floo RES uns). The mineral scheelite is fluorescent. Figure 8 shows several minerals with special properties.

# Section 1 Assessment

**Target Reading Skill** Outlining Use the information in your outline about the properties of minerals to help you answer the questions.

### Reviewing Key Concepts

1. **a. Defining** Write a definition of "mineral" in your own words.
   **b. Explaining** What does it mean to say that a mineral is inorganic?
   **c. Classifying** Amber is a precious material used in jewelry. It forms when the resin of pine trees hardens into stone. Is amber a mineral? Explain.
2. **a. Listing** Name eight properties that can be used to identify minerals.
   **b. Comparing and Contrasting** What is the difference between fracture and cleavage?

   **c. Predicting** Graphite is a mineral made up of carbon atoms that form thin sheets. But the sheets are only weakly held together. Predict whether graphite will break apart with fracture or cleavage. Explain.

## Math Practice

3. **Calculating Density** The mineral platinum is an element that often occurs as a pure metal. If a sample of platinum has a mass of 430 g and a volume of 20 cm³, what is its density?

# Finding the Density of Minerals

## Problem

How can you compare the density of different minerals?

## Skills Focus

measuring

## Materials (per student)

- graduated cylinder, 100-mL
- 3 mineral samples: pyrite, quartz, and galena
- water
- balance

## Procedure

1. Check to make sure the mineral samples are small enough to fit in the graduated cylinder.

2. Copy the data table into your notebook. Place the pyrite on the balance and record its mass in the data table.

3. Fill the cylinder with water to the 50-mL mark.

4. Carefully place the pyrite in the cylinder of water. Try not to spill any of the water.

5. Read the level of the water on the scale of the graduated cylinder. Record the level of the water with the pyrite in it.

6. Calculate the volume of water displaced by the pyrite. To do this, subtract the volume of water without the pyrite from the volume of water with the pyrite. Record your answer.

7. Calculate the density of the pyrite by using this formula.

$$\text{Density} = \frac{\text{Mass of mineral}}{\text{Volume of water displaced by mineral}}$$

(Note: Density is expressed as $g/cm^3$. One mL of water has a volume of 1 $cm^3$.)

8. Remove the water and mineral from the cylinder.

9. Repeat Steps 2–8 for quartz and galena.

## Analyze and Conclude

1. **Interpreting Data** Which mineral had the highest density? The lowest density?

2. **Measuring** How does finding the volume of the water that was displaced help you find the volume of the mineral itself?

3. **Drawing Conclusions** Does the shape of a mineral sample affect its density? Explain.

4. **Predicting** Would the procedure you used in this lab work for a substance that floats or one that dissolves in water?

## Designing Experiments

Pyrite is sometimes called "fool's gold" because its color and appearance are similar to real gold. Design an experiment to determine if a sample that looks like gold is in fact real gold.

| Data Table | | | |
|---|---|---|---|
| | Pyrite | Quartz | Galena |
| Mass of Mineral (g) | | | |
| Volume of Water Without Mineral (mL) | 50 | 50 | 50 |
| Volume of Water With Mineral (mL) | | | |
| Volume of Water Displaced (mL) | | | |
| Volume of Water Displaced ($cm^3$) | | | |
| Density ($g/cm^3$) | | | |

# How Minerals Form

## Reading Focus

### Key Concepts
- How do minerals form from magma and lava?
- How do minerals form from water solutions?

### Key Terms
- geode • crystallization
- solution • vein

### Target Reading Skill

**Asking Questions** Before you read, preview the red headings. In a graphic organizer like the one below, ask a *how* or *what* question for each heading. As you read, write answers to your questions.

**Formation of Minerals**

| Question | Answer |
|----------|--------|
| How do minerals form from magma? | |
| | |

Amethyst geode ▼

---

**Lab zone** **Discover Activity**

### How Does the Rate of Cooling Affect Crystals?

1. ☠ Put on your goggles. Use a plastic spoon to place a small amount of salol near one end of each of two microscope slides. You need just enough to form a spot 0.5 to 1.0 cm in diameter.

2. 🔥 🧤 Carefully hold one slide with tongs. Warm it gently over a lit candle until the salol is almost completely melted. **CAUTION:** *Move the slide in and out of the flame to avoid cracking the glass.*

3. Set the slide aside to cool slowly. While the first slide is cooling, hold the second slide with tongs and heat it as in Step 2.

4. Cool the second slide quickly by placing it on an ice cube. Carefully blow out the candle.

5. Observe the slides under a hand lens. Compare the appearance of the crystals that form on the two slides.

6. Wash your hands when you are finished.

### Think It Over

**Developing Hypotheses** Which sample had larger crystals? If a mineral forms by rapid cooling, would you expect the crystals to be large or small?

---

On a rock-collecting field trip, you spot an egg-shaped rock about the size of a football. No, it's not a dinosaur egg—but what is it? You collect the rock and bring it to a geologic laboratory. There, you carefully split the rock open. The rock is hollow! Its inside surface sparkles with large, colorful amethyst crystals.

You have found a geode (JEE ohd). A **geode** is a rounded, hollow rock that is often lined with mineral crystals. Crystals form inside a geode when water containing dissolved minerals seeps into a crack or hollow in a rock. Slowly, crystallization occurs, lining the inside with large crystals that are often perfectly formed. **Crystallization** is the process by which atoms are arranged to form a material with a crystal structure. In general, minerals can form in two ways: by crystallization of magma and lava or by crystallization of materials dissolved in water.

# Minerals From Magma and Lava

Many minerals form from magma and lava. **Minerals form as hot magma cools inside the crust, or as lava hardens on the surface. When these liquids cool to a solid state, they form crystals.** The size of the crystals depends on several factors. The rate at which the magma cools, the amount of gas the magma contains, and the chemical composition of the magma all affect crystal size.

When magma remains deep below the surface, it cools slowly over many thousands of years. Slow cooling leads to the formation of large crystals, like the amethyst crystals in a geode. If the crystals remain undisturbed while cooling, they grow by adding atoms according to a regular pattern.

Magma closer to the surface cools much faster than magma that hardens deep below ground. With more rapid cooling, there is no time for magma to form large crystals. Instead, small crystals form. If magma erupts to the surface and becomes lava, the lava will also cool quickly and form minerals with small crystals.

 **Reading Checkpoint** What size crystals form when magma cools rapidly?

# Minerals From Solutions

Sometimes the elements and compounds that form minerals can be dissolved in water to form solutions. A **solution** is a mixture in which one substance is dissolved in another. **When elements and compounds that are dissolved in water leave a solution, crystallization occurs.** Minerals can form in this way underground and in bodies of water on Earth's surface.

## Lab zone Try This Activity

### Crystal Hands

1. Put on your goggles.
2. ☠ Pour a solution of table salt into one shallow pan and a solution of Epsom salts into another shallow pan.
3. Put a large piece of black construction paper on a flat surface.

   Dip one hand in the table salt solution. Shake off the excess liquid and make a palm print on the paper. Repeat with the other hand and the Epsom salt solution, placing your new print next to the first one. Wash your hands after making your hand prints. **CAUTION:** *Do not do this activity if you have a cut on your hand.*
4. Let the prints dry overnight.

**Observing** Use a hand lens to compare the shape of the crystals. Which hand prints have more crystals?

**FIGURE 9**
**Selenite Crystals**
These huge selenite crystals in a cave in Mexico formed from the crystallization of minerals in a solution.

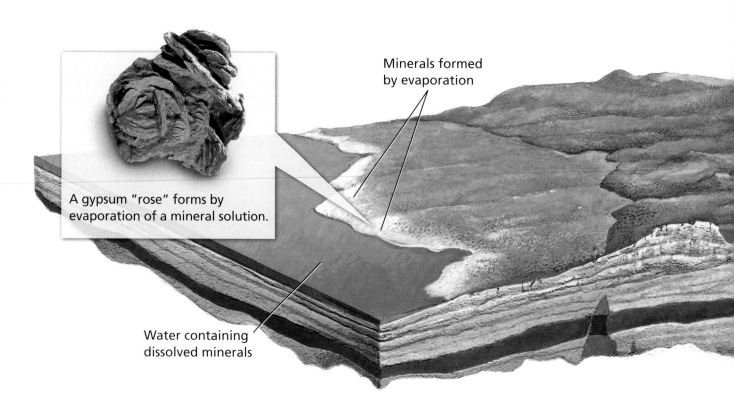

Minerals formed
by evaporation

A gypsum "rose" forms by
evaporation of a mineral solution.

Water containing
dissolved minerals

## Minerals Formed by Evaporation

Some minerals form when solutions evaporate. If you stir salt crystals into a beaker of water, the salt dissolves, forming a solution. But if you allow the water in the solution to evaporate, it will leave salt crystals on the bottom of the beaker. In a similar way, deposits of the mineral halite formed over millions of years when ancient seas slowly evaporated. In the United States, such halite deposits are found in the Midwest, the Southwest, and along the Gulf Coast. Other useful minerals that can form by evaporation include gypsum and calcite.

## Minerals From Hot Water Solutions

Deep underground, magma can heat water to a high temperature. Sometimes, the elements and compounds that form a mineral dissolve in this hot water. When the water solution begins to cool, the elements and compounds leave the solution and crystallize as minerals. The silver in Figure 10 was deposited from a hot water solution.

Pure metals that crystallize from hot water solutions underground often form veins. A **vein** is a narrow channel or slab of a mineral that is different from the surrounding rock. Solutions of hot water and metals often flow through cracks within the rock. Then the metals crystallize into veins that resemble the streaks of fudge in vanilla fudge ice cream.

 **Reading Checkpoint** What is a vein?

**Go Online**
PHSchool.com

**For:** More on mineral formation
**Visit:** PHSchool.com
**Web Code:** cfd-1042

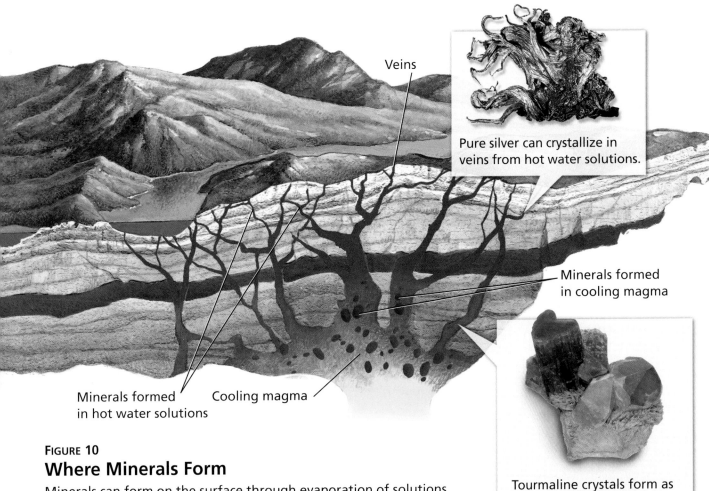

Veins

Pure silver can crystallize in veins from hot water solutions.

Minerals formed in cooling magma

Minerals formed in hot water solutions

Cooling magma

Tourmaline crystals form as magma cools deep beneath the surface.

**FIGURE 10**
## Where Minerals Form
Minerals can form on the surface through evaporation of solutions containing dissolved minerals. Minerals can form beneath the surface when dissolved elements and compounds leave a hot water solution or when magma cools and hardens.
**Interpreting Diagrams** *What process can form veins of underground minerals?*

# Section 2 Assessment

**Target Reading Skill** Asking Questions Use your chart to explain two ways in which minerals can form on Earth's surface.

## Reviewing Key Concepts

1. a. **Defining** What is crystallization?
   b. **Relating Cause and Effect** What factors affect the size of the crystals that form as magma cools?
   c. **Predicting** Under what conditions will cooling magma produce minerals with large crystals?
2. a. **Defining** What is a solution?
   b. **Explaining** What are two ways in which minerals can form from a solution?
   c. **Relating Cause and Effect** Describe the process by which a deposit of rock salt, or halite, could form from a solution.

## Writing in Science

**Dialogue** Suppose that you are a scientist exploring a cave. The light on your helmet suddenly reveals a wall covered with large crystals. Scientists on the surface ask you about your observations. Write a dialogue made up of their questions and your replies. Include the different ways in which the minerals you see might have formed.

# Who Owns the Ocean's Minerals?

Rich mineral deposits lie on and just beneath the ocean floor. Coastal nations have the right to mine deposits near their shores. Today, they are mining minerals from the continental shelf. But mineral deposits on the ocean floor beyond are open for all nations. Who owns these valuable underwater minerals?

## The Issues

### Who Can Afford to Mine?

Mining the ocean floor will cost a huge amount of money. New technologies must be developed to obtain mineral deposits from the ocean floor. Only wealthy industrial nations will be able to afford the costs. Industrial nations that have spent money on mining think that they should keep the profits. But developing nations that lack money and technology and landlocked nations disagree.

### What Rights Do Nations Have?

By 2003, 157 nations had signed the Law of the Sea treaty. Among other things, this treaty stated that ocean mineral deposits are the common property of all people. It also stated that mining profits must be shared among all nations. Some people think that, because of the treaty, wealthy nations should share their technology and any profits they get from mining the ocean floor.

**Ocean-Floor Mining**
Mining on the continental shelf is relatively easy. New technologies will be needed to mine the deep ocean beyond.

**Continental Shelf**
Diamonds are found near the shores of southwest Africa.

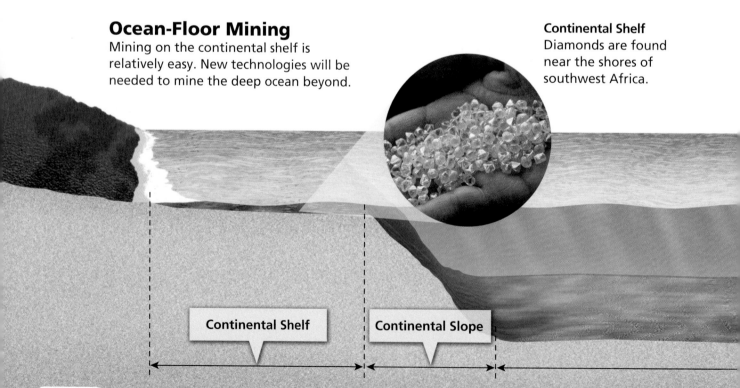

Continental Shelf

Continental Slope

Remotely operated vehicles like this one can be used to search the ocean floor for minerals.

## How Can the Wealth Be Shared?

What can nations do to prevent conflict over mining the ocean floor? They might arrange a compromise. Perhaps wealthy nations should contribute part of their profits to help developing or landlocked nations. Developing nations could pool their money for ocean-floor mining. Whatever nations decide, some regulations for ocean-floor mining are necessary. In the future, these resources will be important to everyone.

## What Would You Do?

### 1. Identify the Problem
Summarize the controversy about ocean mineral rights.

### 2. Analyze the Options
Research this topic at the library or on the Internet. Then compare the concerns of wealthy nations with those of developing nations. How could you reassure developing nations that they will not be left out?

### 3. Find a Solution
Look at a map of the world. Who should share the mineral profits from the Pacific Ocean? From the Atlantic Ocean? Write one or two paragraphs stating your opinion. Support your ideas with facts.

**Go Online**
PHSchool.com

**For:** More on who owns the ocean's minerals
**Visit:** PHSchool.com
**Web Code:** cfh-1040

**Abyssal Plain**
Minerals called manganese nodules form on the deep ocean floor. The metals cobalt, iron, nickel, and copper are also found here.

**Mid-Ocean Ridge**
Rich mineral deposits form from hot water solutions near mid-ocean ridges. Mining for gold, silver, copper, and other minerals might be possible here.

Abyssal Plain

Mid-Ocean Ridge

# Using Mineral Resources

## Reading Focus

### Key Concepts
- How are minerals used?
- How are ores processed to obtain metals?

### Key Terms
- gemstone
- ore
- smelting
- alloy

### Target Reading Skill

**Using Prior Knowledge** Before you read, look at the section headings and visuals to see what this section is about. Then write what you know about mineral resources in a graphic organizer like the one below. As you read, write what you learn.

| What You Know |
|---|
| 1. The gems used in jewelry are minerals. |
| 2. |

| What You Learned |
|---|
| 1. |
| 2. |

### Lab zone Discover **Activity**

## How Are Minerals Processed Before They Are Used?

1. Examine a piece of the mineral bauxite carefully. Use your knowledge of the properties of minerals to describe it.
2. Examine an aluminum can. (The metal aluminum comes from bauxite.) Compare the properties of the aluminum can with the properties of bauxite.
3. Examine a piece of the mineral graphite and describe its properties.
4. Examine the lead in a pencil. (Pencil lead is made from graphite.) Compare the properties of the pencil lead with the properties of graphite.

**Think It Over**

**Posing Questions** How does each mineral compare to the object made from it? To understand how bauxite and graphite are made into useful materials, what questions would you need to answer?

More than a thousand years ago, the Hopewell people lived in the Ohio River valley. These ancient Native Americans are famous for the mysterious earthen mounds they built near the river. There these people left beautiful objects made from minerals. Some of these objects are tools chipped from flint (a variety of quartz). Others are animals made from thin sheets of copper, like the fish in Figure 11.

To obtain these minerals, the Hopewell people traded with peoples across North America. The copper, for example, came from near Lake Superior. There, copper could be found as a pure metal. Because pure copper is soft, it was easy to shape into ornaments or weapons.

**FIGURE 11**
**Hopewell Fish**
The ancient Hopewell people used a thin sheet of copper to make this fish.

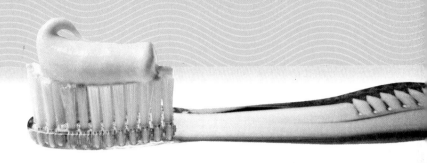

5. **Controlling Variables** What was the independent variable in this experiment? What was the dependent variable? Why did you use the same amount of toothpaste, force, and number of brushstrokes in each trial?

6. **Drawing Conclusions** How do the minerals in toothpaste affect the toothpaste's cleaning ability? Explain.

7. **Developing Hypotheses** Your teeth have the same composition as apatite, which has a hardness of 5 on the Mohs scale. What would be the advantages and disadvantages of using a toothpaste containing a mineral that is harder than apatite? Softer than apatite? Explain.

8. **Communicating** Write a lab report for this experiment. In your report, describe your predictions, your procedure, how you controlled variables, and whether or not your results supported your predictions.

## Design Your Own Experiment

Some brands of toothpaste claim that they whiten teeth. Design an experiment to test the effectiveness of different kinds of whitening toothpaste. Make a data table to organize your findings. *Obtain your teacher's permission before carrying out your investigation.*

## 1 Properties of Minerals

**Key Concepts**

- A mineral is a naturally occurring, inorganic solid that has a crystal structure and a definite chemical composition.

- Each mineral has characteristic properties that can be used to identify it.

- Density can be determined with the following formula:

$$\text{Density} = \frac{\text{Mass}}{\text{Volume}}$$

**Key Terms**

mineral
inorganic
crystal
streak
luster
Mohs hardness scale
cleavage
fracture

## 2 How Minerals Form

**Key Concepts**

- Minerals form as hot magma cools inside the crust, or as lava hardens on the surface. When these liquids cool to a solid state, they form crystals.

- When elements and compounds that are dissolved in water leave a solution, crystallization of minerals occurs.

**Key Terms**

geode
crystallization
solution
vein

## 3 Mineral Resources

**Key Concepts**

- Minerals are the source of gemstones, metals, and a variety of materials used to make many products.

- To produce metal from a mineral, a rock containing the mineral must be located through prospecting and mined, or removed from the ground. Then the rock must be processed to extract the metal.

**Key Terms**

gemstone
ore
smelting
alloy

# Review and Assessment

## Organizing Information

**Comparing and Contrasting** Fill in the Venn diagram to compare the characteristics of a mineral and a material that is not a mineral.

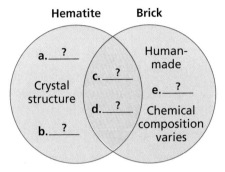

Hematite      Brick

a.___?___

Crystal structure

c.___?___

d.___?___

b.___?___

Human-made

e.___?___

Chemical composition varies

## Reviewing Key Terms

**Choose the letter of the best answer.**

1. Because minerals do not come from once-living material, they are said to be
   a. crystalline.
   b. solid.
   c. colorful.
   d. inorganic.

2. In a mineral, the particles line up in a repeating pattern to form a(n)
   a. element.
   b. crystal.
   c. mixture.
   d. compound.

3. Which characteristic is used to determine the color of a mineral's powder?
   a. luster
   b. fracture
   c. cleavage
   d. streak

4. Halite is a mineral formed through the evaporation of
   a. magma.
   b. a vein.
   c. a solution.
   d. lava.

5. Minerals from which metals can be removed in usable amounts are called
   a. gemstones.      b. crystals.
   c. alloys.         d. ores.

**If the statement is true, write *true*. If it is false, change the underlined word or words to make the statement true.**

6. A hollow rock lined with crystals is a <u>geode</u>.

7. <u>Fracture</u> is the term that describes how a mineral reflects light from its surface.

8. Mineral deposits beneath Earth's surface that are different from the surrounding rocks are called <u>veins</u>.

9. Hard, shiny crystals used in jewelry are called <u>ores</u>.

10. Steel is an example of a(n) <u>alloy</u>.

## Writing in Science

**Descriptive Paragraph** Choose a mineral such as gold or jade. Write a paragraph about the properties of this mineral. Explain why it is valuable and how it is useful to society.

**Discovery** CHANNEL **SCHOOL**

**Minerals**

Video Preview
Video Field Trip
▶ Video Assessment

# Review and Assessment

## Checking Concepts

11. How does the composition of most minerals differ from a pure element?

12. How can the streak test be helpful in identifying minerals?

13. How do geologists use different types of crystal shapes to classify minerals?

14. Describe two ways that minerals can form.

15. Which mineral in the table below would make the best gemstone? Explain your answer.

| Properties of Minerals | | | |
|---|---|---|---|
| Mineral | Hardness | Density (g/cm³) | Luster |
| Galena | 2.5 | 7.5 | metallic |
| Fluorite | 4.0 | 3.3 | glassy |
| Corundum | 9.0 | 4.0 | glassy |
| Talc | 1.0 | 2.8 | pearly |

16. Describe what happens to a mineral during smelting.

## Thinking Critically

17. **Classifying** Obsidian is a solid that occurs in volcanic areas. Obsidian forms when magma cools very quickly, creating a type of glass. In glass, the particles are not arranged in an orderly pattern as in a crystal. Should obsidian be classified as a mineral? Explain why or why not.

18. **Comparing and Contrasting** Color and luster are both properties of minerals. How are they similar? How are they different? How can each be used to help identify a mineral?

19. **Relating Cause and Effect** Describe how a vein of ore forms underground. What is the energy source for this process?

20. **Predicting** What would happen if steel-makers forgot to add enough chromium and nickel to a batch of stainless steel?

## Math Practice

21. **Calculating** A platinum ring has a volume of 0.8 cm³ and a mass of 15.2 g. What is its density?

22. **Calculating** A diamond has a mass of 10.56 g and a volume of 3 cm³. Calculate the density of the diamond.

## Applying Skills

**Use the photograph below to answer Questions 23–25.**

*You have found a sample of the mineral wulfenite. The wulfenite has a hardness of about 3 on the Mohs hardness scale and a density of 6.8 g/cm³. The mineral contains oxygen as well as the metals lead and molybdenum.*

23. **Observing** Describe wulfenite's color and luster and the shape of its crystals.

24. **Inferring** Did the wulfenite form slowly or quickly? Explain your answer.

25. **Drawing Conclusions** Is wulfenite hard enough for use as a gem? What would you use these crystals for? Explain.

## Lab zone Chapter **Project**

**Performance Assessment** Share your crystal garden with a classmate. Can your classmate identify which solution created which crystals? Do your data show differences in crystal growth rates? Which materials worked best for crystals to grow on? Share the answers to these questions when you present your project.

# Standardized Test Prep

**Choose the letter of the best answer.**

1. Which of the following is a mineral?
   A salt
   B pearl
   C coal
   D cement

2. You could distinguish gold from pyrite (fool's gold) by
   F comparing their hardness.
   G testing their chemical composition.
   H comparing their density.
   J all of the above

3. Veins of silver can be found in rock. These veins formed when
   A hot water solutions escaped from cracks in the rock.
   B hot water solutions crystallized in cracks in the rock.
   C magma crystallized in cracks in the rock.
   D hot water solutions evaporated in cracks in the rock.

4. An ore is a mineral that
   F is beautiful and rare.
   G can be mined at a profit.
   H is dense and metallic.
   J is light and durable.

5. The following diagrams show four different mineral samples. Based on these diagrams, what property is the same for all four minerals?

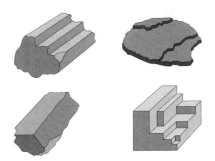

   A crystal structure
   B cleavage
   C hardness
   D color

## Constructed Response

6. A geologist finds an unknown mineral while working in a national park. The geologist is carrying a kit that contains a geologic hammer, a jackknife, a hand lens, a piece of tile, and a penny. In a paragraph, describe how the geologist could use these items to determine some of the mineral's properties.

# Chapter

# 5

# Rocks

Rock climbers need to know the ▶
characteristics of rock.

Rocks

▶ Video Preview
Video Field Trip
Video Assessment

## Lab zone™ Chapter **Project**

### Collecting Rocks

Each rock, whether a small pebble or a mountain peak, tells a story. The rocks in your own community tell part of the story of Earth's crust.

In this chapter, you will learn how three different types of rocks form. You can apply what you learn about rocks to create your own rock collection and explore the properties of your rocks.

**Your Goal** To make a collection of the rocks in your area

To complete this project, you must

- collect samples of rocks, keeping a record of where you found each sample
- describe the characteristics of your rocks, including their color, texture, and density
- classify each rock as igneous, sedimentary, or metamorphic
- create a display for your rock collection
- follow the safety guidelines in Appendix A

**Plan It!** With your classmates and teacher, brainstorm locations in your community where rocks are likely to be found. Are there road cuts, outcroppings of bedrock, riverbanks, or beaches where you could safely and legally collect your rocks? Plan your rock-hunting expeditions. Collect your rocks, and then describe, test, and classify your rock collection.

# Classifying Rocks

## Reading Focus

### Key Concepts
- What characteristics do geologists use to identify rocks?
- What are the three main groups of rocks?

### Key Terms
- rock-forming mineral • granite
- basalt • grains • texture
- igneous rock
- sedimentary rock
- metamorphic rock

### ⊙ Target Reading Skill

**Asking Questions** Before you read, preview the red headings. In a graphic organizer like the one below, ask a *what* or *how* question for each heading. As you read, write answers to your questions.

| Question | Answer |
|----------|--------|
| What does a rock's color tell about the rock? | |
| | |

## Lab zone Discover **Activity**

### How Do Rocks Compare?

1. Look at samples of conglomerate and marble with a hand lens.
2. Describe the two rocks. What is the color and texture of each?
3. Try scratching the surface of each rock with the edge of a penny. Which rock seems harder?
4. Hold each rock in your hand. Allowing for the fact that the samples aren't exactly the same size, which rock seems denser?

**Think It Over**

**Observing** Based on your observations, how would you compare the physical properties of marble and conglomerate?

**Conglomerate**

**Marble**

If you were a geologist, how would you examine a rock for the first time? You might use a camera or notebook to record information about the setting where the rock was found. Then, you would use a chisel or the sharp end of a rock hammer to remove samples of the rock. Finally, you would break open the samples with a hammer to examine their inside surfaces. You must look at the inside of a rock because the effects of ice, liquid water, and weather can change the outer surface of a rock.

You can find interesting rocks almost anywhere. The rock of Earth's crust forms mountains, hills, valleys, beaches, even the ocean floor. **When studying a rock sample, geologists observe the rock's mineral composition, color, and texture.**

**FIGURE 1**
**Inspecting a Rock**
This geologist is using a hand lens to observe a piece of shale.

Quartz

Feldspar

Hornblende

Mica

Granite

# Mineral Composition and Color

Rocks are made of mixtures of minerals and other materials. Some rocks contain only a single mineral. Others contain several minerals. For example, the granite in Figure 2 is made up of the minerals quartz, feldspar, hornblende, and mica. About 20 minerals make up most of the rocks of Earth's crust. These minerals are known as **rock-forming minerals.** Appendix B at the back of this book lists some of the most common rock-forming minerals.

A rock's color provides clues to the rock's mineral composition. For example, **granite** is generally a light-colored rock that has high silica content. **Basalt,** shown in Figure 3, is a dark-colored rock that is low in silica. But as with minerals, color alone does not provide enough information to identify a rock.

Geologists observe the shape and color of crystals in a rock to identify the minerals that the rock contains. In identifying rocks, geologists also use some of the tests that are used to identify minerals. For example, testing the surface of a rock with acid determines whether the rock includes minerals made of compounds called carbonates.

**Reading Checkpoint** How would you define "rock-forming mineral"?

**FIGURE 2**
**Minerals in Granite**
Granite is made up of quartz, feldspar, hornblende, and mica. It may also contain other minerals.
**Observing** *Which mineral seems most abundant in the sample of granite shown?*

**FIGURE 3**
**Basalt**
Basalt is a dark-colored rock that has low silica content. Unlike granite, basalt has mineral crystals that are too small to be seen without a hand lens.

# Texture

As with minerals, color alone does not provide enough information to identify a rock. But a rock's texture is very useful in identifying a rock. Most rocks are made up of particles of minerals or other rocks, which geologists call **grains.** Grains give the rock its texture. To a geologist, a rock's **texture** is the look and feel of the rock's surface. Some rocks are smooth and glassy. Others are rough or chalky. To describe a rock's texture, geologists use terms based on the size, shape, and pattern of the grains.

**FIGURE 4**
**Rock Textures**
Texture helps classify rocks.
**Comparing and Contrasting** *How would you compare the texture of diorite with the texture of gneiss?*

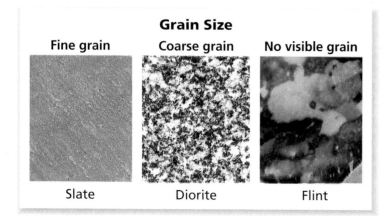

**Grain Size**

| Fine grain | Coarse grain | No visible grain |
| --- | --- | --- |
| Slate | Diorite | Flint |

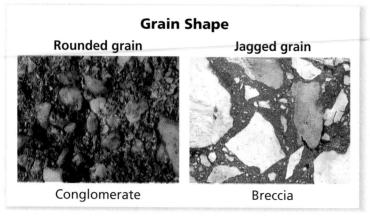

**Grain Shape**

| Rounded grain | Jagged grain |
| --- | --- |
| Conglomerate | Breccia |

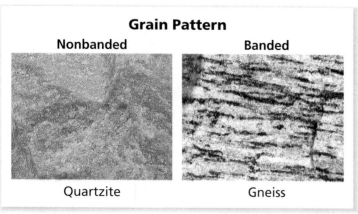

**Grain Pattern**

| Nonbanded | Banded |
| --- | --- |
| Quartzite | Gneiss |

**Grain Size** Often, the grains in a rock are large and easy to see. Such rocks are said to be coarse-grained. In other rocks, the grains are so small that they can only be seen with a microscope. These rocks are said to be fine-grained. Notice the difference in texture between the fine-grained slate and the coarse-grained diorite in Figure 4 at left. Some rocks have no visible grain even when they are examined under a microscope.

**Grain Shape** The grains in a rock vary widely in shape. Some grains look like tiny particles of sand. Others look like small seeds or exploding stars. In some rocks, such as granite, the grain results from the shapes of the crystals that form the rock. In other rocks, the grain shape results from fragments of several rocks. These fragments can be smooth and rounded or they can be jagged.

**Grain Pattern** The grains in a rock often form patterns. Some grains lie in flat layers that look like a stack of pancakes. Other grains form swirling patterns. Some rocks have grains of different colors in bands, like the gneiss (NYS) in Figure 4. In other rocks, the grains occur randomly throughout.

 **Reading Checkpoint** What does it mean to say that a rock is coarse-grained?

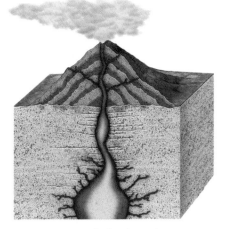

**Igneous Rock** forms when magma or lava cools and hardens.

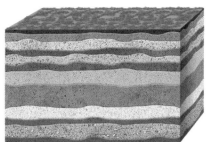

**Sedimentary Rock** forms when pieces of rock are pressed and cemented together.

**Metamorphic Rock** forms from other rocks that are changed by heat and pressure.

## How Rocks Form

Using color, texture, and mineral composition, geologists can classify a rock according to its origin. A rock's origin is how the rock formed. **Geologists classify rocks into three major groups: igneous rock, sedimentary rock, and metamorphic rock.**

Each of these groups of rocks forms in a different way. **Igneous rock** (IG nee us) forms from the cooling of magma or lava. Most **sedimentary rock** (sed uh MEN tur ee) forms when particles of other rocks or the remains of plants and animals are pressed and cemented together. Sedimentary rock forms in layers that are buried below the surface. **Metamorphic rock** (met uh MAWR fik) forms when an existing rock is changed by heat, pressure, or chemical reactions. Most metamorphic rock forms deep underground.

**FIGURE 5**
**Kinds of Rocks**
Rocks can be igneous, sedimentary, or metamorphic, depending on how the rock formed.

**For:** More on rock identification
**Visit:** PHSchool.com
**Web Code:** cfd-1051

---

## Section 1 Assessment

**Target Reading Skill** **Asking Questions** Work with a partner to check the answers in your graphic organizer about the section headings.

### Reviewing Key Concepts

1. **a. Naming** What three characteristics do geologists use to identify rocks?
   **b. Defining** What are the grains of a rock?
   **c. Comparing and Contrasting** In your own words, compare the grain size, shape, and pattern of the conglomerate and breccia in Figure 4.
2. **a. Reviewing** What are the three main groups of rocks?
   **b. Explaining** How do igneous rocks form?
   **c. Classifying** Gneiss is a kind of rock that forms when heat and pressure inside Earth change granite. To what group of rocks does gneiss belong?

### Writing in Science

**Wanted Poster** Write a paragraph for a wanted poster in which you describe the characteristics of granite. In your wanted poster, be sure to describe granite's mineral composition, color, and texture. Also mention the group of rocks to which granite belongs.

# Igneous Rocks

## Reading Focus

### Key Concepts
- What characteristics are used to classify igneous rocks?
- How are igneous rocks used?

### Key Terms
- extrusive rock • intrusive rock

### Target Reading Skill
**Identifying Main Ideas** As you read Classifying Igneous Rocks, write the main idea in a graphic organizer like the one below. Then write three supporting details that further explain the main idea.

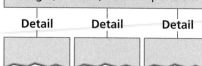

**Main Idea**

Igneous rocks are classified by origin, texture, and composition.

**Detail**   **Detail**   **Detail**

**Go Online**
SciLINKS NSTA

For: Links on igneous rocks
Visit: www.SciLinks.org
Web Code: scn-1052

**Obsidian**

**Granite**

### Lab zone Discover **Activity**

#### How Do Igneous Rocks Form?
1. Use a hand lens to examine samples of granite and obsidian.
2. Describe the texture of both rocks using the terms coarse, fine, or glassy.
3. Which rock has coarse-grained crystals? Which rock has no crystals or grains?

**Think It Over**
**Inferring** Granite and obsidian are igneous rocks. From your observations, what can you infer about how each type of rock formed?

The time is 4.6 billion years ago. You are in a spacecraft orbiting Earth. Do you see the blue and green globe of Earth that astronauts today see from space? No—instead, Earth looks like a charred and bubbling marshmallow heated over hot coals.

Soon after Earth formed, the planet's interior became so hot that magma formed. Lava repeatedly flowed over the surface. The lava quickly hardened, forming a rocky crust. Because this early crust was denser than the material beneath it, chunks of crust sank into Earth's interior. This allowed more lava to erupt over the surface and harden to form rock.

## Classifying Igneous Rocks

The first rocks to form on Earth probably looked like the igneous rocks that can be seen today. Igneous rock is any rock that forms from magma or lava. The name *igneous* comes from the Latin word *ignis*, meaning "fire." **Igneous rocks are classified according to their origin, texture, and mineral composition.**

**Origin** Igneous rock may form on or beneath Earth's surface. **Extrusive rock** is igneous rock formed from lava that erupted onto Earth's surface. Basalt is the most common extrusive rock. Basalt forms much of the crust, including the oceanic crust, shield volcanoes, and lava plateaus.

Igneous rock that formed when magma hardened beneath Earth's surface is called **intrusive rock.** The most abundant intrusive rock in continental crust is granite. Batholiths made of granite form the core of many mountain ranges.

**Texture** The texture of an igneous rock depends on the size and shape of its mineral crystals. The only exceptions to this rule are the different types of volcanic glass—igneous rock that lacks a crystal structure.

Igneous rocks may be similar in mineral composition and yet have very different textures. Rapidly cooling lava forms fine-grained igneous rocks with small crystals. Slowly cooling magma forms coarse-grained rocks with large crystals. Therefore, intrusive and extrusive rocks usually have different textures.

Intrusive rocks have larger crystals than extrusive rocks. If you examine a coarse-grained rock such as granite, you can easily see that the crystals vary in size and color. Some intrusive rocks, like the porphyry in Figure 6, have a texture that looks like a gelatin dessert with chopped-up fruit mixed in.

Extrusive rocks have a fine-grained or glassy texture. Basalt is a fine-grained extrusive rock. It consists of crystals too small to be seen without a microscope. Obsidian is an extrusive rock that cooled very rapidly without forming crystals. As a result, obsidian has the smooth, shiny texture of a thick piece of glass.

**FIGURE 6**
**Igneous Rock Textures**
Igneous rocks such as rhyolite, pegmatite, and porphyry can vary greatly in texture depending on whether they are intrusive or extrusive.
**Relating Cause and Effect** *What conditions caused rhyolite to have a fine-grained texture?*

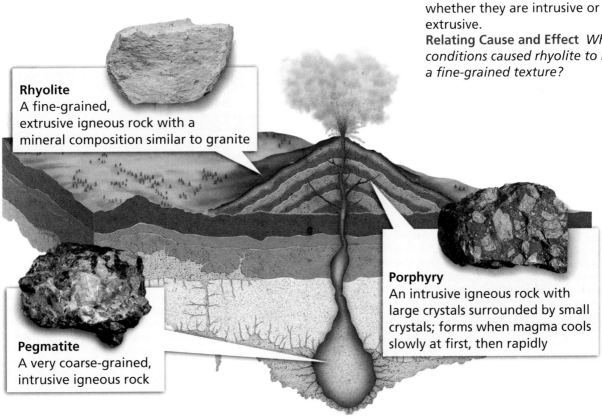

**Rhyolite**
A fine-grained, extrusive igneous rock with a mineral composition similar to granite

**Pegmatite**
A very coarse-grained, intrusive igneous rock

**Porphyry**
An intrusive igneous rock with large crystals surrounded by small crystals; forms when magma cools slowly at first, then rapidly

**F ◆ 149**

# Math ► Analyzing Data

## Mineral Mixture

Granite is a mixture of light-colored minerals such as feldspar and quartz and dark-colored minerals including hornblende and mica. But, granite can vary in mineral composition, affecting its color and texture.

Study the circle graph and then answer the questions.

1. **Reading Graphs** What mineral is most abundant in granite?

2. **Reading Graphs** About what percentage of granite is made up of dark minerals?

3. **Calculating** If the amount of quartz increases to 35 percent and the amount of dark-colored minerals stays the same, what percentage of the granite will be made up of feldspar?

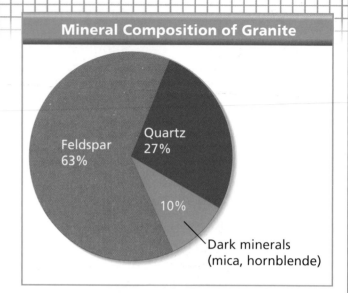

**Mineral Composition of Granite**

Feldspar 63%
Quartz 27%
10%
Dark minerals (mica, hornblende)

4. **Predicting** How would the color of the granite change if it contained less feldspar and more mica and hornblende?

**Mineral Composition** You may recall that the silica content of magma and lava can vary. Lava that is low in silica usually forms dark-colored rocks such as basalt. Basalt contains feldspar as well as certain dark-colored minerals, but does not contain quartz.

Magma that is high in silica usually forms light-colored rocks, such as granite. Granite's mineral composition determines its color—light gray, red, pink, or nearly black. Granite that is rich in reddish feldspar is a speckled pink. But granite rich in hornblende and dark mica is light gray with dark specks. Quartz crystals in granite add light gray or smoky specks.

Geologists can make thin slices of a rock, such as the gabbro in Figure 7. They study the rock's crystals under a microscope to determine the rock's mineral composition.

 **Reading Checkpoint** How can mineral composition affect a rock's color?

**FIGURE 7**
**Thin Section of a Rock**
This thin slice of gabbro, viewed under a microscope, contains olivine, feldspar, and other minerals.

# Uses of Igneous Rocks

Many igneous rocks are hard, dense, and durable. **People throughout history have used igneous rock for tools and building materials.**

**Building Materials** Granite has a long history as a building material. More than 3,500 years ago, the ancient Egyptians used granite for statues like the ones shown in Figure 8. About 600 years ago, the Incas of Peru carefully fitted together great blocks of granite and other igneous rocks to build a fortress near Cuzco, their capital city. In the United States during the 1800s and early 1900s, granite was widely used to build bridges and public buildings and for paving streets with cobblestones. Today, thin, polished sheets of granite are used in curbstones, floors, and kitchen counters. Basalt is crushed to make gravel that is used in construction.

**Other Uses** Igneous rocks such as pumice and obsidian also have important uses. The rough surface of pumice makes it a good abrasive for cleaning and polishing. Ancient native Americans used obsidian to make sharp tools for cutting and scraping. Perlite, formed from the heating of obsidian, is often mixed with soil for starting vegetable seeds.

**FIGURE 8**
**Durable Granite**
The ancient Egyptians valued granite for its durability. These statues from a temple in Luxor, Egypt, were carved in granite.

 **Reading Checkpoint** What igneous rock is most often used as a building material?

## Section 2 Assessment

**Target Reading Skill** **Identifying Main Ideas** Use your graphic organizer about the characteristics of igneous rock to help you answer Question 1 below.

### Reviewing Key Concepts

1. a. **Explaining** How are igneous rocks classified?
   b. **Defining** What are extrusive rocks and intrusive rocks?
   c. **Comparing and Contrasting** Compare granite and basalt in terms of their origin and texture. Which is extrusive? Which is intrusive?
2. a. **Summarizing** What are two common uses of igneous rocks?
   b. **Reviewing** What characteristics make igneous rocks useful?
   c. **Making Judgments** Would pumice be a good material to use to make a floor? Explain.

**Lab zone** **At-Home Activity**

**The Rocks Around Us** Many common household products contain minerals found in igneous rock. For example, glass contains quartz, which is found in granite. Research one of the following materials and the products in which it is used: garnet, granite, perlite, pumice, or vermiculite. Explain to family members how the rock or mineral formed and how it is used.

# 3 Sedimentary Rocks

## Reading Focus

### Key Concepts
• How do sedimentary rocks form?
• What are the three major types of sedimentary rocks?
• How are sedimentary rocks used?

### Key Terms
• sediment • erosion
• deposition • compaction
• cementation • clastic rock
• organic rock • chemical rock

### Target Reading Skill
**Outlining** As you read, make an outline about sedimentary rocks. Use the red section headings for the main topics and the blue headings for the subtopics.

| Sedimentary Rocks |
|---|
| I. From sediment to rock |
|   A. Erosion |
|   B. |
| II. |
|   A. |

### Lab zone Discover **Activity**

#### How Does Pressure Affect Particles of Rock?

1. Place a sheet of paper over a slice of soft bread.
2. Put a stack of several heavy books on top of the paper. After 10 minutes, remove the books. Observe what happened to the bread.
3. Slice the bread so you can observe its cross section.
4. Carefully slice a piece of fresh bread and compare its cross section to that of the pressed bread.

**Think It Over**
**Observing** How did the bread change after you removed the books? Describe the texture of the bread. How does the bread feel? What can you predict about how pressure affects the particles that make up sedimentary rocks?

Visitors to Badlands National Park in South Dakota see some of the strangest scenery on Earth. The park contains jagged peaks, steep cliffs, and deep canyons sculpted in colorful rock that is layered like a birthday cake. The layers of this cake are red, orange, pink, yellow, or tan. These rocks formed over millions of years as particles of mud, sand, and volcanic ash were deposited in thick layers. The mud and sand slowly changed to sedimentary rock. Then, uplift of the land exposed the rocks to the forces that wear away Earth's surface.

**Badlands National Park** ▲

## From Sediment to Rock

If you have ever walked along a stream or beach you may have noticed tiny sand grains, mud, and pebbles. These are particles of sediment. **Sediment** is small, solid pieces of material that come from rocks or living things. In addition to particles of rock, sediment may include shells, bones, leaves, stems, and other remains of living things. Sedimentary rocks form when sediment is deposited by water and wind. **Most sedimentary rocks are formed through a series of processes: erosion, deposition, compaction, and cementation.** Figure 9 shows how sedimentary rocks form.

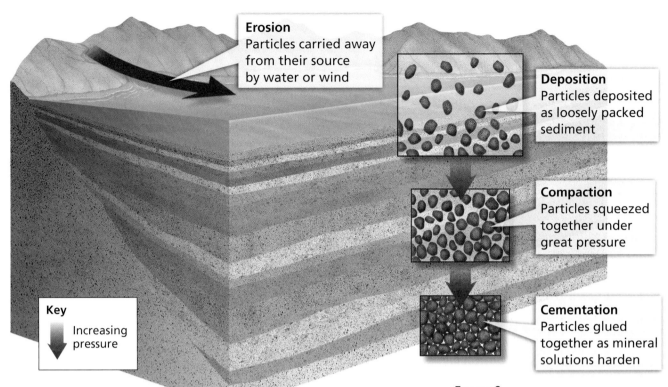

**Erosion**
Particles carried away from their source by water or wind

**Deposition**
Particles deposited as loosely packed sediment

**Compaction**
Particles squeezed together under great pressure

**Cementation**
Particles glued together as mineral solutions harden

**Key**
Increasing pressure

**Erosion** Destructive forces are constantly breaking up and wearing away, or weathering, all the rocks on Earth's surface. These forces include heat and cold, rain, waves, and grinding ice. The forces of erosion form sediment. In **erosion,** running water, wind, or ice loosen and carry away fragments of rock.

**Deposition** Eventually, the moving water, wind, or ice slows and deposits the sediment in layers. If water is carrying the sediment, rock fragments and other materials sink to the bottom of a lake or ocean. **Deposition** is the process by which sediment settles out of the water or wind carrying it.

**Compaction** The process that presses sediments together is **compaction.** Thick layers of sediment build up gradually over millions of years. These heavy layers press down on the layers beneath them. The weight of new layers further compacts the sediments, squeezing them tightly together. The layers often remain visible in sedimentary rock.

**Cementation** While compaction is taking place, the minerals in the rock slowly dissolve in the water. **Cementation** is the process in which dissolved minerals crystallize and glue particles of sediment together. In cementation, dissolved minerals seep into the spaces between particles and then harden.

 **Reading Checkpoint** What is deposition?

**FIGURE 9**
**How Sedimentary Rocks Form**
Sedimentary rocks form through the deposition, compaction, and cementation of sediments over millions of years.
**Relating Cause and Effect** *What conditions are necessary for sedimentary rocks to form?*

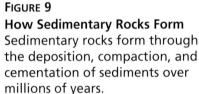

**For:** Links on sedimentary rocks
**Visit:** www.SciLinks.org
**Web Code:** scn-1053

**Shale**
Fossils are often found in shale, which splits easily into flat pieces.

**Sandstone**
Many small holes between sand grains allow sandstone to absorb water.

**Conglomerate**
Rock fragments with rounded edges make up conglomerate.

FIGURE 10
**Clastic Rocks**
Clastic rocks such as shale, sandstone, conglomerate, and breccia are sedimentary rocks that form from particles of other rocks.

**Lab zone** Try This **Activity**

### Rock Absorber

Here's how to find out if water can soak into rock.

1. Using a hand lens, compare samples of sandstone and shale.

2. Use a balance to measure the mass of each rock.

3. Place the rocks in a pan of water and watch closely. Which sample has bubbles escaping? Predict which sample will gain mass.

4. Leave the rocks submerged in the pan overnight.

5. The next day, remove the rocks from the pan and find the mass of each rock.

**Drawing Conclusions** How did the masses of the two rocks change after soaking? What can you conclude about each rock?

# Types of Sedimentary Rock

Geologists classify sedimentary rocks according to the type of sediments that make up the rock. **There are three major groups of sedimentary rocks: clastic rocks, organic rocks, and chemical rocks.** Different processes form each of these types of sedimentary rocks.

**Clastic Rocks** Most sedimentary rocks are made up of broken pieces of other rocks. A **clastic rock** is a sedimentary rock that forms when rock fragments are squeezed together. These fragments can range in size from clay particles that are too small to be seen without a microscope to large boulders that are too heavy for you to lift. Clastic rocks are grouped by the size of the rock fragments, or particles, of which they are made. Common clastic rocks include shale, sandstone, conglomerate, and breccia (BRECH ee uh), shown in Figure 10.

Shale forms from tiny particles of clay. Water must deposit the clay particles in thin, flat layers. Sandstone forms from the sand on beaches, the ocean floor, riverbeds, and sand dunes. Most sand particles consist of quartz.

Some sedimentary rocks contain a mixture of rock fragments of different sizes. If the fragments have rounded edges, they form a clastic rock called conglomerate. A rock made up of large fragments with sharp edges is called breccia.

**Organic Rocks** Not all sedimentary rocks are made from particles of other rocks. **Organic rock** forms where the remains of plants and animals are deposited in thick layers. The term "organic" refers to substances that once were part of living things or were made by living things. Two important organic sedimentary rocks are coal and limestone, shown in Figure 11.

**Breccia**
Rock fragments with sharp edges form breccia.

**Coal**
Swamp plants that formed millions of years ago slowly changed to form coal.

**Limestone**
Coquina is a form of limestone in which the shells that makeup the rock are easy to see.

Coal forms from the remains of swamp plants buried in water. As layer upon layer of plant remains build up, the weight of the layers squeezes the decaying plants. Over millions of years, they slowly change into coal.

Limestone forms in the ocean, where many living things, such as coral, clams, and oysters, have hard shells or skeletons made of calcite. When these animals die, their shells pile up on the ocean floor. Over millions of years, these layers of sediment can grow to a depth of hundreds of meters. Slowly, compaction and cementation change the sediment to limestone.

**Chemical Rocks**  When minerals that are dissolved in a solution crystallize, **chemical rock** forms. For example, limestone can form when calcite that is dissolved in lakes, seas, or underground water comes out of solution and forms crystals. This kind of limestone is considered a chemical rock. Chemical rocks can also form from mineral deposits left when seas or lakes evaporate. For example, rock salt is made of the mineral halite, which forms by evaporation.

 **How does coal form?**

**FIGURE 11**
**Organic Rocks**
Organic rocks such as coal and limestone are sedimentary rocks that form from the remains of living things.

**FIGURE 12**
**Chemical Rocks**
These rock "towers" in Mono Lake California, are made of tufa, a form of limestone. Tufa is a chemical rock that forms from solutions containing dissolved materials.  **Classifying** *What type of sedimentary rock is tufa?*

## Uses of Sedimentary Rocks

**People have used sedimentary rocks throughout history for many different purposes, including building materials and tools.** For example, people made arrowheads out of flint for thousands of years. Flint is a hard rock, yet it can be shaped to a point. Flint is formed when small particles of silica settle out of water.

Sedimentary rocks such as sandstone and limestone have been used as building materials for thousands of years. Both types of stone are soft enough to be cut easily into blocks or slabs. You may be surprised to learn that the White House in Washington, D.C., is built of sandstone. Builders today use sandstone and limestone on the outside walls of buildings. Limestone also has many industrial uses. For example, limestone is used in making cement and steel.

**FIGURE 13**
**Carving Limestone**
This stone carver is sculpting designs on a sphere of white limestone.

 **Reading Checkpoint** Why are sandstone and limestone useful as building materials?

## Section 3 Assessment

**Target Reading Skill** Outlining Use the information in your outline about sedimentary rocks to help you answer the questions below.

### Reviewing Key Concepts

1. **a. Defining** What is sediment?
   **b. Sequencing** Place these steps in the formation of sedimentary rock in the proper sequence: compaction, erosion, cementation, deposition.
   **c. Inferring** In layers of sedimentary rock, where would you expect to find the oldest sediment? Explain your answer.
2. **a. Listing** What are the three main types of sedimentary rock?
   **b. Explaining** Which type of sedimentary rock forms from the remains of living things? Explain how this sedimentary rock forms.
   **c. Relating Cause and Effect** What process causes deposits of rock salt to form? What type of sedimentary rock is rock salt?

3. **a. Listing** What are some uses of sedimentary rocks?
   **b. Predicting** The particles of sediment that make up shale are not usually well cemented. Would shale be a good choice of building material in a wet climate?

## Writing in Science

**Explaining a Process** Suppose that a large mass of granite lies exposed on Earth's surface. Explain the steps in the process by which the granite could become sedimentary rock. Your answer should also state which of the main types of sedimentary rock will result from this process.

# Rocks From Reefs

## Reading Focus

### Key Concepts
- How do coral reefs form?
- What evidence do limestone deposits from coral reefs provide about Earth's history?

### Key Term
- coral reef

### Target Reading Skill
**Using Prior Knowledge**
Before you read, look at the section headings to see what this section is about. Then write what you know about coral reefs in a graphic organizer like the one below. As you read, write what you learn.

| What You Know |
|---|
| 1. Coral reefs grow in the oceans. |
| 2. |

| What You Learned |
|---|
| 1. |
| 2. |

## Lab zone Discover **Activity**

### How Does a Rock React to Acid?

1. Using a hand lens, observe the color and texture of limestone and coquina.
2. Put on your goggles and apron.
3. Obtain a small amount of dilute hydrochloric acid from your teacher. Hydrochloric acid is used to test rocks for the presence of the mineral calcite.

   Using a plastic dropper, place a few drops of dilute hydrochloric acid on the limestone. **CAUTION:** *Hydrochloric acid can cause burns.*
4. Record your observations.
5. Repeat Steps 2 through 4 with the sample of coquina and observe the results.
6. Rinse the rock samples with lots of water before returning them to your teacher. Wash your hands.

**Think It Over**
**Drawing Conclusions** How did the two rocks react to the test? A piece of coral reacts to hydrochloric acid the same way as limestone and coquina. What could you conclude about the mineral composition of coral?

Off the coast of Florida lies a "city" in the sea. It is a coral reef providing both food and shelter for many sea animals. The reef shimmers with life—clams, sponges, sea urchins, starfish, marine worms and, of course, fish. Schools of brilliantly colored fish dart in and out of forests of equally colorful corals. Octopuses lurk in underwater caves, scooping up crabs that pass too close. A reef forms a sturdy wall that protects the shoreline from battering waves. This city was built by billions of tiny, soft-bodied animals that have skeletons made of calcite.

**FIGURE 14**
**A City in the Sea**
A coral reef provides food and shelter for many different kinds of living things.

**FIGURE 15**
**Coral Animals and Reefs**
The coral animals in the close-up feed on tiny organisms carried their way by the movement of ocean water. (The view has been magnified to show detail.) The aerial photograph shows an island in the South Pacific Ocean that is ringed by a coral reef (light blue areas). **Inferring** *Why are there no coral reefs in the dark blue areas of ocean water?*

# Coral Reefs

Coral animals are tiny relatives of jellyfish that live together in vast numbers. They produce skeletons that grow together to form a structure called a **coral reef.**

**How Coral Animals Live** Most coral animals are smaller than your fingernail. Each one looks like a small sack with a mouth surrounded by tentacles. These animals use their tentacles to capture and eat microscopic creatures that float by.

Tiny algae grow within the body of each coral animal. The algae provide substances that the coral animals need to live. In turn, the coral animals provide a framework for the algae to grow on. Like plants, algae need sunlight. Below 40 meters, there is not enough light for the algae to grow. For this reason, almost all coral growth occurs within 40 meters of the water's surface.

**How a Coral Reef Forms** To form their skeletons, coral animals absorb the element calcium from the ocean water. The calcium is then combined with carbon and oxygen to form calcite. Recall that calcite is a mineral. **When coral animals die, their skeletons remain. More corals build on top of them, gradually forming a coral reef.**

Coral animals cannot grow in cold water. As a result, coral reefs form only in the warm, shallow water of tropical oceans. Reefs are most abundant around islands and along the eastern coasts of continents. In the United States, only the coasts of southern Florida and Hawaii have coral reefs.

Over thousands of years, reefs may grow to be hundreds of kilometers long and hundreds of meters thick. Reefs usually grow outward toward the open ocean. If the sea level rises or if the sea floor sinks, the reef will grow upward, too.

 **Reading Checkpoint** What conditions of light and temperature do coral animals require?

# Limestone From Coral Reefs

A coral reef is really organic limestone. **Limestone deposits that began as coral reefs provide evidence of how plate motions have changed Earth's surface. These deposits also provide evidence of past environments.**

Limestone from coral reefs has been forming in Earth's oceans for more than 400 million years. The limestone formed when shallow seas covered the low-lying parts of the continents. The limestone was exposed when the seas retreated. Later, plate motions slowly moved these limestone deposits far from the tropical oceans where they formed. In the United States, reefs that formed millions of years ago are exposed in Wisconsin, Illinois, Indiana, Texas, New Mexico, and many other places.

Deposits of organic limestone help geologists understand past environments. Where geologists find fossils of an ancient coral reef, they know that the reef formed in an area with a warm climate and shallow ocean water. In North America, these conditions existed for millions of years when much of the continent lay closer to the equator than it does today. Shallow seas covered the central part of North America, allowing large coral reefs to form. Today, the reefs are thick deposits of sedimentary rock.

**FIGURE 16**
**Limestone From Coral**
A band of light-colored limestone marks an ancient reef that forms part of Guadalupe Peak in Texas. This reef is now 2,600 meters above sea level!

---

## Section 4 Assessment

**Target Reading Skill** Using Prior Knowledge Review your graphic organizer about coral reefs and revise it based on what you just learned.

### Reviewing Key Concepts

1. **a. Describing** What is a coral animal?
   **b. Summarizing** How do coral animals build a coral reef?
   **c. Predicting** If sea level rises above a coral reef, what may happen to the reef?
2. **a. Identifying** What type of rock is made up of ancient coral?
   **b. Inferring** A geologist finds an area where the rocks were formed from an ancient coral reef. What can the geologist infer about the ancient environment where the rocks formed?

### Lab zone At-Home **Activity**

**Earth's Coral Reefs** Obtain a globe or world map. Find the lines that represent the tropic of Cancer and the tropic of Capricorn. The area that lies between these two lines, called the Tropics, is where most coral reefs form in warm ocean water. Locate the northeast coast of Australia, the Red Sea, and groups of tropical islands in the Caribbean Sea, Indian Ocean, and Pacific Ocean. Point out these features to family members and explain that these are areas where coral reefs occur today.

# Metamorphic Rocks

## Reading Preview

### Key Concepts
- Under what conditions do metamorphic rocks form?
- How do geologists classify metamorphic rocks?
- How are metamorphic rocks used?

### Key Term
- foliated

### Target Reading Skill
**Previewing Visuals** Before you read, preview Figure 17. Then write two questions that you have about metamorphic rocks in a graphic organizer like the one below. As you read, answer your questions.

**Metamorphic Rocks**

| Q. | Why do the crystals in gneiss line up in bands? |
|---|---|
| A. | |
| Q. | |

**For:** Links on metamorphic rocks
**Visit:** www.SciLinks.org
**Web Code:** scn-1055

---

**Lab zone Discover Activity**

### How Do Grain Patterns Compare?

1. Using a hand lens, observe samples of gneiss and granite. Look carefully at the grains or crystals in both rocks.
2. Observe how the grains or crystals are arranged in both rocks. Draw a sketch of both rocks and describe their textures.

**Think It Over**
**Inferring** Within the crust, some granite becomes gneiss. What do you think must happen to cause this change?

---

Every metamorphic rock is a rock that has changed its form. In fact, the word *metamorphic* comes from the Greek words *meta*, meaning "change," and *morphosis*, meaning "form." But what causes a rock to change into metamorphic rock? The answer lies inside Earth.

**Heat and pressure deep beneath Earth's surface can change any rock into metamorphic rock.** When rock changes into metamorphic rock, its appearance, texture, crystal structure, and mineral content change. Metamorphic rock can form out of igneous, sedimentary, or other metamorphic rock.

Collisions between Earth's plates can push the rock down toward the heat of the mantle. Pockets of magma rising through the crust also provide heat that can produce metamorphic rocks. The deeper a rock is buried in the crust, the greater the pressure on that rock. Under high temperature and pressure many times greater than at Earth's surface, the minerals in a rock can be changed into other minerals. The rock has become a metamorphic rock.

## Types of Metamorphic Rocks

While metamorphic rocks are forming, high temperatures change the size and shape of the grains, or mineral crystals, in the rock. Extreme pressure squeezes rock so tightly that the mineral grains may line up in flat, parallel layers. **Geologists classify metamorphic rocks according to the arrangement of the grains that make up the rocks.**

**Foliated Rocks** Metamorphic rocks that have their grains arranged in parallel layers or bands are said to be **foliated.** The term *foliated* comes from the Latin word for "leaf." It describes the thin, flat layering found in most metamorphic rocks. Foliated rocks—including slate, schist, and gneiss—may split apart along these bands. In Figure 17, notice how the crystals in granite have been flattened to create the foliated texture of gneiss.

One common foliated rock is slate. Heat and pressure change the sedimentary rock shale into slate. Slate is basically a denser, more compact version of shale. During the change, new minerals such as mica form in the slate.

**Nonfoliated Rocks** Some metamorphic rocks are nonfoliated. The mineral grains in these rocks are arranged randomly. Metamorphic rocks that are nonfoliated do not split into layers. Marble and quartzite are two metamorphic rocks that have a nonfoliated texture. Quartzite forms out of sandstone. The weakly cemented quartz particles in the sandstone recrystallize to form quartzite, which is extremely hard. Notice in Figure 17 how much smoother quartzite looks than sandstone.

**Reading Checkpoint** What is a foliated rock?

**FIGURE 17**
**Forming Metamorphic Rocks**
Great heat and pressure can change one type of rock into another. **Observing** *How does slate differ from shale?*

**Lab zone Try This Activity**

**A Sequined Rock**
1. Make three balls of clay about 3 cm in diameter. Gently mix about 25 sequins into one ball.
2. Use a 30-cm piece of string to cut the ball in half. How are the sequins arranged?
3. Roll the clay with the sequins back into a ball. Stack the three balls with the sequin ball in the middle. Set these on a block of wood. With another block of wood, press slowly down until the stack is about 3 cm high.
4. Use the string to cut the stack in half. How are the sequins arranged?

**Making Models** What do the sequins in your model rock represent? Is this rock foliated or nonfoliated?

**Granite**
igneous

**Sandstone**
sedimentary

**Shale**
sedimentary

Heat and pressure

Heat and pressure

Heat and pressure

**Gneiss**
metamorphic, foliated

**Quartzite**
metamorphic, nonfoliated

**Slate**
metamorphic, foliated

## Uses of Metamorphic Rock

**Certain metamorphic rocks are important materials for building and sculpture.** Marble and slate are two of the most useful metamorphic rocks. Marble usually forms when limestone is subjected to heat and pressure deep beneath the surface. Because marble has a fine, even grain, it can be cut into thin slabs or carved into many shapes. And marble is easy to polish. These qualities have led architects and sculptors to use marble for many buildings and statues. For example, one of America's most famous sculptures is in the Lincoln Memorial in Washington, D.C. Sculptor Daniel Chester French carved this portrait of Abraham Lincoln in gleaming white marble.

Like marble, slate comes in a variety of colors, including gray, black, red, and purple. Because it is foliated, slate splits easily into flat pieces. These pieces can be used for flooring, roofing, outdoor walkways, chalkboards, and as trim for stone buildings.

**FIGURE 18**
**The Lincoln Memorial**
The statue of Abraham Lincoln in the Lincoln Memorial in Washington, D.C., is made of gleaming white marble.

 **Reading Checkpoint** **What characteristics of slate make it useful?**

---

## Section 5 Assessment

**Target Reading Skill** **Previewing Visuals** Compare your questions and answers about Figure 17 with those of a partner.

### Reviewing Key Concepts

1. **a. Explaining** What does *metamorphic* mean?
   **b. Relating Cause and Effect** Where and under what conditions are metamorphic rocks formed?
2. **a. Identifying** What characteristic of metamorphic rocks do geologists use to classify them?
   **b. Explaining** How does a foliated metamorphic rock form?
   **c. Classifying** Which of the rocks in Figure 17 is foliated? How can you tell?
3. **a. Identifying** What is the main use of metamorphic rocks?
   **b. Making Judgments** Which might be more useful for carving chess pieces—marble or slate? Explain your answer.

### Lab zone At-Home Activity

**Rocks Around the Block** How are rocks used in your neighborhood? Take a walk with your family to see how many uses you can observe. Identify statues, walls, and buildings made from rocks. Can you identify which type of rock was used? Look for limestone, sandstone, granite, and marble. Share a list of the rocks you found with your class. For each rock, include a description of its color and texture, where you observed the rock, and how it was used.

# Mystery Rocks

## Problem

What properties can be used to classify rocks?

## Skills Focus

inferring, classifying

## Materials

- 1 "mystery rock"
- 2 unknown igneous rocks
- 2 unknown sedimentary rocks
- 2 unknown metamorphic rocks
- hand lens

## Procedure

1. For this activity, you will be given six rocks and one sample that is not a rock. They are labeled A through G.
2. Copy the data table into your notebook.
3. Using the hand lens, examine each rock for clues that show the rock formed from molten material. Record the rock's color and texture. Observe if there are any crystals or grains in the rock.
4. Use the hand lens to look for clues that show the rock formed from particles of other rocks. Observe the texture of the rock to see if it has any tiny, well-rounded grains.
5. Use the hand lens to look for clues that show the rock formed under heat and pressure. Observe if the rock has a flat layer of crystals or shows colored bands.
6. Record your observations in the data table.

## Analyze and Conclude

1. **Inferring** Infer from your observations the group in which each rock belongs.
2. **Classifying** Which of the samples could be classified as igneous rocks? What physical properties do these rock share with the other samples? How are they different?
3. **Classifying** Which of the samples could be classified as sedimentary rocks? How do you think these rocks formed? What are the physical properties of these rocks?
4. **Classifying** Which of the samples could be classified as metamorphic rocks? What are their physical properties?
5. **Drawing Conclusions** Decide which sample is not a rock. How did you determine that the sample you chose is not a rock? What do you think the "mystery rock" is? Explain.
6. **Communicating** What physical property was most useful in classifying rocks? Which physical property was least useful? Explain your answer.

## More to Explore

Can you name each rock? Use a field guide to rocks and minerals to find the specific name of each rock sample.

| Data Table | | | | |
|---|---|---|---|---|
| Sample | Color | Texture (fine, medium, or coarse-grained) | Foliated or Banded | Rock Group (igneous, metamorphic, sedimentary) |
| A | | | | |
| B | | | | |

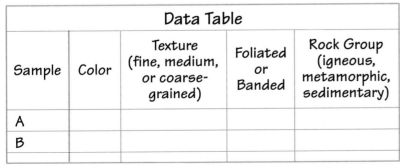

## Reading Preview

### Key Concepts
- What is the rock cycle?
- What is the role of plate tectonics in the rock cycle?

### Key Term
- rock cycle

### Target Reading Skill

**Sequencing** As you read, make a cycle diagram that shows the stages in the rock cycle. Write each stage of the rock cycle in a separate circle in your diagram.

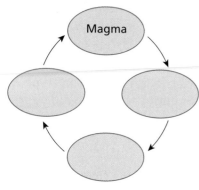

Rock Cycle

Magma

## Lab zone Discover Activity

### Which Rock Came First?

1. Referring to the photos below, make sketches of quartzite, granite, and sandstone on three index cards.
2. Observe the color and texture of each rock. Look for similarities and differences.
3. To which major group does each rock belong?

**Think It Over**

**Developing Hypotheses** How are quartzite, granite, and sandstone related? Arrange your cards in the order in which these three rocks formed. Given enough time in Earth's crust, what might happen to the third rock in your series?

Sandstone          Quartzite          Granite

Earth's rocks are not as unchanging as they seem. **Forces deep inside Earth and at the surface produce a slow cycle that builds, destroys, and changes the rocks in the crust.** The **rock cycle** is a series of processes on Earth's surface and in the crust and mantle that slowly change rocks from one kind to another.

## A Cycle of Many Pathways

Here's one possible pathway through the rock cycle, shown in Figure 19. The igneous rock granite formed beneath the surface. Then, the forces of mountain building slowly pushed the granite upward, forming a mountain. Slowly, water and wind wore away the granite. These granite particles became sand, carried by streams to the ocean. Over millions of years, layers of sandy sediment piled up on the ocean floor. Slowly, the sediment changed to sandstone, a sedimentary rock. Over time, the sandstone became deeply buried. Heat and pressure changed the rock's texture from gritty to smooth. The sandstone changed into the metamorphic rock quartzite. But metamorphic rock does not end the rock cycle, which continues for millions of years.

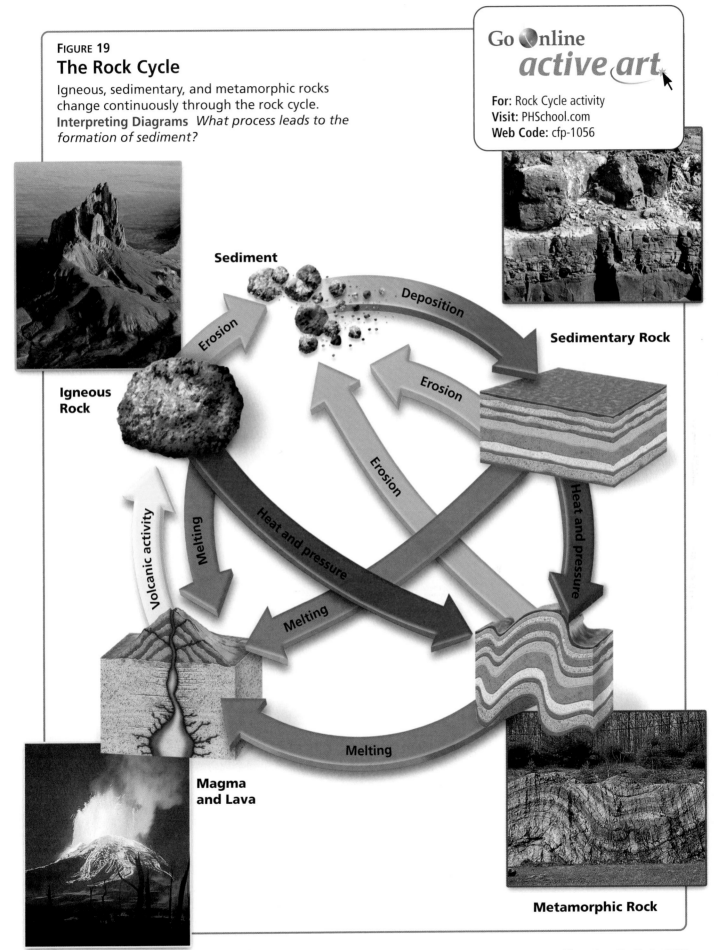

FIGURE 19
**The Rock Cycle**
Igneous, sedimentary, and metamorphic rocks change continuously through the rock cycle.
**Interpreting Diagrams**  *What process leads to the formation of sediment?*

Go Online
*active art*
**For:** Rock Cycle activity
**Visit:** PHSchool.com
**Web Code:** cfp-1056

**Sediment**

Erosion

Deposition

**Sedimentary Rock**

Erosion

**Igneous Rock**

Erosion

Heat and pressure

Volcanic activity

Melting

Heat and pressure

Melting

Melting

**Magma and Lava**

**Metamorphic Rock**

# The Rock Cycle and Plate Tectonics

The changes of the rock cycle are closely related to plate tectonics. **Plate movements start the rock cycle by helping to form magma, the source of igneous rocks. Plate movements also cause faulting, folding, and other motions of the crust that help to form sedimentary and metamorphic rocks.**

**Igneous Rocks** Where oceanic plates move apart, magma formed from melted mantle rock moves upward and fills the gap with new igneous rock. Where an oceanic plate is subducted beneath a continental plate, magma forms and rises. The result is a volcano made of igneous rock. A collision of continental plates may push rocks so deep that they melt and form magma. This magma slowly cools and hardens to form igneous rock.

**Sedimentary and Metamorphic Rocks** The collision of continental plates produces faults, folds, and uplift of the crust. Eventually, the collision could push up a mountain range. Then, erosion begins. The mountains eventually are worn away, leading to the formation of sedimentary rock.

A collision between continental plates can also push rocks down deep into the mantle. There, heat and pressure could change the rocks to metamorphic rock. And so the rock cycle continues, for hundreds of millions of years.

 **Reading Checkpoint** How can plate movements help to form metamorphic rock?

**FIGURE 20**
**Moving Up in the World**
This fossil trilobite lived on an ocean floor about 500 million years ago. As plate tectonics moved pieces of Earth's crust, the rock containing this fossil became part of a mountain.

---

## Section 6 Assessment

**Target Reading Skill** Sequencing Review your cycle diagram about the rock cycle with a partner. Add any necessary information.

### Reviewing Key Concepts

1. a. **Defining** Write a definition of the rock cycle in your own words.
   b. **Sequencing** Begin with igneous rock and explain how it could change through two more steps in the rock cycle.
2. a. **Reviewing** How do plate movements help to form igneous rocks?
   b. **Relating Cause and Effect** How can the collision of plates lead to the formation of sedimentary rock?
   c. **Predicting** What would be likely to happen to the rock cycle if Earth's interior cooled so much that plate motions stopped?

### Writing in Science

**Rock Legend** Pick one type of rock and write a possible "biography" of the rock as it moves through the rock cycle. Your story should state the type of rock, how the rock formed, and how it might change.

# Testing Rock Flooring

## Problem

What kind of building stone makes the best flooring?

## Skills Focus

designing experiments, controlling variables, drawing conclusions

## Suggested Materials

- steel nail • wire brush • water
- plastic dropper • hand lens
- samples of igneous, sedimentary, and metamorphic rocks with flat surfaces
- greasy materials such as butter and crayons
- materials that form stains, such as ink and paints

## Procedure

1. Brainstorm with your partner the qualities of good flooring. For example, good flooring should resist stains, scratches, and grease marks, and be safe to walk on when wet.

2. Predict what you think is the best building stone for a kitchen floor. Why is it the best?

3. Write the steps you plan to follow in answering the problem question. As you design your plan, consider the following factors:
   - What igneous, sedimentary, and metamorphic rocks will you test? (Pick at least one rock from each group.)
   - What materials or equipment will you need to acquire, and in what amounts?
   - What tests will you perform on the samples?
   - How will you control the variables in each test?
   - How will you measure each sample's resistance to staining, grease, and scratches?
   - How will you measure slipperiness?

4. Review your plan. Will it lead to an answer to the problem question?

5. Check your procedure and safety plan with your teacher.

6. Create a data table that includes a column in which you predict how each material will perform in each test.

## Analyze and Conclude

1. **Interpreting Data** Which material performed the best on each test? Which performed the worst on each test?

2. **Drawing Conclusions** Which material is best for the kitchen flooring? Which material would you least want to use?

3. **Drawing Conclusions** Do your answers support your initial prediction? Why or why not?

4. **Applying Concepts** The person installing the floor might want stone that is easy to cut to the correct size or shape. What other qualities would matter to the flooring installer?

5. **Communicating** Based on your results, write an advertisement for the building stone that performed best as a flooring material.

## Design an Experiment

Suppose you are trying to select flooring material for a laboratory where heavy equipment is frequently moved across the floor. Make a hypothesis predicting which type of stone flooring will be strongest. Then design an experiment to compare how well each type resists breakage.

## ① Classifying Rocks

**Key Concepts**

- When studying a rock sample, geologists observe the rock's mineral composition, color, and texture.
- Geologists classify rocks into three major groups: igneous rock, sedimentary rock, and metamorphic rock.

**Key Terms**

| | |
|---|---|
| rock-forming mineral | texture |
| granite | igneous rock |
| basalt | sedimentary rock |
| grains | metamorphic rock |

## ② Igneous Rocks

**Key Concepts**

- Igneous rocks are classified according to their origin, texture, and mineral composition.
- People throughout history have used igneous rock for tools and building materials.

**Key Terms**

extrusive rock
intrusive rock

## ③ Sedimentary Rocks

**Key Concepts**

- Most sedimentary rocks are formed through a series of processes: erosion, deposition, compaction, and cementation.
- There are three major groups of sedimentary rocks: clastic rocks, organic rocks, and chemical rocks.
- People have used sedimentary rocks throughout history for many different purposes, including building materials and tools.

**Key Terms**

| | |
|---|---|
| sediment | cementation |
| erosion | clastic rock |
| deposition | organic rock |
| compaction | chemical rock |

## ④ Rocks From Reefs

**Key Concepts**

- When coral animals die, their skeletons remain. More corals build on top of them, gradually forming a reef.
- Limestone deposits that began as coral reefs provide evidence of how plate motions have changed Earth's surface. These deposits also provide evidence of past environments.

**Key Term**

coral reef

## ⑤ Metamorphic Rocks

**Key Concepts**

- Heat and pressure deep beneath Earth's surface can change any rock into metamorphic rock.
- Geologists classify metamorphic rocks according to the arrangement of the grains that make up the rocks.
- Certain metamorphic rocks are important materials for building and sculpture.

**Key Term**

foliated

## ⑥ The Rock Cycle

**Key Concepts**

- Forces deep inside Earth and at the surface produce a slow cycle that builds, destroys, and changes the rocks in the crust.
- Plate movements start the rock cycle by helping to form magma, the source of igneous rocks. Plate movements also cause faulting, folding, and other motions of the crust that help to form sedimentary and metamorphic rocks.

**Key Term**

rock cycle

## Organizing Information

**Concept Mapping** Copy the concept map about classifying rocks onto a separate sheet of paper. Then complete it and give it a title. (For more on concept maps, see the Skills Handbook.)

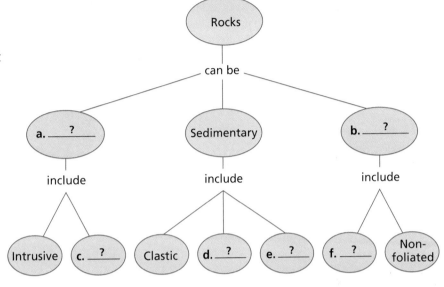

## Reviewing Key Terms

**Choose the letter of the best answer.**

1. A rock formed from fragments of other rocks is a(n)
   **a.** metamorphic rock.  **b.** extrusive rock.
   **c.** sedimentary rock.  **d.** igneous rock.

2. An igneous rock containing large crystals is most likely a(n)
   **a.** chemical rock.  **b.** extrusive rock.
   **c.** foliated rock.  **d.** intrusive rock.

3. A sedimentary rock formed from pieces of other rocks is called a(n)
   **a.** organic rock.  **b.** chemical rock.
   **c.** clastic rock.  **d.** compacted rock.

4. A deposit of organic limestone on land probably formed millions of years ago as a(n)
   **a.** extrusive rock.  **b.** coral reef.
   **c.** chemical rock.  **d.** metamorphic rock.

5. A metamorphic rock in which the grains line up in parallel bands is a
   **a.** clastic rock.  **b.** nonclastic rock.
   **c.** nonfoliated rock.  **d.** foliated rock.

6. In the rock cycle, the process by which an igneous rock changes to a sedimentary rock must begin with
   **a.** cementation.
   **b.** deposition.
   **c.** erosion.
   **d.** compaction.

## Writing in Science

**Field Guide** Research and write a field guide for geologists and visitors to an area such as the Grand Canyon. Describe the types of rocks you might find there, what the rocks look like, and what their properties are. Briefly explain the kinds of forces that shaped the rocks in the area you chose.

**Rocks**

Video Preview
Video Field Trip
▶ Video Assessment

# Review and Assessment

## Checking Concepts

7. What is the relationship between an igneous rock's texture and where it was formed?

8. Why can water pass easily through sandstone but not through shale?

9. Describe how a rock can form by evaporation. What type of rock is it?

10. How do the properties of a rock change when it becomes a metamorphic rock?

11. What are the sources of the heat that helps metamorphic rocks to form?

12. What are two things that could happen to a metamorphic rock to continue the rock cycle?

## Thinking Critically

13. **Developing Hypotheses** The sedimentary rocks limestone and sandstone are used as building materials. However, they wear away more rapidly than marble and quartzite, the metamorphic rocks that are formed from them. Why do you think this is so?

14. **Inferring** A geologist finds an area where the rocks are layers of coal and shale as shown in the diagram below. What kind of environment probably existed in this area millions of years ago when these rocks formed?

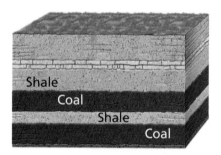

15. **Comparing and Contrasting** How are clastic rocks and organic rocks similar? How are they different?

16. **Predicting** Would you be less likely to find fossils in metamorphic rocks than in sedimentary rocks? Explain your answer.

## Applying Skills

**Answer Questions 17–20 using the photos of three rocks.**

Ⓐ                    Ⓑ

Ⓒ

17. **Observing** How would you describe the texture of each rock?

18. **Classifying** Which of the three rocks would you classify as a metamorphic rock? Why?

19. **Inferring** A rock's texture gives clues about how the rock formed. What can you infer about the process by which Rock B formed?

20. **Relating Cause and Effect** What conditions led to the formation of the large crystals in Rock C? Explain your answer.

### Lab zone Chapter **Project**

**Performance Assessment** Construct a simple display for your rocks. It should show your classification for each rock sample. In your presentation, describe where you hunted and what kinds of rocks you found. Were any rocks hard to classify? Did you find rocks from each of the three major groups? Can you think of any reason why certain types of rocks would not be found in your area?

# Standardized Test Prep

**Choose the letter of the best answer.**

**1.** You find a rock in which the grains are arranged in parallel bands of white and black crystals. The rock is probably a(n)

   **A** igneous rock.

   **B** sedimentary rock.

   **C** metamorphic rock.

   **D** reef rock.

**2.** Many sedimentary rocks have visible layers because of the process of

   **F** eruption.

   **G** deposition.

   **H** intrusion.

   **J** crystallization.

**3.** Rock salt, made of the mineral halite, is an organic sedimentary rock. A deposit of rock salt is most likely to be formed when

   **A** magma cools and hardens inside Earth.

   **B** hot water solutions form veins of rock salt.

   **C** the minerals form a solution in magma.

   **D** a solution of halite and water evaporates.

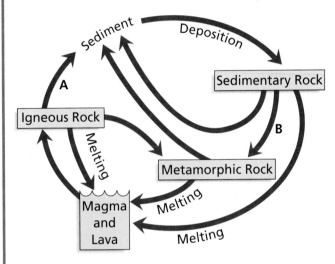

*Use the diagram above to answer Questions 4 and 5.*

**4.** If the heat and pressure inside Earth cause a rock to melt, the material that formed would be

   **F** metamorphic rock.

   **G** magma.

   **H** sedimentary rock.

   **J** igneous rock.

**5.** How can a metamorphic rock change into a sedimentary rock?

   **A** erosion and deposition

   **B** melting and crystallization

   **C** heat and pressure

   **D** all of the above

## Constructed Response

**6.** You are studying some moon rocks. Some of the moon rocks are made up of jagged pieces of other rocks. The pieces are cemented together by fine, dust-sized particles called rock powder. How would you classify this type of moon rock? Explain how you used the rock's characteristics to classify it.

# Pompeii–
# In the Shadow of Vesuvius

### Which ancient city . . .
- was destroyed in one day?
- lay buried for centuries?
- is a window on ancient Roman life?

Nearly 2,000 years ago, the city of Pompeii prospered on the fertile slopes near the volcano Vesuvius. About 100 kilometers north of Pompeii was the city of Rome. Rome was the capital of a vast empire that stretched across Europe and around the Mediterranean Sea.

Pompeii was a small but popular trading center and site for luxury Roman villas. When Vesuvius erupted violently in A.D. 79, thousands of Pompeians were caught unawares. Ash, hot gases, and rocks trapped and preserved this ancient city and its inhabitants. Today, excavations at Pompeii reveal the daily life of a bustling city at the height of the Roman Empire.

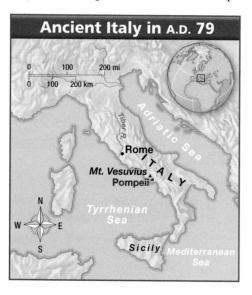

**Ancient Italy in A.D. 79**

**The Forum**
Mount Vesuvius looms behind the ruins of the Forum at Pompeii.

**Fresco From Pompeii**
This fresco portrays an educated couple. Here the wife holds a stylus and wax tablet, and the husband holds a scroll.

# Daily Life in Pompeii

Excavations at Pompeii began in the mid-1700s and continue today. The findings have been astounding. Life stopped abruptly that fateful day. Thousands abandoned their meals or left food simmering on the fire. A baker had just placed the day's round loaves of bread in the oven. A jeweler left his work unfinished on a bench. Houses and public buildings that remained intact reveal daily life through frescoes (wall paintings), sculpture, mosaic floors, and expansive indoor courtyards.

At the center of city life was the Forum, a large, rectangular open space where Pompeians conducted business and politics. Here people sold meat and fish as well as fruits, vegetables, grapes, and olives grown on the fertile slopes of Vesuvius. Some merchants sold cloth made from the wool of sheep raised nearby. Others sold copper pots, oil lamps, furniture, and glassware. People of all classes gathered at the Forum to exchange ideas, notices, and gossip. Some even wrote graffiti on the walls!

**Bakery and Bread**
This fresco, found in Pompeii, shows a man purchasing bread. A carbonized loaf of bread, below, indicates how bread was cut into wedges.

## Social Studies Activity

The Forum was central to life in Pompeii. Research another structure in Pompeii. Write a short report that describes its structure and function. Explain the building's importance to Roman society. Possible topics include

- amphitheater
- basilica
- city walls
- public baths
- temples
- water system

# Vesuvius Erupts!

Most volcanoes and earthquakes occur along plate boundaries where Earth's crust is fractured and weak. Unknown to the people of Pompeii, their city and surrounding areas rested directly over a subduction zone where the Eurasian plate meets the African plate. Although Mount Vesuvius had erupted in the past, the volcano had lain dormant for hundreds of years.

Around noon on August 24, A.D. 79, the volcano suddenly exploded. Volcanic ash and gases shot 27 kilometers into the air. During the rest of the day and into the night, 3 meters of ash blanketed the city. But the destruction wasn't over. Around midnight, a deadly pyroclastic flow poured over the entire area, trapping about 2,000 Pompeians who had not yet escaped. Afterward, an additional 3 meters of volcanic debris rained down on Pompeii. This layer of material sealed the city, preserving it nearly intact for centuries.

***The Great Eruption of Mt. Vesuvius***
This eighteenth-century painting is by Louis-Jean Desprez.

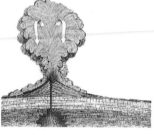

**1** Magma explodes from the vent in Mount Vesuvius. A column of pumice and ash rises.

**2** Pumice and ash blow southeast and fall on Pompeii.

**3** The column of ash collapses and pyroclastic flows cover the region.

## Science Activity

Different kinds of lava vary in silica content and temperature and therefore spread at different rates. Use molasses to model lava flow rates.

1. Measure one tablespoon of molasses, and slowly pour it onto a plastic plate. Time and record how long it takes for the molasses to stop spreading.

2. Add one tablespoon of sand to one tablespoon of molasses. Stir the mixture thoroughly. Repeat the pouring and timing of Step 1.

How does the sand affect the viscosity of the molasses? What does the sand represent in your model? How would a volcano with this type of lava be likely to erupt?

3. Heat one tablespoon of molasses over a hot plate. Repeat Step 1. How does the viscosity of the heated molasses compare with the viscosity of the molasses in Step 1? What can you conclude about the effect of temperature on the flow rate of lava?

## Eyewitness Account

Pliny the Younger (circa A.D. 62–113) was a nephew of the scholar and historian Pliny the Elder. When he was about 17 years old, he witnessed the eruption of Mount Vesuvius while visiting a city across the bay from Pompeii. Some 25 years later, Pliny the Younger described the terrifying scene in a letter to the historian Tacitus.

### *Excerpt from Pliny the Younger's letter to Tacitus, circa A.D. 104*

▲ Pliny the Younger

"I look back: a dense cloud looms behind us, following us like a flood poured across the land. . . . A darkness came that was not like a moonless or cloudy night, but more like the black of closed and unlighted rooms. You could hear women lamenting, children crying, men shouting. Some were calling for parents, others for children or spouses. . . . There were some so afraid of death that they prayed for death. . . . It grew lighter, though that seemed not a return of day, but a sign that the fire was approaching. The fire itself actually stopped some distance away, but darkness and ashes came again, a great weight of them. We stood up and shook the ash off again and again, otherwise we would have been covered with it and crushed by the weight. . . .

"At last the cloud thinned out and dwindled to no more than smoke or fog. Soon there was real daylight. The sun was even shining, though with the lurid glow it has after an eclipse. The sight that met our still terrified eyes was a changed world, buried in ash like snow."

## Language Arts Activity

An eyewitness account is a firsthand, factual account of an event or experience. Pliny the Younger filled his letter with vivid sensory details—details that help the reader see, feel, smell, taste, and hear—in order to convey what the Vesuvius eruption was like.

Choose an interesting event that you've witnessed. Write an eyewitness account of it. Provide readers with key facts, such as the time and place of the event, along with interesting and vivid details.

**Dog at Pompeii**
This is a plaster cast of a dog left chained to a post during the eruption of Vesuvius.

# Mathematics

## Roman Calculators

To calculate business trades in the Forum and elsewhere, Pompeians used an abacus. An abacus is a metal or wood box, with counters that slide along grooves or wires. The Romans made abacuses small enough to be portable, rather like today's pocket calculators.

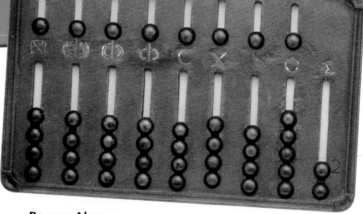

**Roman Abacus**
This Roman abacus could calculate numbers into the millions. The groove on the right was used to calculate fractions.

### Reading the Roman Abacus

A typical Roman abacus could be used to calculate numbers up to 9,999. The ancient Romans used letters to represent numerals. The table below shows the value of the Roman numerals.

**Roman Numerals**

| M | C | X | I |
|---|---|---|---|
| 1,000 | 100 | 10 | 1 |

The Roman numerals divide the abacus into an upper and lower part. Each bead or counter on the upper part stands for five. Each bead on the lower part stands for one.

If you were using a modern calculator, you would start with 0. To set the Roman abacus at 0, move all the counters away from the letters in the middle as shown.

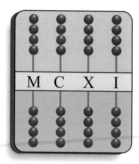

**This abacus reads 0.**

To read a number, count the beads that are closest to the letters in the middle.

3 hundreds (C) + 5 tens (X) + 1 ten (X) + 2 ones (I) = 362

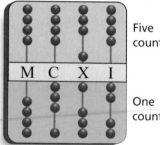

Five counters

One counters

**This abacus reads 362.**

### Using the Roman Abacus

**Adding** Clear the abacus to 0. You are now ready to add 25 + 362 on the abacus. Set up the counters to display 362 as shown above. Then add 25 by moving the counters toward the middle.

1. Go to the X (tens) column. Move 2 tens counters up, so that the tens column displays 2 tens + 6 tens = 8 tens.

2. Go to the I (ones) column. Remember that the upper counters are multiples of 5. Move the counter that stands for 5 ones down to the middle, so that the ones column displays 5 ones + 2 ones = 7 ones.

3. The result is 387, as shown.

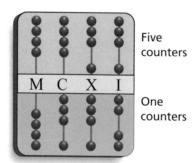

Five counters

One counters

**Subtracting** You use the same steps to subtract. Clear the abacus to 0. To calculate 387 – 180, first set up the abacus to show 387, as shown above. Subtract by moving the counters away from the middle.

1. Go to the C (hundreds) column. Subtract by moving 1 hundreds counter down.

2. Then go to the X (tens) column. Subtract by moving the counter that stands for 5 tens up and the 3 tens counters down.

After performing the calculation, you should get the number shown below. What number is it?

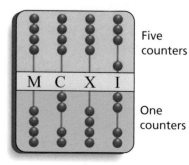

Five counters

One counters

## Math Activity

Create an abacus of your own by drawing heavy lines with a marker or crayon on a sheet of paper. Label each line about halfway up, as shown in the abacus illustrations on these pages. Use beans, pennies, or other small objects as beads. Begin by setting up your abacus to read 0. Perform the following calculations.

| | |
|---|---|
| 801 + 143 | 2,788 − 1,517 |
| 8,754 + 241 | 6,487 − 2,382 |

Check your work using Arabic numerals. Now create two of your own problems for a partner to solve.

**Products From Pompeii**
Colorful glassware and fine jewelry were among the luxury goods traded in ancient Pompeii.

## Tie It Together

### Press Kit

It's A.D. 80. Your class is a group of Pompeians who escaped the eruption and are living at a safe distance south of Mount Vesuvius. To advertise the businesses in your new location, write a "press kit" to distribute in the Roman Empire. Your kit should include

- a map showing your new location in relation to Vesuvius

- a description of your trade, such as a baker, potter, barber, cloth maker, restaurant owner, mason, or jewelry maker

- the products or services you're selling, such as wool, gold and silver jewelry, oil lamps, glassware, mosaic tiles, and so on

- drawings and photos

Research ancient Pompeii, using the library or the Internet.

# Think Like a Scientist

Scientists have a particular way of looking at the world, or scientific habits of mind. Whenever you ask a question and explore possible answers, you use many of the same skills that scientists do. Some of these skills are described on this page.

## Observing

When you use one or more of your five senses to gather information about the world, you are **observing.** Hearing a dog bark, counting twelve green seeds, and smelling smoke are all observations. To increase the power of their senses, scientists sometimes use microscopes, telescopes, or other instruments that help them make more detailed observations.

An observation must be an accurate report of what your senses detect. It is important to keep careful records of your observations in science class by writing or drawing in a notebook. The information collected through observations is called evidence, or data.

## Inferring

When you interpret an observation, you are **inferring,** or making an inference. For example, if you hear your dog barking, you may infer that someone is at your front door. To make this inference, you combine the evidence—the barking dog—and your experience or knowledge—you know that your dog barks when strangers approach—to reach a logical conclusion.

Notice that an inference is not a fact; it is only one of many possible interpretations for an observation. For example, your dog may be barking because it wants to go for a walk. An inference may turn out to be incorrect even if it is based on accurate observations and logical reasoning. The only way to find out if an inference is correct is to investigate further.

## Predicting

When you listen to the weather forecast, you hear many predictions about the next day's weather—what the temperature will be, whether it will rain, and how windy it will be. Weather forecasters use observations and knowledge of weather patterns to predict the weather. The skill of **predicting** involves making an inference about a future event based on current evidence or past experience.

Because a prediction is an inference, it may prove to be false. In science class, you can test some of your predictions by doing experiments. For example, suppose you predict that larger paper airplanes can fly farther than smaller airplanes. How could you test your prediction?

## Activity

**Use the photograph to answer the questions below.**

**Observing** Look closely at the photograph. List at least three observations.

**Inferring** Use your observations to make an inference about what has happened. What experience or knowledge did you use to make the inference?

**Predicting** Predict what will happen next. On what evidence or experience do you base your prediction?

# Classifying

Could you imagine searching for a book in the library if the books were shelved in no particular order? Your trip to the library would be an all-day event! Luckily, librarians group together books on similar topics or by the same author. Grouping together items that are alike in some way is called **classifying.** You can classify items in many ways: by size, by shape, by use, and by other important characteristics.

Like librarians, scientists use the skill of classifying to organize information and objects. When things are sorted into groups, the relationships among them become easier to understand.

**Activity**

Classify the objects in the photograph into two groups based on any characteristic you choose. Then use another characteristic to classify the objects into three groups.

# Making Models

Have you ever drawn a picture to help someone understand what you were saying? Such a drawing is one type of model. A model is a picture, diagram, computer image, or other representation of a complex object or process. **Making models** helps people understand things that they cannot observe directly.

Scientists often use models to represent things that are either very large or very small, such as the planets in the solar system, or the parts of a cell. Such models are physical models—drawings or three-dimensional structures that look like the real thing. Other models are mental models—mathematical equations or words that describe how something works.

**Activity**

This student is using a model to demonstrate what causes day and night on Earth. What do the flashlight and the tennis ball in the model represent?

# Communicating

Whenever you talk on the phone, write a report, or listen to your teacher at school, you are communicating. **Communicating** is the process of sharing ideas and information with other people. Communicating effectively requires many skills, including writing, reading, speaking, listening, and making models.

Scientists communicate to share results, information, and opinions. Scientists often communicate about their work in journals, over the telephone, in letters, and on the Internet.

They also attend scientific meetings where they share their ideas with one another in person.

**Activity**

On a sheet of paper, write out clear, detailed directions for tying your shoe. Then exchange directions with a partner. Follow your partner's directions exactly. How successful were you at tying your shoe? How could your partner have communicated more clearly?

# Making Measurements

By measuring, scientists can express their observations more precisely and communicate more information about what they observe.

## Measuring in SI

The standard system of measurement used by scientists around the world is known as the International System of Units, which is abbreviated as SI (**Système International d'Unités,** in French). SI units are easy to use because they are based on multiples of 10. Each unit is ten times larger than the next smallest unit and one tenth the size of the next largest unit. The table lists the prefixes used to name the most common SI units.

| Common SI Prefixes | | |
| --- | --- | --- |
| **Prefix** | **Symbol** | **Meaning** |
| kilo- | k | 1,000 |
| hecto- | h | 100 |
| deka- | da | 10 |
| deci- | d | 0.1 (one tenth) |
| centi- | c | 0.01 (one hundredth) |
| milli- | m | 0.001 (one thousandth) |

**Length** To measure length, or the distance between two points, the unit of measure is the **meter (m).** The distance from the floor to a doorknob is approximately one meter. Long distances, such as the distance between two cities, are measured in kilometers (km). Small lengths are measured in centimeters (cm) or millimeters (mm). Scientists use metric rulers and meter sticks to measure length.

| Common Conversions | |
| --- | --- |
| 1 km | = 1,000 m |
| 1 m | = 100 cm |
| 1 m | = 1,000 mm |
| 1 cm | = 10 mm |

**Activity**

The larger lines on the metric ruler in the picture show centimeter divisions, while the smaller, unnumbered lines show millimeter divisions. How many centimeters long is the shell? How many millimeters long is it?

**Liquid Volume** To measure the volume of a liquid, or the amount of space it takes up, you will use a unit of measure known as the **liter (L).** One liter is the approximate volume of a medium-size carton of milk. Smaller volumes are measured in milliliters (mL). Scientists use graduated cylinders to measure liquid volume.

**Activity**

The graduated cylinder in the picture is marked in milliliter divisions. Notice that the water in the cylinder has a curved surface. This curved surface is called the *meniscus*. To measure the volume, you must read the level at the lowest point of the meniscus. What is the volume of water in this graduated cylinder?

| Common Conversion |
| --- |
| 1 L = 1,000 mL |

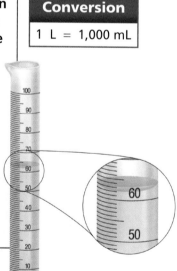

**Mass** To measure mass, or the amount of matter in an object, you will use a unit of measure known as the **gram (g).** One gram is approximately the mass of a paper clip. Larger masses are measured in kilograms (kg). Scientists use a balance to find the mass of an object.

**Common Conversion**

1 kg = 1,000 g

**Activity**

The mass of the potato in the picture is measured in kilograms. What is the mass of the potato? Suppose a recipe for potato salad called for one kilogram of potatoes. About how many potatoes would you need?

0.25 KG

**Temperature** To measure the temperature of a substance, you will use the **Celsius scale.** Temperature is measured in degrees Celsius (°C) using a Celsius thermometer. Water freezes at 0°C and boils at 100°C.

**Time** The unit scientists use to measure time is the **second (s).**

**Activity**

What is the temperature of the liquid in degrees Celsius?

# Converting SI Units

To use the SI system, you must know how to convert between units. Converting from one unit to another involves the skill of **calculating,** or using mathematical operations. Converting between SI units is similar to converting between dollars and dimes because both systems are based on multiples of ten.

Suppose you want to convert a length of 80 centimeters to meters. Follow these steps to convert between units.

1. Begin by writing down the measurement you want to convert—in this example, 80 centimeters.

2. Write a conversion factor that represents the relationship between the two units you are converting. In this example, the relationship is 1 meter = 100 centimeters. Write this conversion factor as a fraction, making sure to place the units you are converting from (centimeters, in this example) in the denominator.

3. Multiply the measurement you want to convert by the fraction. When you do this, the units in the first measurement will cancel out with the units in the denominator. Your answer will be in the units you are converting to (meters, in this example).

*Example*

80 centimeters = ▓ meters

$$80 \text{ centimeters} \times \frac{1 \text{ meter}}{100 \text{ centimeters}} = \frac{80 \text{ meters}}{100}$$

$$= 0.8 \text{ meters}$$

**Activity**

Convert between the following units.

1. 600 millimeters = ▓ meters

2. 0.35 liters = ▓ milliliters

3. 1,050 grams = ▓ kilograms

# Conducting a Scientific Investigation

In some ways, scientists are like detectives, piecing together clues to learn about a process or event. One way that scientists gather clues is by carrying out experiments. An experiment tests an idea in a careful, orderly manner. Although experiments do not all follow the same steps in the same order, many follow a pattern similar to the one described here.

## Posing Questions

Experiments begin by asking a scientific question. A scientific question is one that can be answered by gathering evidence. For example, the question "Which freezes faster—fresh water or salt water?" is a scientific question because you can carry out an investigation and gather information to answer the question.

## Developing a Hypothesis

The next step is to form a hypothesis. A **hypothesis** is a possible explanation for a set of observations or answer to a scientific question. In science, a hypothesis must be something that can be tested. A hypothesis can be worded as an *If . . . then . . .* statement. For example, a hypothesis might be *"If I add salt to fresh water, then the water will take longer to freeze."* A hypothesis worded this way serves as a rough outline of the experiment you should perform.

**geyser** A fountain of water and steam that builds up pressure underground and erupts at regular intervals. (p. 105)
**géiser** Fuente de agua y vapor que acumula presión subterránea y hace erupción a intervalos regulares.

**grains** The particles of minerals or other rocks that give a rock its texture. (p. 146)
**granos** Partículas de minerales o de otras rocas que dan la textura a una roca.

**granite** A usually light-colored igneous rock that is found in continental crust. (p. 10, 145)
**granito** Roca usualmente de color claro que se encuentra en la corteza continental.

**H**

**hanging wall** The block of rock that forms the upper half of a fault. (p. 46)
**labio superior** Bloque de roca que constituye la mitad superior de una falla.

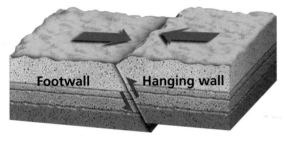
Footwall    Hanging wall

**hot spot** An area where magma from deep within the mantle melts through the crust above it. (p. 85)
**punto caliente** Área por donde el magma de las profundidades del manto atraviesa la corteza.

**I**

**igneous rock** A type of rock that forms from the cooling of molten rock at or below the surface. (p. 147)
**roca ígnea** Tipo de roca que se forma cuando se enfrían las rocas fundidas en la superficie o debajo de la superficie.

**inner core** A dense sphere of solid iron and nickel at the center of Earth. (p. 12)
**núcleo interno** Densa esfera de hierro y níquel situada en el centro de la Tierra.

**inorganic** Not formed from living things or the remains of living things. (p. 115)
**inorgánico** Que no está formado de seres vivos o de los restos de seres vivos.

**intrusive rock** Igneous rock that forms when magma hardens beneath Earth's surface. (p. 149)
**roca intrusiva** Roca ígnea que se forma cuando el magma se endurece bajo la superficie de la Tierra.

**island arc** A string of islands formed by the volcanoes along a deep-ocean trench. (p. 84)
**arco de islas** Cadena de islas formadas por los volcanes que se encuentran a lo largo de una fosa oceánica profunda.

**L**

**lava** Liquid magma that reaches the surface; also the rock formed when liquid lava hardens. (p. 82)
**lava** Magma líquida que sale a la superficie; también, la roca que se forma cuando la lava líquida se solidifica.

**lava flow** The area covered by lava as it pours out of a volcano's vent. (p. 92)
**colada de lava** Área cubierta de lava a medida que ésta sale por la boca del volcán.

**liquefaction** The process by which an earthquake's violent movement suddenly turns loose soil into liquid mud. (p. 70)
**licuefacción** Proceso mediante el que las violentas sacudidas de un terremoto de pronto convierten la tierra suelta en lodo líquido.

**lithosphere** A rigid layer made up of the uppermost part of the mantle and the crust. (p. 11)
**litosfera** Capa rígida constituida por la parte superior del manto y la corteza.

**luster** The way a mineral reflects light from its surface. (p. 117)
**brillo** La manera en la que un mineral refleja la luz en su superficie.

**M**

**magma** The molten mixture of rock-forming substances, gases, and water from the mantle. (p. 82)
**magma** Mezcla fundida de las sustancias que forman las rocas, gases y agua, proveniente del manto.

**magma chamber** The pocket beneath a volcano where magma collects. (p. 92)
**cámara magmática** Bolsa debajo de un volcán en la que se acumula el magma.

**magnitude** The measurement of an earthquake's strength based on seismic waves and movement along faults. (p. 54)
**magnitud** Medida de la fuerza de un sismo basada en las ondas sísmicas y en el movimiento que ocurre a lo largo de las fallas.

**mantle** The layer of hot, solid material between Earth's crust and core. (p. 11)
**manto** Capa de material caliente y sólido entre la corteza terrestre y el núcleo.

**Mercalli scale** A scale that rates earthquakes according to their intensity and how much damage they cause at a particular place. (p. 54)
**escala de Mercalli** Escala con la que se miden los sismos basándose en la intensidad y el daño que ocasionan.

**metamorphic rock** A type of rock that forms from an existing rock that is changed by heat, pressure, or chemical reactions. (p. 147)
**roca metamórfica** Tipo de roca que se forma cuando una roca es transformada por el calor, presión o reacciones químicas.

**mid-ocean ridge** An undersea mountain chain where new ocean floor is produced; a divergent plate boundary. (p. 24)
**dorsal oceánica** Cadena montañosa submarina donde se produce el nuevo suelo oceánico; borde de placa divergente.

**mineral** A naturally occurring, inorganic solid that has a crystal structure and a definite chemical composition. (p. 114)
**mineral** Sólido inorgánico que ocurre en la naturaleza, de estructura cristalina y composición química definida.

**Mohs hardness scale** A scale ranking ten minerals from softest to hardest; used in testing the hardness of minerals. (p. 118)
**escala de dureza de Mohs** Escala en la que se clasifican diez minerales del más blando al más duro; se usa para probar la dureza de los minerales.

**moment magnitude scale** A scale that rates earthquakes by estimating the total energy released by an earthquake. (p. 55)
**escala de magnitud del momento** Escala con la que se miden los sismos estimando la cantidad total de energía liberada por un terremoto.

**normal fault** A type of fault where the hanging wall slides downward; caused by tension in the crust. (p. 46)
**falla normal** Tipo de falla en la cual el labio superior se desliza hacia abajo como resultado de la tensión en la corteza.

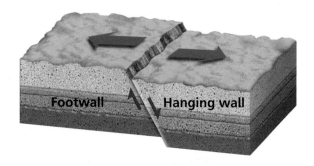

Footwall    Hanging wall

**ore** Rock that contains a metal or other economically useful mineral. (p. 132)
**mena** Roca que contiene un metal u otro mineral de importancia económica.

**organic rock** Sedimentary rock that forms from remains of organisms deposited in thick layers. (p. 154)
**roca orgánica** Roca sedimentaria que se forma cuando los restos de organismos se depositan en capas gruesas.

**outer core** A layer of molten iron and nickel that surrounds the inner core of Earth. (p. 12)
**núcleo externo** Capa de hierro y níquel fundidos que rodea el núcleo interno de la Tierra.

**pahoehoe** A hot, fast-moving type of lava that hardens to form smooth, ropelike coils. (p. 90)
**cordada** Tipo de lava caliente de movimiento muy veloz que al endurecerse forma espirales lisas en forma de cuerda.

**Pangaea** The name of the single landmass that broke apart 200 million years ago and gave rise to today's continents. (p. 19)
**Pangea** Nombre de la masa terrestre única que se dividió hace 200 millones de años, dando origen a los continentes actuales.

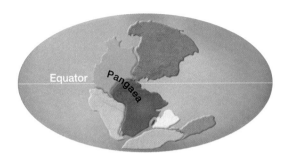

**physical property** Any characteristic of a substance that can be observed or measured without changing the composition of the substance. (p. 88)
**propiedad física** Cualquier característica de una sustancia que se puede observar o medir sin que cambie la composición de la misma.

**pipe** A long tube through which magma moves from the magma chamber to Earth's surface. (p. 92)
**chimenea** Largo tubo por el que el magma sube desde la cámara magmática hasta la superficie de la Tierra.

**plate** A section of the lithosphere that slowly moves over the asthenosphere, carrying pieces of continental and oceanic crust. (p. 32)
**placa** Sección de la litosfera que se desplaza lentamente sobre la astenosfera, llevando consigo trozos de la corteza continental y de la oceánica.

**plateau** A large area of flat land elevated high above sea level. (p. 50)
**meseta** Zona extensa de tierra plana elevada por encima del nivel del mar.

**plate tectonics** The theory that pieces of Earth's lithosphere are in constant motion, driven by convection currents in the mantle. (p. 33)
**tectónica de placas** Teoría según la cual las partes de la litosfera de la Tierra están en continuo movimiento, impulsadas por las corrientes de convección del manto.

**pressure** The force exerted on a surface divided by the area over which the force is exerted. (p. 9)
**presión** Fuerza que actúa sobre una superficie, dividida por el área sobre la que la fuerza actúa.

**P wave** A type of seismic wave that compresses and expands the ground. (p. 53)
**onda P** Tipo de onda sísmica que comprime y expande el suelo.

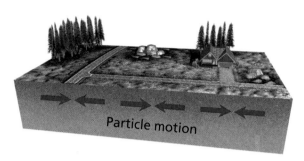

Particle motion

**pyroclastic flow** The expulsion of ash, cinders, bombs, and gases during an explosive volcanic eruption. (p. 95)
**flujo piroclástico** Emisión de ceniza, escoria, bombas y gases durante una erupción volcánica explosiva.

**R**

**radiation** The transfer of energy through space. (p. 15)
**radiación** Transferencia de energía a través del espacio.

**reverse fault** A type of fault where the hanging wall slides upward; caused by compression in the crust. (p. 47)
**falla inversa** Tipo de falla en la cual el labio superior se desliza hacia arriba como resultado de compresión en la corteza.

**Richter scale** A scale that rates an earthquake's magnitude based on the size of its seismic waves. (p. 54)
**escala de Richter** Escala con la que se mide la magnitud de un terremoto basándose en el tamaño de sus ondas sísmicas.

**rift valley** A deep valley that forms where two plates move apart. (p. 34)
**valle de fisura** Valle profundo que se forma cuando dos placas se separan.

**Ring of Fire** A major belt of volcanoes that rims the Pacific Ocean. (p. 83)
**Cinturón de Fuego** Gran cadena de volcanes que rodea el océano Pacífico.

**rock** A solid mixture of minerals and other materials. (p. 145)
**roca** Mezcla sólida de minerales y otros materiales.

**rock cycle** A series of processes on the surface and inside Earth that slowly changes rocks from one kind to another. (p. 164)
**ciclo de las rocas** Serie de procesos en la superficie y dentro de la Tierra que lentamente transforman las rocas de un tipo de roca a otro.

**rock-forming minerals** One of the common minerals that make up most of the rocks of Earth's crust. (p. 145)
**minerales formadores de rocas** Uno de los minerales comunes de los que están compuestas la mayoría de las rocas de la corteza de la Tierra.

**scientific theory** A well-tested concept that explains a wide range of observations. (p. 32)
**teoría científica** Concepto bien comprobado que explica una amplia gama de observaciones.

**sea-floor spreading** The process by which molten material adds new oceanic crust to the ocean floor. (p. 25)
**expansión del suelo oceánico** Proceso mediante el cual la materia fundida añade nueva corteza oceánica al suelo oceánico.

**sediment** Small, solid pieces of material that come from rocks or organisms. (p. 152)
**sedimento** Partículas sólidas de materiales que provienen de rocas u organismos.

**sedimentary rock** A type of rock that forms when particles from other rocks or the remains of plants and animals are pressed and cemented together. (p. 147)
**roca sedimentaria** Tipo de roca que se forma cuando las partículas de otras rocas o los restos de plantas y animales son presionados y cementados.

**seismic waves** Vibrations that travel through Earth carrying the energy released during an earthquake. (p. 8)
**ondas sísmicas** Vibraciones que se desplazan por la Tierra, llevando la energía liberada durante un terremoto.

**seismogram** The record of an earthquake's seismic waves produced by a seismograph. (p. 61)
**sismograma** Registro producido por un sismógrafo de las ondas sísmicas de un terremoto.

**seismograph** A device that records ground movements caused by seismic waves as they move through Earth. (p. 54)
**sismógrafo** Aparato con el que se registran los movimientos del suelo ocasionados por las ondas sísmicas a medida que éstas se desplazan por la Tierra.

**shearing** Stress that pushes masses of rock in opposite directions, in a sideways movement. (p. 45)
**cizallamiento** Esfuerzo que presiona masas de roca en sentidos opuestos.

**shield volcano** A wide, gently sloping mountain made of layers of lava and formed by quiet eruptions. (p. 100)
**volcán en escudo** Montaña ancha de pendientes suaves, compuesta por capas de lava y formada durante erupciones no violentas.

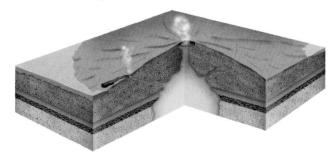

**silica** A material found in magma that is formed from the elements oxygen and silicon. (p. 89)
**sílice** Material presente en el magma, compuesto por los elementos oxígeno y silicio.

**sill** A slab of volcanic rock formed when magma squeezes between layers of rock. (p. 103)
**dique concordante** Placa de roca volcánica formada cuando el magma se mete entre las capas de roca.

**smelting** The process by which ore is melted to separate the useful metal from other elements. (p. 134)
**fundición** Proceso mediante el que una mena se funde para separar el mineral útil de otros elementos.

**solution** A mixture in which one substance is dissolved in another. (p. 125)
**solución** Mezcla en la que una sustancia se halla disuelta en otra.

**sonar** A device that determines the distance of an object under water by recording echoes of sound waves. (p. 24)
**sonar** Aparato con el cual se determina la distancia de un objeto sumergido en el agua mediante el registro del eco de las ondas sonoras.

**streak** The color of a mineral's powder. (p. 117)
**raya** El color del polvo de un mineral.

**stress** A force that acts on rock to change its shape or volume. (p. 44)
**esfuerzo** Fuerza que al actuar sobre una roca cambia su forma o volumen.

**strike-slip fault** A type of fault in which rocks on either side move past each other sideways with little up or down motion. (p. 47)
**falla transcurrente** Tipo de falla en la cual las rocas a ambos lados se deslizan horizontalmente en sentidos opuestos, con poco desplazamiento hacia arriba o abajo.

**subduction** The process by which oceanic crust sinks beneath a deep-ocean trench and back into the mantle at a convergent plate boundary. (p. 28)
**subducción** Proceso mediante el cual la corteza oceánica se hunde debajo de una fosa oceánica profunda y vuelve al manto por el borde de una placa convergente.

**surface wave** A type of seismic wave that forms when P waves and S waves reach Earth's surface. (p. 53)
**onda superficial** Tipo de onda sísmica que se forma cuando las ondas P y las ondas S llegan a la superficie de la Tierra.

**S wave** A type of seismic wave that moves the ground up and down or side to side. (p. 53)
**onda S** Tipo de onda sísmica que hace que el suelo se mueva de arriba abajo o de lado a lado.

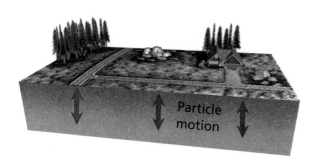

Particle motion

**syncline** A downward fold in rock formed by compression in Earth's crust. (p. 48)
**sinclinal** Pliegue de la roca hacia abajo ocasionado por la compresión de la corteza terrestre.

**T**

**tension** Stress that stretches rock so that it becomes thinner in the middle. (p. 45)
**tensión** Esfuerzo que estira una roca, haciéndola más delgada en el centro.

**texture** The look and feel of a rock's surface, determined by the size, shape, and pattern of a rock's grains. (p. 146)
**textura** Apariencia y sensación producida por la superficie de una roca, determinadas por el tamaño, forma y patrón de los granos de la roca.

**transform boundary** A plate boundary where two plates move past each other in opposite directions. (p. 35)
**borde de transformación** Borde de placa donde dos placas se deslizan una respecto a la otra, pero en sentidos opuestos.

**tsunami** A large wave produced by an earthquake on the ocean floor. (p. 71)
**tsunami** Gran ola producida cuando un terremoto sacude el suelo oceánico.

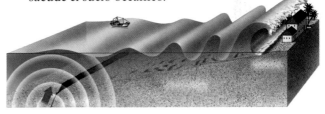

**V**

**vein** A narrow deposit of a mineral that is sharply different from the surrounding rock. (p. 126)
**vena** Acumulación delgada de un mineral que es marcadamente distinta de la roca que la rodea.

**vent** The opening through which molten rock and gas leave a volcano. (p. 92)
**boca** Abertura a través de la que la roca en fusión y los gases salen de un volcán.

**viscosity** The resistance of a liquid to flowing. (p. 88)
**viscosidad** La resistencia que presenta un líquido al fluir.

**volcanic neck** A deposit of hardened magma in a volcano's pipe. (p. 103)
**cuello volcánico** Depósito de magma solidificada en la chimenea de un volcán.

**volcano** A weak spot in the crust where magma has come to the surface. (p. 82)
**volcán** Punto débil en la corteza por donde el magma escapa hacia la superficie.

# Index

Page numbers for key terms are printed in **boldface** type.
Page numbers for illustrations, maps, and charts are printed in *italics*.

# Index

## S

safety in the laboratory 198–199
St. Helens, Mount *94, 97,* 101
San Andreas fault 47, *64,* 69
sandstone 154, 156, 161, 164
satellites, GPS 62, *63*
scheelite 122
schist 161
scientific notation 193
scientific theory 33
scratch test of hardness 119
sea-floor spreading 23–24, *25*–29
  at divergent boundary 34
  evidence for 26–27
  at mid-ocean ridges 25, *26*
  subduction at trenches *28*–29
second (SI unit of time) **181**
sediment 152
sedimentary rocks *147,* 152–156
  formation of 152–153
  metamorphic rock from *161*
  in rock cycle 164, *165*
  types of *154–155*
  uses of *156*
seismic-safe building *74–75. See
  also* **earthquake safety**
seismic waves 8, *52*–57
  evidence of Earth's interior from *8*
  measuring 54, 55, 61
  shaking produced by 70
  types of 52–*53*
seismogram *61*
seismograph 54, 55, *61*
seismographic data, using 64–65
shaft mines 133
shale 154, 161
shearing *45*
  strike-slip faults created by 47
shield volcanoes **100,** *101*
significant figures 193
silica **89,** 150
  in magma 89, 94, 95, 150
sill *103*
silver 88, 126, *127*
SI units of measurement **180**
slag 134
slate 161, 162
smelting *134*
soils, volcanic 102
solution 125
  minerals formed from *125–126*
sonar 24
special physical properties of
  minerals *122*

## T

streak *117*
stress *44*
  along fault 64, 65
  faults created by *46–47,* 51
  types of *45*
strike-slip faults **47**
strip mines 133
subduction *28*–29, 33, 69, 84
  collision of oceanic and
    continental plate and *34,* 35
sulfur *120*
supercontinents 36
surface waves 52, *53, 61*
S waves 52, *53,* 56
  damage from 70
  on seismogram 61
syncline *48*

talc *118,* 131
temperature
  convection currents and *16*
  and depth in Earth's interior 9
  viscosity and 90
tension *45*
  normal faults caused by 46
texture of rocks **146**
  igneous rock *149*
theory, scientific 33
tiltmeters 62, *63,* 98
topaz *119*
trade-off **185**
transform boundary **34,** *35*
  strike-slip faults forming 47
troubleshoot **185**
tsunami *71*

## U

utilities, earthquake-safe 73

## V

variable (in an experiment) **183**
vein (mineral) 126, *127,* 133
vent (volcano) 92, *93*
viscosity **88,** *89*
  of magma 89–90
volcanic ash 95, 96
  landforms from 100–102
volcanic belts 83
volcanic eruptions 6, 7, 91–**93,**
  94–98

  kinds of 94–96
  landforms from 99–105
  lava *82*
  stages of volcanic activity 97–98
volcanic glass 149
volcanic landforms 99–105
  from lava and ash 100–102
  from magma 103–104
volcanic neck *103*
volcanoes **82**–105
  cinder cone **100,** 101
  composite *100,* **101**
  Earth's active *83*
  hot spot *85*
  life cycle of 97
  monitoring 98
  plate boundaries and *83*–84
  plate tectonics and 82–85
  shield **100,** *101*
  structure of 92, *93*
volcano hazards 96

## W

Wegener, Alfred *19*–22, 23, 25
Wilson, J. Tuzo 32

## Y

Yellowstone National Park 85

## Z

Zhang Heng 60

# Acknowledgments

"Gelatin Volcanoes" by R. Fisk and D. Jackson from *Exploring Planets in the Classroom*. Copyright by Hawaii Space Grant Consortium, based on experiments done by R. Fisk and D. Jackson, U.S. Geological Survey.

"Pliny Letter 6.16" by Pliny the Younger from **www.amherst.edu** *(classics/class36/sylcl36.html)*. Copyright © 2003 by Dr. Cynthia Damon, Associate Professor at Amherst College. Reprinted with permission.

## Staff Credits

Diane Alimena, Scott Andrews, Jennifer Angel, Michele Angelucci, Laura Baselice, Carolyn Belanger, Barbara A. Bertell, Suzanne Biron, Peggy Bliss, Stephanie Bradley, James Brady, Anne M. Bray, Sarah M. Carroll, Kerry Cashman, Jonathan Cheney, Joshua D. Clapper, Lisa J. Clark, Bob Craton, Patricia Cully, Patricia M. Dambry, Kathy Dempsey, Leanne Esterly, Emily Ellen, Thomas Ferreira, Jonathan Fisher, Patricia Fromkin, Paul Gagnon, Kathy Gavilanes, Holly Gordon, Robert Graham, Ellen Granter, Diane Grossman, Barbara Hollingdale, Linda Johnson, Anne Jones, John Judge, Kevin Keane, Kelly Kelliher, Toby Klang, Sue Langan, Russ Lappa, Carolyn Lock, Rebecca Loveys, Constance J. McCarty, Carolyn B. McGuire, Ranida Touranont McKneally, Anne McLaughlin, Eve Melnechuk, Natania Mlawer, Janet Morris, Karyl Murray, Francine Neumann, Baljit Nijjar, Marie Opera, Jill Ort, Kim Ortell, Joan Paley, Dorothy Preston, Maureen Raymond, Laura Ross, Rashid Ross, Siri Schwartzman, Melissa Shustyk, Laurel Smith, Emily Soltanoff, Jennifer A. Teece, Elizabeth Torjussen, Amanda M. Watters, Merce Wilczek, Amy Winchester, Char Lyn Yeakley. **Additional Credits:** Tara Alamilla, Louise Gachet, Allen Gold, Andrea Golden, Terence Hegarty, Etta Jacobs, Meg Montgomery, Stephanie Rogers, Kim Schmidt, Adam Teller, Joan Tobin.

## Illustration

**Articulate Graphics:** 120, 121; **Carol Barber:** 15, 16; **Morgan Cain & Associates:** 8, 11r, 13r, 17, 25, 26, 40, 45, 46, 47, 48, 61, 63, 79r, 84, 100, 101, 103, 110l, 111, 147, 149, 153, 165, 170; **Kerry Cashman:** 18, 19, 36, 64, 115, 141; **Dorling Kindersley:** 10, 11l, 55, 93; **John Edwards:** 74; **Forge FX:** 52, 53; **Chris Forsey:** 28, 34, 35, 85; **Dale Gustafson:** 74, 75; **Robert Hynes:** 126, 127, 138; **Kevin Jones Associates:** 128, 129; **Martucci Design:** 110r; **Steve McEntee:** 102; **Matthew Pippin:** 75, 134; **Brucie Rosch:** 29; **J/B Woolsey Associates:** 49, 78, 79l; **XNR Productions:** 20, 21, 24, 33, 57, 59, 69, 83, 104. **All charts and graphs by Matt Mayerchak.**

## Photography

**Photo Research** John Judge **Cover Image top,** David Trood/Getty Images; **bottom,** Roger Ressmeyer/Corbis.

**Page vi,** G. Brad Lewis/Getty Images, Inc.; **vii,** Richard Haynes; **viii,** Richard Haynes, **x,** Douglas Peebles/Corbis; **1,** Ben Hankins/USGS; **2,** Kaj R. Svensson/SPL/Photo Researchers, Inc.; **2–3,** C. Heliker/USGS.

**Chapter 1 Pages 4–5,** Mats Wibe Lund; **5 inset,** Richard Haynes; **6–7,** David Briscoe/AP/Wide World Photos; **7l,** Jeff Greenberg/PhotoEdit; **7r,** Michael Nichols/Magnum; Tracy Frankel/Getty Images, Inc.; **10,** Dorling Kindersley; **11,** Getty Images, Inc.; **13,** Runk/Schoenberger/Grant Heilman Photography, Inc.; **14,** Richard Haynes; **15,** Richard Haynes; **16,** Randy Faris/Corbis; **18,** Dorling Kindersley/Stephen Oliver; **21,** Ken Lucas/Visuals Unlimited; **22,** Bettmann/Corbis; **23,** Jeffrey L. Rotman/Corbis; **26–27,** SIO Archives/UCSD; **30 all,** Richard Haynes; **31,** Richard Haynes; **32,** Russ Lappa; **37,** Russ Lappa.

**Chapter 2 Pages 42–43,** AP/Wide World Photos; **43 inset,** Richard Haynes; **44b,** Wang Yuan-Mao/AP/Wide World Photos; **44t,** Russ Lappa; **46,** Tom & Susan Bean Inc.; **47l,** Martin Miller/Visuals Unlimited; **47r,** W. Kenneth Hamblin; **48,** E.R. Degginger/Animals Animals/Earth Scenes; **49,** Jim Wark/Airphoto; **50,** Tom Bean; **51,** Richard Haynes; **52l,** Wesley K. Wallace/Geophysical Institute, University of Alaska Fairbanks; **52r,** Kevin Fleming/Corbis; **54b,** AP/Wide World Photos; **54m,** Tim Crosby/Getty Images, Inc.; **54t,** Lauren McFalls/AP/Wide World Photos; **55,** Dorling Kindersley/Peter Griffiths; **56,** Roger Ressmeyer/Corbis; **58b,** Richard Haynes; **58t,** Russ Lappa; **60b,** Michael Holford; **60t,** Russ Lappa; **65,** Reuters NewMedia Inc./Corbis; **66,** Richard Haynes; **67,** Richard Haynes; **68b,** Tom Szlukovenyi/Reuters/Corbis; **68t,** Richard Haynes; **70,** Roger Ressmeyer/Corbis; **75,** IFA/eStock Photography/PictureQuest; **76,** AP/Wide World Photos.

**Chapter 3 Pages 80–81,** Richard A. Cooke/Corbis; **81 inset,** Richard Haynes; **82,** Bettmann/Corbis; **87,** Richard Haynes; **88,** Russ Lappa; **89,** Roger Ressmeyer/Corbis; **90b,** Tui De Roy/Minden Pictures; **90t,** Dave B. Fleetham/Tom Stack & Associates, Inc.; **91b,** Dorling Kindersley; **91m,** E.R. Degginger/Color Pic, Inc.; **91t,** Breck P. Kent; **92,** G. Brad Lewis/Getty Images, Inc.; **93,** Dorling Kindersley; **94 inset r,** P. Lipman/U.S. Geological Survey/Geologic Inquiries Group; **94–95,** Richard Thom/Visuals Unlimited; **96l,** North Wind Picture Archives; **96m,** Robert Fried Photography; **96r,** Kim Heacox/Peter Arnold, Inc.; **97bl,** Alberto Garcia/Saba Press; **97m,** Alberto Garcia/Saba Press; **97ml,** Alberto Garcia/Saba Press; **97r,** Fabrizio Villa/AP/Wide World Photos; **97 all others,** Alberto Garcia/Saba Press; **98,** Hawaiian Volcano Observatory/USGS; **99b,** Helga Lade/Peter Arnold, Inc.; **99t,** Richard Haynes;

**100–101,** AFP/Corbis; **101b,** Manfred Gottschalk/Tom Stack & Associates, Inc.; **101t,** Earth Observatory/NASA; **102t,** Greg Vaughn/Tom Stack & Associates, Inc.; **102–103,** Danny Lehman/Corbis; **103 inset,** David Hosking/Photo Researchers, Inc.; **104,** David J. Boyle/Animals Animals/Earth Scenes; **105,** Linda Bailey/Animals Animals/Earth Scenes; **106,** Richard Haynes; **107,** Breck P. Kent; **108,** Alberto Garcia/Saba Press.

**Chapter 4 Pages 112–113,** Kevin Downey; **113 inset,** Richard Haynes; **114,** Richard Haynes; **114–115,** Anthony Bannister/Gallo Images/Corbis; **115t,** Tim Wright/Corbis; **115b,** Dorling Kindersley; **116tl,** Dorling Kindersley/Colin Keates; **116tm,** Breck P. Kent; **116tr,** Breck P. Kent; **116b,** AFP/Corbis; **117t,** Russ Lappa; **117ml,** Breck P. Kent; **117m,** Charles D. Winters/Photo Researchers, Inc.; **117mr,** Charles D. Winters/Photo Researchers, Inc.; **117bl,** Ken Lucas/Visuals Unlimited; **117bm,** Breck P. Kent; **117br,** Barry Runk/Grant Heilman Photography, Inc.; **118 all,** Dorling Kindersley; **119 all except topaz,** Dorling Kindersley; **119 topaz,** Charles D. Winters/Photo Researchers, Inc.; **120 all,** Breck P. Kent; **121tl,** Chip Clark; **121tr,** E.R. Degginger/Color Pic. Inc.; **121m,** Breck P. Kent **121bl,** Breck P. Kent; **121br,** Charles D. Winters/Photo Researchers, Inc.; **122t both,** E.R. Degginger/Color Pic., Inc.; **122br,** Ken Lucas/Visuals Unlimited; **122bm,** Dorling Kindersley/Colin Keates; **122bl,** Breck P. Kent/Animals Animals/Earth Scenes; **124t,** Richard Haynes; **124b,** Breck P. Kent/Animals Animals/Earth Scenes; **125,** Kevin Downey; **126,** Jane Burton/Bruce Coleman, Inc.; **127t,** Ken Lucas/Visuals Unlimited; **127b,** Dorling Kindersley/Colin Keates; **128–129t,** Dan Fornari/WHOI; **128b,** Cary S. Wolinsky/IPN/Aurora Photos; **129bl,** Peter Ryan/Science Photo Library/Photo Researchers, Inc.; **129br,** Dudley Foster/WHOI; **130,** © 1986 The Field Museum/Ron Testa; **131,** Art Resource, NY; **132l,** C. M. Dixon; **132m,** Scala/Art Resource, NY; **132r,** C. M. Dixon; **133t,** The Granger Collection, NY; **133b,** Mark Mainz/Getty Images, Inc.; **135,** Bettmann/Corbis; **137b,** Richard Haynes; **137t,** Getty Images, Inc.; **138,** Russ Lappa; **140,** Breck P. Kent.

**Chapter 5 Pages 142–143,** Corbis; **143 inset,** Richard Haynes; **144t both,** Breck P. Kent; **144b,** Jonathan Blair/Corbis; **145tl,** E.R. Degginger/Color Pic, Inc.; **145tm,** Breck P. Kent; **145tr,** Barry Runk/Grant Heilman Photography, Inc.; **145ml,** Breck P. Kent; **145mr,** E.R. Degginger/Color Pic, Inc.; **145b,** David Reed/Corbis; **146tl,** E.R. Degginger/Color Pic, Inc.; **146tm,** Breck P. Kent; **146tr,** Breck P. Kent; **146ml,** Breck P. Kent; **146mr,** Breck P. Kent; **146bl,** Jeff Scovil; **146br,** Breck P. Kent; **148t,** Doug Martin/Photo Researchers, Inc.; **148b,** Barry Runk/Grant Heilman Photography, Inc.; **149 all,** Breck P. Kent; **150,** Jan Hinsch/SPL/Photo Researchers, Inc.; **151,** Michele & Tom Grimm/Getty Images, Inc.; **152,** Tom Lazar/Animals Animals/Earth Scenes; **154l,** Runk/Schoenberger/Grant Heilman Photography, Inc.; **154m,** Jeff Scovil; **154r,** North Museum/Franklin and Marshall College/Grant Heilman Photography, Inc.; **155b,** Mark Newman/Photo Researchers, Inc.; **155tl,** Charles R. Belinky/Photo Researchers, Inc.; **155 tm,** E.R. Degginger/Color Pic, Inc.; **155tr,** Breck P. Kent; **156,** Jeff Greenberg/Photo Agora; **157t,** Ted Clutter/Photo Researchers, Inc.; **157b,** Dave Fleetham/Tom Stack & Associates; **158t,** Stuart Westmorland/Corbis; **158b,** Jean-Marc Trucher/Stone/Getty Images, Inc.; **159,** Richard Thom/Visuals Unlimited; **161tl,** Barry Runk/Grant Heilman Photography, Inc.; **161tm,** Jeff Scovil; **161tr,** Runk/Schoenberger/Grant Heilman Photography, Inc.; **161bl,** Andrew J. Martinez/Photo Researchers, Inc.; **161bm,** Barry Runk/Grant Heilman Photography, Inc.; **161br,** Breck P. Kent; **162,** Catherine Karnow/Corbis; **163,** Richard Haynes; **164l,** Jeff Scovil; **164m,** Jeff Scovil; **164r,** Breck P. Kent; **165tl,** Francois Gohier/Photo Researchers, Inc.; **165tr,** David J. Wrobel/Visuals Unlimited; **165bl,** Breck P. Kent; **165br,** N.R. Rowan/Stock Boston; **166,** Breck P. Kent; **167 all,** Russ Lappa; **168,** Richard Haynes; **170tl,** Andrew J. Martinez/Photo Researchers, Inc.; **170tr,** Breck P. Kent; **170b,** E.R. Degginger/Color Pic, Inc.

**Pages 172–173,** Roger Ressmeyer/Corbis; **173b,** Erich Lessing/Art Resource, NY; **173m,** Scala/Art Resource, NY; **173t,** Museo Archeologico Nazionale, Naples, Italy/Scala/Art Resource, NY; **174b,** Dorling Kindersley; **174t,** Private Collection/Bridgeman Art Library; **175b,** Sean Sexton Collection/Corbis; **175t,** Dorling Kindersley; **176,** Dorling Kindersley/Dave King; **177b,** Corbis; **177t,** Richard Haynes; **178,** Tony Freeman/PhotoEdit; **179b,** Russ Lappa; **179m,** Richard Haynes; **179t,** Russ Lappa; **180,** Richard Haynes; **182,** Richard Haynes; **184,** Morton Beebe/Corbis; **185,** Catherine Karnow/Corbis; **187b,** Richard Haynes; **187t,** Dorling Kindersley; **202,** David J. Boyle/Animals Animals/Earth Scenes; **204,** Breck P. Kent/Animals Animals/Earth Scenes; **205,** Breck P. Kent; **206,** Dave B. Fleetham/Tom Stack & Associates, Inc.

**Skills Handbook**
**Page 178,** Tony Freeman/PhotoEdit; **179b,** Russ Lappa; **179m,** Richard Haynes; **179t,** Russ Lappa; **180,** Richard Haynes; **182,** Richard Haynes; **184,** Tanton Yachts; **185,** Richard Haynes; **187b,** Richard Haynes; **187t,** Dorling Kindersley; **189,** Image Stop/Phototake; **192,** Richard Haynes; **199,** Richard Haynes.

**English/Spanish Glossary**
**Page 202,** David J. Boyle/Animals Animals/Earth Scenes; **204,** Breck P. Kent/Animals Animals/Earth Scenes; **205,** Breck P. Kent; **206,** Dave B. Fleetham/Tom Stack & Associates, Inc.